Eugene S. Willard

A Son of Israel

An original Story

Eugene S. Willard

A Son of Israel
An original Story

ISBN/EAN: 9783743368750

Manufactured in Europe, USA, Canada, Australia, Japa

Cover: Foto ©ninafisch / pixelio.de

Manufactured and distributed by brebook publishing software (www.brebook.com)

Eugene S. Willard

A Son of Israel

CONTENTS

CHAPTER	PAGE
I.—David Rheba, the Jew	5
II.—The Hand reveals itself	18
III.—He was a Jew	26
IV.—Michael Volkenoff	33
V.—Morning Time	53
VI.—In Bondage	61
VII.—Judith Manuelli	69
VIII.—"La Meldola"	73
IX.—Fine Feathers	81
X.—The Dance	88
XI.—Belah's Dream comes true	95
XII.—Between Jew and Christian	101
XIII.—The Marriage	113
XIV.—Housemates	120
XV.—According to Jewish Law	126
XVI.—A Man's Wit against a Woman's	132
XVII.—Concerning Michael and Marya	141
XVIII.—The Arrest	153
XIX.—Russian Justice	163
XX.—The Little Mannikin	168
XXI.—Compensation	174
XXII.—What will it be?	182
XXIII.—Spring-Time	192
XXIV.—The Princess Czartoryski	198
XXV.—A Woman's Creed	206
XXVI.—On the Way to David	219
XXVII.—Followers of Christ	224

CONTENTS

CHAPTER	PAGE
XXVIII.—In Danger	230
XXIX.—Anna's Husband	243
XXX.—Olga	249
XXXI.—The Woman Kezia	255
XXXII.—Out of Suffering comes Strength	270
XXXIII.—The Child	278
XXXIV.—David comes Home	294
XXXV.—The Redemption of Michael Volkenoff	300

A SON OF ISRAEL

CHAPTER I.

DAVID RHEBA, THE JEW.

DAVID RHEBA was a silversmith; he was what the trade calls "an all round man," meaning that he began and finished his work even from the smelting down of the silver to the last polish with the ball of his thumb. He was known throughout Odessa and to all the export merchants as the most ingenious and clever workman in the whole of Russia. His skill was beyond question; his originality in design as delicate and fine as his execution and finish.

His smithy was in the room that served him both for living- and sleeping-room, and was up on the third floor of a house at the corner of a street in the Jews' Quarter. The windows faced north and east, so that he got the steady north light to work by, and the morning sun to rouse him from sleep the moment it shot up from the edge of the earth. Over the window looking east was a wooden disc with green trees, and a temple far away in the distance, painted upon it, and round it, in black letters, the word Mirzach, in Hebrew.

David had built out the wide window northwards, and in that stood his bench, anvil, and to the right of it his forge with its smelting-pots. A narrow wooden bedstead, with a straw mattress and pillow, and a few clean rugs thrown over it, was at the side of the wall near the door; a half-dozen earthenware crocks and plates, and two copper pans for cooking, were on a shelf over the stove; a roughly made oak table stood in the middle of the room, and on it was a bowl of lentils steaming hot, just taken from the charcoal fire that was smouldering on the forge. In a corner near the stove was an old painted chest where David kept some bits of linen, the last he had of his mother's weaving, his father's old caftan, and his own only other and best blouse, a blouse such as the Russian peasants wear, and a fur-lined pelisse for winter use. David said that as he found the blouse more handy for working in, so he found it more useful for out-door wear in summer-time, and that was why he had discarded the caftan in favour of it. Upon a shelf slung against the wall over the chest were some books and two tall silver candlesticks.

David was sitting in front of his work-bench rolling up a cigarette. He was about thirty, somewhat above middle height, with long, thick, wavy, red-gold hair and a close curling beard which showed the outline of a strong, masterful chin and finely shaped mouth. His eyes were a warm hazel color; his nose delicate and clear cut; the whole face was of the highest Eastern type, with all its fire and mysticism; and in the movements of his hands, his body; in the quick changes of light in his eyes, was something which said he might as easily be made devil as angel. He was talking to John Pemberton, a buyer of curios for one of the largest retail houses in the west of London. He was saying,—

"There, my friend, is some of the sweetest tobacco in the whole world. Smoke! for the love of peace, and let's hear no more of this word work!"

"Confound it all, Rheba, I must speak of work! You've had the order for that ewer and basin since last January twelvemonth: we are now nearly in the middle of February and you are as far from finishing as you were when I called five months ago. Look at them!" John Pemberton pointed with cigarette to a silver basin and ewer pushed away to the back of the bench among unfinished candlesticks, boxes, and many other things, all in the same unfinished condition. They were exquisitely moulded and of perfect shape, but there were the marks of the hammer all over them; they were still in the rough.

"Yes, as you say, look at them!" said David, ruefully, and rubbing his broad hand through his hair. "But what shall we do? The inspiration will not come to me: so my fingers are dumb."

"Well, our client won't wait after June——"

"No; then someone else will do the work for him, and it will be all right."

"No, it will be all wrong. He wants a David Rheba piece, and he won't take any other. Why on earth must you wait for what you call inspiration?"

"This is the how—I mean—no, what is the little word which I do want? 'How' is not it. I cannot understand your Russian, and my English puzzles you because I have so little of him." He watched the smoke floating over his head for a second or two. "Ah! so now I have him!" he exclaimed. "I mean the how-with. In Nazareth, where I lived with my father before we came to this Russia, we only worked when our fingers had something to say, and thus it will be always with me, and I can do no other. Why, if that my eyes could see now what God means me to carve upon that basin and ewer, they would be finished by the third or fourth week from to-day."

"Yes, I know how you can work when the fit is on you. But why—— Now see here, David Rheba, why not teach your craft to some of the boys round about? Why not take an apprentice,—two or three? then we shouldn't have to wait a whole year, sometimes two, before an order is turned out."

"Teach!" David stared at him. "Well, so; I could hammer what I know into the head, but the mystery; the divine part; the originality; they must come from the heart, and only the Great God of all can give that. Look hither now; you say I have been lazy, but what's that?" He smiled with his eyes and held up a slender little thimble which it had been his whim to make since the day before.

"Well, do you like it?" he asked, laughing heartily at the expression on John Pemberton's face, as he turned the thimble about with his fingers, uttering a contemptuous "Ye gods!" But John began to laugh, too, when he looked more closely at it and saw chubby, winged little loves peeping out at him through clusters of roses and leaves.

"Is not that what nearly all the girls think of when they are sewing, or why do their eyes shine so? or why do they sigh and let the work fall while they twist the little thimble round and round and dream?" asked David, as he took back the thimble and laughed again softly, while he rubbed it with his sleeve, and stuck it on the top of his little finger.

"But think of the money you might make!"

"Ah, so!" The smile died out of David's eyes, and he looked through his window at some half-starved Jewish children who were playing with some dirty snow in the street below. "Then I should have more to give to those. Yes, that is so."

"No, for yourself, man! Why, you are no more like the regulation Jew than I am like the real thing in Christians?"

"Well, of course, there are Christians and Christians," said David, with a queer look, "and in Russia there are many kinds of Jews; but in Nazareth I knew but of one kind, praise be to God—— Come in!" he called suddenly in Russian, turning his face towards the door.

"I didn't hear any one."

"No? then listen."

"Oh, my poor legs!" came in a faint, quavering voice from outside the door.

"Come in, thou little rogue!"

"What! didst thou not think it was old Isaac?" a sweet, childish voice cried out, and in another moment the door was thrown open and a beautiful face with wide, dark, clear eyes, and soft, black hair in waves and curls fluttering about it, was thrust into the room just above the threshold.

"Come in, little rogue," cried David, "and let me see the whole of thee. How do I know what mischief thou art hiding below there on the stairs?"

"Well, then, here I am, and now what dost thou say?" laughed the child, dancing into the room, her ragged frock flapping against her bare legs. She stopped when she saw John Pemberton, and stood eyeing him curiously from the middle of the room. Suddenly she turned her head and darted away to the table in the corner where the bowl of lentils was standing. She grasped the bowl in both small hands, and turning, she said triumphantly to David,—

"I thought I could smell them."

Both the men laughed outright; there was such an air of defiant possession and ownership about her small face and thin arms holding the bowl of lentils close to her fragile little body as though she would say,—

"Touch it if you dare!"

"Well, little mother, the lentils are thine, and they have been waiting for thee since an hour ago."

"Thou hast cooked some garlic with them!" she cried, tasting the lentils, which she dug out with her finger. "Mother will be glad."

"Ah! thou must not do that! Away with thee or there'll be none left for thy brother." And David laughingly drove her from the room, calling after her, "Bring back the basin or there'll be none for thee tomorrow!"

"And who may that bag of bones with the wonderful eyes and face be?" asked John Pemberton when the child was gone.

"Salome Manuelli. She lives in the lower part of the house with her people, Italian Jews. She has a marvellous talent for dancing; at least so Kezia, the Meldola, has discovered."

"Meldola! Meldola!" said John Pemberton. "Not La Meldola, the famous dancer? The beautiful Italian Jewess who turned every male head in London, mine included, during 1817. More than twenty years ago now," he added, with a rueful grimace.

"I have heard that she was famous," answered David, and turned away with an expression of disgust. "But now she is poor and is teaching Salome Manuelli."

"Poor! Not dancing, then."

"Man, she is like the rest of my poor brothers here in Odessa, half starved. But she deserved her sufferings."

"Then why on earth don't your poor brothers leave the place!" cried John, forgetting La Meldola in the question that was always involving him in disputes and arguments when at home in England. "One would think they could see by this time the government doesn't want them."

"Ah! it is so easy for you outside the pale to talk; but do you know how they are treated? do you know how they are compelled to live? Do you know that they haven't one farthing to rub against the other? They are crushed down, brutalized. Think you now! could you leave Russia if you had no shoes on your feet? if your wife, family, yourself were starving and hadn't one whole garment between you? Eh? Ah! you have nothing to say. You judge things from the inside of a warm fur coat. How can you now, I ask this, scarcely risen from what you call your real English breakfast, judge of what a man should do whose one meal a day is a piece of bread rubbed with garlic! Some days not even the bread, only the smell of the garlic in his neighbour's house!" David began to walk up and down his room, speaking now in Russian, now in English, with his hands thrust into the belt of his blouse, his eyes flashing, flame-coloured, angry.

"Why, when a poor Jew wants to get away from Russia, he has to wait months, sometimes years, for a passport, because the officials demand such enormous bribes before they will give it into his hands that he has perforce to stay here and sit down under his load, or sell everything he possesses and go from hence without one kopeck in his pocket. Then after all this he may fall into the hands of some rascally official, who, finding it impossible to squeeze more bribes from a moneyless man, will invent some plausible excuse to fling him into prison after a good sound flogging; and then if my poor brother hasn't the good fortune to die while he is there, he comes out again at the end of some months only to go through the same torture over again."

"Well, it's a question I can't solve." John Pemberton took up the unfinished ewer as he spoke, tested the weight, and rubbed the silver with his thumb while he was speaking. " When I venture to speak of the sights I see here in these streets on my way to you, my friends in England jump at me with, ' Then why do they stop there ?' So the next time I'm jumped at I shall tell them what you say."

"But they won't understand you!" cried David. "How can they, unless they lived here and looked on these things till the misery and horror of it burnt into their blood and half paralyzed them, as it most does me at times."

"Then why do you stay? Come now, you can't plead that you haven't two farthings to rub one against the other; you have only to work to get as much money as you please. Come to England and share my home." John Pemberton grasped David hard by the shoulder, "Say you'll come. You've told me you haven't a relation in the whole world. Come to England, and in the words of your Book, my people shall be your people. You needn't be afraid to trust yourself to them; they're not like me, commonplace, commercial. only the very best in music, and art, and poetry satisfies them; stuff that's beyond me. But I love you, David Rheba, for your genius and for that something in yourself which is greater than your genius, and which has made me, as you see, half womanish. Come now, say you'll leave this."

David shook his head.

"I must stay here."

"What for, in the name of Heaven ?"

"I hardly know," answered David, simply; "I seem to be waiting for a revelation. It kept me here even after my father died, though his last words to me were, 'Return to Judea, to the hills looking towards Lebanon.' But I tarried here, held by an invisible hand, and until the Hand reveals itself to me I must stay."

John Pemberton had no more to say. A lump rose up in his throat, part disappointment, part shame, that he had allowed himself to show what he had felt, and got entangled with a strange feeling of awe and foreboding for David. He took his hat and walked slowly to the door. "Good-bye," he said, huskily; "I'll see you to-morrow."

David was staring at his work-bench.

"Good-bye," said John again.

"Good-bye," answered David, dreamily, and John went slowly down-stairs, while David went as slowly to his bench and began to make a rough sketch on a piece of paper. After a few rapid strokes he cried,—

"So that will do. Look you hither now, John Pemberton, the ewer and basin shall be ready within a month. It has come to me!" He looked round. "Gone! I remember now he said 'Good-bye.'" He sat down again at his bench and took the ewer in his hands, turning it round and round, comparing its shape with the sketch.

"Yes, you will do," he murmured. "The hills looking towards Lebanon. Here in the concave of the bowl shall be one of the western valleys, surrounded by the hills; on the convex side the vine, olive, and fig-tree shall put forth their branches and shall come up to the edge with rich bosses of fruit and leaf." He pulled a bar of silver from a drawer in his bench and began shaving it into his smelting-pot. "I shall need a lining to my basin to make the design perfect. The bosses of vine and fruit round the edge I'll contrive so cunningly the most clever smith shall not be able to detect the join."

He put the smelting-pot into the forge fire and worked away at the bellows.

"On the ewer I'll carve a cedar-tree with a woman of Israel seated under the branches carding wool."

He gathered the tools he would need into a heap close by his hand; tied on his leathern apron and began to draw the design on the basin while the silver was smelting. He looked up once when the sun shone out on the houses opposite and smiled. He knew that old Isaac in the garret facing his room was stretching out his bony hands to the glow and saying,—

"It warms me, it warms me."

Sounds came up from the street; a man was crying out salted cucumbers for sale, another was selling fresh water. About two in the afternoon Salome came quietly up the stairs and put her head round the open door. Seeing that he was so engrossed she sat down on the threshold with the basin in her lap, and there she sat for full an hour watching him, nor did she stir until David paused and stretched his arms to relieve them, then she said,—

"Does the work go well?"

"What, little rogue, art thou there?"

"Yes and here's thy basin, washed clean this time."

She ran across the room and set it on the table. "What art thou about now?"

"The ewer and basin," he answered, smiling.

"Hath God spoken to thee, then?"

"Yea, He hath spoken." David put out his hand and drew the child to his side, and showed her what progress he had made. He had marked out the design in pencil on the basin, and already the leaves and bunches of fruit were beginning to show under his hammer.

"I have something to tell thee!" she suddenly cried. "Just before I carried back thy basin a carriage came into the street and the coachman asked for David Rheba, the silversmith. He set us laughing at first because he made to be so fine, and held his nose thus and sniffed; but when mother told him where he might find thee, he said, 'Tell him my mistress will call about the hour of two.' Now who can it be?"

David rose, poured out the smelted silver from the smelting-pot into a tray to cool, then sat down again to his work, saying, "I know not, little one."

"And he threw us a piece of money; that's how the basin comes to be clean this time, because we were able to buy some water."

"Thou shouldst not have wasted the water, my pigeon; I have plenty."

"Hark! some one is coming. Perhaps it is the lady!" The child's quick ear had caught the rustle of a woman's dress against the stairs.

"Who dost thou mean?" asked David, absorbed in his work.

"The coachman's mistress!" she cried, darting away to the door.

"Then the end of the world is come if a Russian lady takes the trouble to climb those stairs.'

"I am right and thou art wrong!" cried Salome, in a loud whisper from the landing, whence she was peeping down the stairs. "There are two,—a tall one and one not so high as the other. Now the tall one has stopped, and the little one is coming up alone." Salome rushed over to David and stood by him all eyes and curiosity.

CHAPTER II.

THE HAND REVEALS ITSELF.

Now David heard the soft rustle of the woman's dress, and with the sound a fresh, sweet smell of flowers seemed to come into the room. It made him shiver and close his eyes with a sensation of exquisite pain. What did it remind him of? It seemed to pervade and fill the air, and he rose with his hands stretched out as though asking a question. They as suddenly fell again to his side, for a young woman about eighteen years of age stood in the doorway gazing mildly at him with lustrous, tender eyes from under a smooth, white forehead and straight, dark brows. Ineffable sweetness breathed from her: an atmosphere of womanliness and strength surrounded her and made the air vibrate as it were with mystic, wonderful music, which filled the room, and filled full to overflowing David's heart. He strove to speak, but he could only look and wonder with his heart beating, his pulses throbbing from the swift rush of joyous blood which went swinging and singing through his veins, and drawing in with deep, full breath the sweet, fresh smell which came from her. It was a smell of leaves, and flowers, and grasses; of pure, clear air which had sung lightly in the tree-tops the golden summer through, had rustled through hedges and over fields of ripe corn and orchards of rosy fruit to find its home and resting-place in the hair and clothes of this one woman. It was for her that he had waited. The Hand had revealed itself.

The young woman made an almost imperceptible movement towards him; her lips parted as though to speak; her eyes overflowing with glad, quick tears; her soul in a tumult of joy, and pain, and delight. Earth no longer existed for her, she had left it and was treading a world of love and peace with the man who was facing her.

Salome looked on, her eyes wide with wonder and half with fear. Presently a pale, slight woman in a long cloak lined with sables appeared on the landing and rested there awhile with her hand on the doorpost. She was about twenty-seven years of age, with delicate, dark brows and thick, sunny hair, a sensitive mouth, and earnest, dark-grey eyes. She looked at the young woman and smiled; then seeing her abstraction, she said, in a soft, gentle voice,—

"Olga, hast thou told David Rheba I wish to speak with him?"

The young woman heaved a deep sigh and moved backwards, leaving the entrance free, saying, in a low voice,—

"My mistress wishes to speak to thee."

"Thee!" David whispered to himself. "Thee!"

And Salome wondered to herself, whispering, "She said 'Thee.'"

David moved towards the door, saying,—

"Will you please enter, madam?"

"Thank you. My name is Marya; I am the wife of

Michael Volkenoff, and I have come to talk to you about a little commission that I wish you to undertake for me."

Olga took Marya's cloak and laid it over the end of David's bed, together with her own. David saw that her hand touched his pillow, and a mist came over his eyes so that he could scarce see the stool he placed for Marya Volkenoff in the window by his work-bench. Olga stood behind her mistress with her hands loosely clasped; her face was pale and her lips tremulous; her lustrous eyes were half veiled under her eyelids.

Salome fidgeted with her feet and longed to know what it all meant. The tension, the magnetism in the air, made her blood tingle and prick, but she was resolved to stay and fathom it out spite of the trial it was to remain quiet. Why should a stranger call David "Thee"? Thee and thou were only used by friends and lovers. Why had she not said "You"?

Marya Volkenoff, calm, serene, and self-contained, was quite undisturbed by the vibration in the air. She was looking enquiringly round the room.

"Are you married?" she said at last to David, and wondering a little that he had not spoken.

Olga looked at him, question and fear in her face. David smiled at her, and shook his head, answering,—

"No."

Marya, seeing the direction of his eyes, turned and looked at Olga, who on David's answer drooped her face till her hair overshadowed it, but Marya could see there was a colour on the girl's cheeks like the colour at the heart of a June rose.

"Pardon my question," said Marya, she too now smiling, "but your room is so fresh—and yes, there is no other word for it, but sweet; so I imagined you must have a wife."

She looked once more at the well-scrubbed floor and whitewashed walls with not a speck of dust on them.

David did not speak; he had picked up the little thimble and was trying to measure with his eyes the size of Olga's second finger and wondering whether the thimble would fit it.

Salome crept up to him and nudged him with her elbow; she didn't want her friend to lose one jot of praise. Why couldn't he say that he had whitewashed the room and made it look "sweet"?

Marya divined the child's thought; she smiled and said to David,—

"So it was you yourself?"

Salome gave her one grateful look, then said, vehemently, "Yes, it was, wasn't it, David?"

"What is it, my pigeon?" asked David.

"The lady was speaking to thee."

"I beg your pardon," he said, confusedly, and put the thimble in his blouse pocket. "You wished me to —to——" He rubbed his hand through his hair; he had forgotten what it was she came for.

"I wish you to make something for me, something which must be original, unique; though many of the same kind have been made; that is why I wish you to undertake the work; that is why I wished to see you myself and explain, because the work may prove objectionable, and I want to overcome that objection if possible."

David bowed to her and said, " Please excuse me one moment;" then taking up his work-stool, he put it down by Olga, saying,—

"Wilt thou not rest?"

Olga flushed and looked at her mistress.

"Yes, be seated, child," Marya nodded to her.

David's eyes shone when Olga sat down trembling upon his stool with her hands folded lightly in her lap. How could he ever put the stool to common use again now that she, the one woman on all God's earth for him, had honoured it? He turned to Marya with his face glowing, and said,—

"If you please, I am ready."

Marya looked at him intently for a moment. He was not the type of Jew she was used to meeting in Odessa. He was as original in appearance as in his work, which she had often seen. She began to feel more hopeful of getting her commission carried out, and less timid of telling him the nature of it; so she took her courage in both hands and simply said,—

"I wish you to make a silver crucifix for me."

David looked at her in doubt for a moment, then his brows contracted and his firm mouth trembled as a child's will when it is about to weep; but after a pause and a movement of the muscles of his throat as though they had gripped hold of and conquered some trouble which had climbed up into it from its heart, he said, gravely,—

"I hear."

"I wish it for a very dear sister of mine in France. I have been to every silversmith in Odessa, but I cannot obtain exactly what I want, believe me, for they will not make the cross of the Roman Church, or I would not trouble you."

"Trouble!" David looked at Olga. Had not this brought her to him?

"But I fear that I have pained you," said Marya, self-reproach in her eyes.

"Do not grieve at that," he answered, simply. "It is nothing; it is passed. I will do what you desire."

He turned away to the table between the windows, and took a sheet of drawing-paper from a shelf which was fixed to the wall above it and a lead-pencil.

Olga touched Marya's arm and whispered,—

"Why should it pain him to make an image of our Lord Christ?"

"Because he is a Jew," whispered Marya in reply.

Olga drew in her breath and sighed. "A Jew——!"

David heard the sigh and the words, and there went a thrill through his heart; he had forgotten in the overwhelming ecstasy which had laid hold on him at sight of her that she might be a Christian. He turned now and faced her with the thought in his soul, "Do not shrink from me, thy Christ was a Jew." She had risen from the stool, and was standing gazing intently at him, and he almost cried out for very joy, for there was neither shrinking nor horror in her eyes; in her as in him Love had overthrown all lesser things; they were man and woman made by God to be mate each to each; no creed, no obstacle set up by man, could separate them one from the other; they had met by apparent chance only to discover that they were one perfect whole and that they had been so from all time.

Marya, too, rose from her seat and stared at them. She now felt the magnetism pulsing backwards and forwards through the air of the room, and she was bewildered by it: something wonderful had happened; what it was she knew not; she only knew that Olga, who had always shrunk away trembling at the mere word "Jew," was looking at David Rheba as though she had forgotten all else in the world but this one man.

"Come, child, we must go," she said, quickly, a sensation of fear creeping over her. "Give me my cloak."

Olga mechanically took up the cloak and fastened it round her mistress' throat; then she took up her own cloak while Marya walked slowly to the door. She was following with the cloak hanging loosely from her arm, when David, who had moved with her step by step, laid his hand upon it and said in Hebrew,—

"The day is cold; thou must not go forth uncovered."

She turned to him and lifted up her chin as a child will when it is being dressed, while David fastened the clasp and drew the warm hood over her dark hair; then he let her go.

"When will the work be finished?" asked Marya from the landing.

"In a few days," answered David.

Marya felt some surprise that it should be finished so soon, but she simply said,—

"Thank you; good-day," and went down the stairs.

"May the night but increase thy peace," said Olga, softly; then she went slowly down, one stair at a time, loath to go.

David gave a great, happy sigh and watched her slight body and trailing cloak. Suddenly he darted after her. He had remembered the thimble.

"Stay, madam," he called. "Wilt that fit thy finger?" he whispered, eagerly, when he had caught her up.

"Surely, right well! See!" answered Olga, with a happy little laugh, holding up her hand with the thimble perfectly fitting her second finger.

"So it doth!" He smiled and ventured to touch her hand for one moment; then he said, fervently,—

"The Father of All Good bless thee."

"And thee," murmured Olga, her hand going out to his. Midway she suddenly grew shy, remembering that she had met him that day for the first time, and she snatched it back, blushing rosy-red, turned away, and sped down the rest of the stairs, with the thimble held close to her heart, and into the carriage, which set off at once. She flung herself down on the rug, with her arms round Marya's waist, her face hidden in her lap, and she wept and laughed,—

"Little Mother! Little Mother! mistress! I love him! I love him! and I think that he loves me."

Marya stroked the girl's hair and prayed that all might be well, but she was in fear and trembling for her.

CHAPTER III.

HE WAS A JEW.

David waited on the stairs till the sound of the carriage-wheels had quite died away; then he went up the stairs three at a time, and into his room, and there he stood looking about him. The place seemed to be full of light, and radiance, and warmth. The sweet, fresh smell from Olga's hair and clothes was still there, pervading the air, and again he said,—

"Of what doth it remind me?" He paused, thinking, pulling at his beard. Suddenly he struck his hands together and cried, "The cedars of Lebanon!" Then he fell to thinking again, lost to everything.

Salome watched him in silence. Presently she crept over to him and put her head in under his arm and looked up in his face.

"Nay, nay, it is not possible!" he murmured after a while to himself. "She is a Russian girl; it is my imagination. It must be the odour of her own native pine-trees; they love her and give her of all their sweetness to add to her own."

Salome's head began to grow impatient; would he never notice her?

"Ah, my pigeon!" he said, dreamily, and drew her with him over to his bench, where he sat down on the stool he had given to Marya.

"So the Hand hath revealed itself," he said, softly; "it was for her that I waited. God be thanked for all His goodness to me."

"Thou hast the wrong stool!" cried Salome; "this is thy work-stool," and she was darting over to the stool Olga had sat upon.

"Stay!" said David, springing up and taking it before she could touch it. "This is Hers!" He strode with it to the oak chest and stood it on the top, out of reach; then he turned, smiled at Salome, and sat down on the other stool.

"But thou canst not work on that one; it is too high for thee."

"Well, then, there!" and David took a measure and a saw, and in two minutes he had sawn off a few inches from each leg. "Now what dost thou say?" and he sat down once more and laughed at her.

"Nothing," answered Salome, "only that I liked thy old stool better; it was broader, and I am sure it rested thee more than this will do."

"Well, thou shalt go to Amos Linski. Take to him this sketch,"—David began a rough sketch of a stool, —"and tell him to make me a stool of oak. Stay thee now till I get the measurements." He took his old work-stool from the shelf and measured it, dotted down the inches, put it back again, then gave the plan to Salome.

Salome stood twisting it round and round on her finger. She was puzzled. Some change had come over David just in the little time between the coming and going of the young woman, Olga. It was as though he had grown younger. And the stool! why should it be treated like a relic?

David was bending over a sketch that he was making. He had entirely forgotten her. She tucked the plan into the bosom of her frock, then she crept up behind him and peeped over his shoulder. He had drawn the outline of a cross, and was now sketching the figure of a man with the arms stretched out and the palms of the hands nailed to the cross-beam. A tear had rolled down David's cheek on to the paper and blistered it.

Salome leaned over him, interested and wondering.

"Who is that thou art drawing?" she asked.

"Jesus of Nazareth," he answered.

"The Jesus my father talks of?"

"Yea," he answered, not pausing in his work.

Salome drew back from him, trembling, with her eyes blazing. How many and many a time had she seen her father spit at the name, declaring that all their sufferings, all their wrongs and oppressions, were caused by this one man. This man, Jesus!

"Why hast thou nailed him to that?" she asked eagerly, pointing to the cross.

David put her round till she stood facing him. There was a glad light dancing in her eyes, her cheeks were hot and flushed. He looked sadly at her.

"Because that was the manner of his death."

"Was it?" Her lips parted; her white teeth began to shine between them.

"Hast thou not heard? Dost thou not know that our forefathers crucified him?"

"No!" with breathless eagerness. "Did they?"

"And that he was a Jew, one of our own race?"

"Nay, there thou art wrong. Father says he was the God of the Christians."

"He was a Jew," said David.

"I tell thee father says he was the God of the Christians!"

"That was so; but at first he was a Jew."

Salome struck her hands passionately together.

"Then how"—she puckered her brows—"how could he be a Jew, a God, and a Christian? Dost thou know?"

"Not clearly, but I will try to explain to thee," answered David. "He was a Jew because he was born of a Jewess named Mary, a sweet, pure woman, as the sweetness and purity of his life testify. He was the brother and friend of all the poor and of those who were sick or afflicted in mind or body. He had friends who after his death, out of their great love for him, called themselves Christians, that is to say, Followers of Christ, and they lived after his teaching; but in time, as the hearers of his word died, he was worshipped as the God he was inspired to teach of. Then his beautiful creed was degraded by ritual and ceremony. His followers no longer looked to the Deed, but the Letter of his word; and now, as thou knowest, they persecute us his People, yet read our Holy Book of Laws in their churches on the day they have chosen for their Sabbath."

Salome stared at him; still she could not understand.

"Is this"—she touched the sketch with her finger—"what the lady wanted you to make?"

"Yea, this is a sketch of what she wants. This is what the Christians worship in the Roman Church."

"But is not that a graven image?" whispered Salome.

"No, it is a symbol. Here in Russia the Christian church is Greek, and the cross is shaped thus." As he spoke he marked out a Grecian cross on his leathern apron with a piece of chalk.

"That is like what the priests carry sometimes through the streets. Why should it be a different shape from that one?" Salome pointed to the sketch of the crucifix which David held in his right hand.

David shook his head,—

"I know not."

"Why did our forefathers crucify him?"

"His book says that the high priest and priests feared him, and that they sought to put him to death."

"Feared him! because of the evil he would bring upon us?" exclaimed Salome.

"Nay, it was not Jesus of Nazareth who brought all these sufferings upon us; he was good. If one can believe what is written, there has been no man like him either before or since."

"Thou lovest him!" cried Salome, fiercely.

"Wherefore not? He was a Jew and loved his people; why should we not love him?"

Salome drew in her breath with a sharp hiss and lifted her hand to strike David. He caught it firmly in his and looked sternly at her. She snatched it away and cast herself down on the floor beside his stool, screaming wildly, with her hands gripping her thick, black hair,—

"I hate him! I hate him! Mother, father, hate him! I have never heard anything but hate and curses for him, and now thee, because a Christian woman but comes and looks at thee, say that thou lovest him."

David let her cry. When she was tired of dragging at her hair she beat her hands passionately against the floor. He was used to her lightning-like moods and tempers. He laid down the drawing and went on with his work on the silver bowl. Salome gave one last piercing scream, then came a pause, and presently a muffled voice asked,—

"Art thou not going to speak to me?"

David smiled, and made no answer.

Salome sat up with her feet under her and looked at him: her face was white and stained with tears.

"Well?" she said, making a little grimace.

"Well?" he said, smiling, without looking round. "What did you do with the lentils?"

"Gave them to mother and father; Belah was out."

"Well? and thyself?"

"I wasn't hungry," answering his look with another little grimace. "But I am now."

"So am I," he said, cheerfully, and began to unfasten his leathern apron. "It's nigh supper-time. There's some soup in the stove, set it out with the bowls and bread, then call Belah; I can hear his voice in the street."

Salome darted hither and thither, singing, light as a

bird, all her rage forgotten. When she had put out the soup she sprang down the stairs, returning in a few seconds with Belah, who was a smaller likeness of herself, and in a few moments David and the children were seated round the stove with their bowls on their knees, eating the bean and onion soup with infinite relish and chatting away merrily. When it was finished David sent them away with a thick piece of bread for each, lighted his lamp and worked on again till past midnight. Once he rose to cover "Olga's stool" with a piece of a silk waist scarf which had belonged to his mother, then he went on again with his work, and was well pleased with what he had done when at last he lay down to sleep.

CHAPTER IV.

MICHAEL VOLKENOFF.

OLGA IVANNER had lived with Marya since she was seven years of age; since the time she had been bought by Michael Volkenoff as a beautiful present for his girl-wife, to keep her mind from brooding over the death of her first child. He did not tell Marya that he had seen the girl advertised for sale in the *Moscow Gazette* along with several other serfs from the same proprietor; nor did Olga know that she had been sold by the heirs of her old mistress, who had loved the girl and had educated her in a way. It had been impressed upon her mind by the steward of the house that she had been "given" in exchange. Michael knew his wife's prejudices too well to ask her to accept a slave. When he saw Olga, her beautiful, serene face and gentle manners, he resolved to buy her and keep the transaction a secret from Marya. She was exactly what Marya craved: something akin to her, which she could educate and train according to her own refined ideas and theories. That was how it came about that Olga had the power of reasoning things out for herself: a love of everything in Nature, and great sweetness and purity both in her body and in her thoughts.

It was Marya who gave the name of Olga to the child. She said it was a name that she loved, and that the girl should be called by that name, serf though she was. From the first Olga had had her own room in the same wing of the great house as Marya, and she regarded her mistress as mother, family, and confessor, so strong was the love between them.

The house of Michael Volkenoff lay out towards the west, nearly a mile from the town. It stood full south, facing the sea. In the front was a great, paved court-yard, and on the eastern side was another court-yard, where the out-door servants had their quarters. At the other side of the house, and extending away for twenty acres or so at the back, was a beautiful, wild old garden, which an ancestor of Michael Volkenoff had made, bringing the mould for the trees and flowers to be planted in, at great cost, from the Crimea, the soil in and about Odessa being so chalky trees cannot live in it. And on a hill looking down upon the place he had planted a wood of larch and pine in deep wide holes, filled with the same rich soil mixed with sand and dead leaves. This garden and wood were a source of constant self-congratulation to Michael Volkenoff; it marked him as the richest man in the province. Beyond the garden stretched miles of corn-growing land, barren and shadeless.

After leaving the Jews' Quarter, Marya drove home. The coachman pulled up at a door, under the shade of a treble row of pine-trees, on the western side of the house, the door that was known to all the serfs on the estate as "The Little Mother's door." There was not a soul among the many hundred that Michael owned that did not love Marya. She was called "Little Mother" among themselves by one and all, and that was how the door got its name; she always used it to avoid the vast crowd of people that thronged the hall and court-yard from about eight in the morning until five in the evening; for, besides being the owner of the immense tracts of corn-growing land beyond his house, Michael Volkenoff was head and, in many cases, the founder of most of the charitable institutions in Odessa. He loved the popularity and power his good deeds brought him, though no one would have suspected it from his impassive face and cold blue eyes, and though it had been as food to him to see the crowd bow and cringe to Marya when she passed through, yet he had said no word when she began to use the "Little Mother's door" because she shrank from the flattery and many a heart-rending story that she was powerless to help; he only asked himself whether his marriage had been a wise one?—whether the young, simple girl who had been given to him for wife on the day she left the convent was, after all, the proper mate? She had retained all her simplicity and charm, but she cared neither to rule nor lead, nor could he mould her to what he wished his wife to be. Instead of taking the mark of his thumb as he had seen the clay take the potter's, she seemed to be developing in quite another direction, which he could neither understand nor gage. There was something in her which eluded him, and which at last made him coldly suspicious. Her love for him had been helpful and deep, but he was starving it; he had taken all and given nothing in return, and so bitter had grown her resentment and his grudging that they no longer used the sweet, loving "thee" and "thou," but spoke as strangers, using the cold, formal "you." And so a thick growth of misgiving, and doubt, and rancour had sprung up between them, and soon would shut out all that was best and fairest in their sky.

Marya, from the first, found her little door a great comfort; it not only helped her to avoid the crowd, but also the great state staircase, with its lazy porters and servants, and the enormous reception-rooms, which looked more desolate and empty because of the many beautiful things they held with no one to enjoy them, except on a few important days in the year. But once through the "Little Mother's door" and she was in another world. There was old Nicolas, the house-steward, to welcome her; her rough-coated dog, Wolf, grown stiff in his joints and almost blind, but like a puppy in his joy at seeing his mistress; her cozy rooms on one side of the broad hall and Michael's on the other; and at the end, facing south, a large room which was half study, half sitting-room,—a wholly charming room, with silver hanging lamps, cedar-wood ceiling and door and cedar-wood panelling, carved oak book-shelves lining two sides of the room to about the height of five feet, and above them some rare pieces of china and a few etchings; the third side was filled with a big, open fireplace with bright copper hearth and dogs and with copper at the back and sides in place of tiles, so that even with a small log fire in the misty autumn evenings there was a glow like sunset in the place. In the angle on each side of the fireplace were two high-backed oak settees, brown with age, with rose silk damask cushions piled in the corners; and the fourth side of the room was entirely taken up by a wide, deep-set window with a double set of rose silk curtains and a window-seat. This was the room that Marya loved and always used, and this was the room she went to after her visit to David Rheba.

Olga followed and took off her mistress' cloak and little hood-like bonnet and fur-lined overshoes, while Nicolas brought forward her deep elbow chair and a cushion for her feet; then he went away and presently returned with a silver tray bearing dainty white cups and saucers; sweetmeats in a little gold dish, and some white bread and butter; this he set by her on a small oak table, then went again to the door and took a small samovar from the boy Dimitri, who stood there holding it, his round, merry face and twinkling eyes striving to subdue their gaiety and to look as grave and dignified as Nicolas himself.

Olga stood holding Marya's bonnet, and was giving one or two light affectionate touches to the smooth golden-brown hair it had covered. She smiled when she managed to coax a little curl or two down from the thick coils to kiss the nape of her beloved mistress' neck. As soon as Marya was seated, Wolf, the dog, snuggled up close to her side and rested his chin on her lap, blinking his eyes and tapping his tail on the floor.

"Come back, child, when thou hast removed thy cloak," Marya said to Olga; and as Olga ran lightly away old Nicolas muttered,—

"Thou!"

"Why not, Nicolas?" asked Marya, smiling at his grave face, as she had done many a time before when asking the same question, and the old hound turned his head on Marya's knees and looked at Nicolas as though he, too, would ask, "Why not?"

"Because. Well, I know not," replied Nicolas, returning the same answer that he had given to the same question for the last eleven years, since the day Olga first entered the house. But this time he suddenly added, "Nay, I am wrong; I do know. She may marry one of these days and forget you. How will you endure that? for you have made her like a child of your own blood."

Marya started and looked at Nicolas. She had foreseen the possibility of Olga marrying; such a thing, of course, might happen, but that Olga could forget her!

"But she might marry someone on the estate," she replied; but even as she said it her heart sank. It seemed degrading to Olga to think of wedding her to a serf, and then was there not David Rheba? She had forgotten him for the moment.

"Nay!" muttered Nicolas; "she'll never marry a serf! I once told her that my son Foka wished to marry her, and she stared at me as though she thought me mad."

"You spoke to her of marriage without consulting me?"

"Well, well, yes." Nicolas rubbed his hands nervously together and edged nearer to the door. There was a note in Marya's voice which frightened him.

"My son is bright and clever, and, since the master gave him leave to work for himself in the town, is growing rich and will soon have two rooms to live in, and then he will want a wife to keep them clean and cook his food. He fancied Olga, and I spoke to her."

"Please not to do so again, Nicolas, without first telling me. Though Olga is a serf, she has not been trained to a serf's life, nor has she been treated as a serf; and as it is now"—again she thought of David Rheba—"it is best that you speak no more to her of your son. My tea; I am waiting for it." She held out her hand for the cup of tea Nicolas had poured out for her.

He handed the tea, saying, "My Foka is a good boy and loves her——"

"That is sufficient, Nicolas; you may go now."

Instead of going, Nicolas advanced and stood humbly by her chair.

"You are not angry with me, mistress?"

Marya looked at him and smilingly shook her head. "Angry with you, Nicolas. No; I was surprised, that was all."

"My dear mistress," the old man said, somewhat brokenly, and then he bent down and kissed her hand. "Thou art always kind, Little Mother," he whispered to himself under his breath, and rose with his old wrinkled face twitching to keep back his tears, and left the room.

Marya put up her little feet on the fender and sipped her tea. Presently Nicolas returned with a lighted taper in his hand.

"Nay, do not light the lamps," she cried; "but you may put more logs on the fire. Pine logs, Nicolas, not oak. I want the splendid blaze the resin gives."

He put on a few logs deftly here and there among the red embers of the burning wood, and in a moment the flames leapt up and made the room glow like a rosy shell.

"Now, tell Olga to come to me, please."

Nicolas went to the end of the wide corridor, mounted a few steps to the left, and along a short passage to Olga's room. The door was open, and he could see her standing before a small oval looking-glass, gazing at the reflection of the silver thimble, which she was still wearing on her second finger. She moved her hand from right to left, now up, now down, and Nicolas thought she was admiring its firm, fine lines and shape.

"The mistress is waiting for you," he muttered, gruffly. He had always supposed Olga much too good to be in love with her own beauty, and was mightily angry with himself to find he had been mistaken.

"Yes, Nicolas," replied Olga, turning to him for a moment; and then, turning again to the glass, she pressed the thimble against her round, dimpled chin, and smiled and sighed at it.

Nicolas gave a grunt of disgust and strode heavily away, muttering to himself something about the vanity of girls. Olga laughed merrily at him and ran lightly through the corridor, and, laughing, she ran in to Marya.

"What kept thee, child?" asked Marya.

"This, mistress," answered Olga, kneeling down by Wolf and holding up the silver thimble above his head.

"A thimble!"

"Yes. Nicolas caught me looking in my glass at it, and went away growling something about all girls being cursed with vanity."

"But why shouldst thou look in thy glass at it?"

"Because I wanted to see how it would appear to other people, and there is nothing like a looking-glass for telling one that."

"It seems to be a beautiful piece of work. Where didst thou buy it?"

"I didn't buy it. He—David Rheba gave it to me." Olga's head suddenly went down over Wolf's and stayed there.

"David Rheba gave it to thee?"

"Yes, to-day, when I was following thee, Little Mother."

Marya put her hand under Olga's chin and lifted up the girl's face till she could see into her eyes.

"Let us speak seriously of this. Thou saidst to me in the carriage that thou lovest this man——"

"Ah, yes, with all my soul!" cried Olga, with her hands suddenly clasping Marya's.

"But how may that be? Thou hast only seen him to-day for the first time; and what canst thou know of love?"

Olga shook her head. "I know not how I know, but I know that I love him."

"But, child, he is a Jew!"

"Yes, that is so; but didst thou not hear him say that our Christ was a Jew? Think of it! Our Christ was a Jew——" Olga sank back upon her heels, her hands clasped tightly together in her lap, her eager face lifted to Marya's full of question.

"Thy imagination, Olga; I did not hear him say that."

"Surely thou must have heard! When I asked thee, 'Why should he not make an image of our Lord?' and thou saidst, 'Because he is a Jew,' David Rheba turned suddenly and looked at me and said——" Olga paused, her face grew pale. "Nay, he did not speak; but I heard him say here in my heart, 'Do not shrink from me; thy Christ was a Jew,' and I thought it was he speaking aloud to me."

"It was his thought, child, which thou didst hear."

"And was our Christ a Jew?"

Marya nodded "Yes," and wondered at the girl's eyes, they were grown so wide and solemn.

"Then he is one of Christ's own people; and though I should have loved him whatever he might be, but that he is of our Lord's race makes our love seem of heaven." . . . Suddenly Olga's face went deadly white. She had seen Jews kicked like curs, spat upon; hated and reviled; hounded from their homes, beaten, and abused. She herself had shivered if one had touched her in passing. She grasped Marya by the arms and strove to speak, but her speech was broken with sobs; she could only shake and tremble with the vehemence of the grief which suddenly swept over her, and she bowed her head on Marya's knees and wept, stammering, "Why, if they are his people, the people of our Lord, should they be treated so cruelly?"

There was a slight noise at the handle of the door. Wolf crept away under the nearest settee, but neither Marya nor Olga heard the door open; it was the slight change in the air which made Marya turn to see who it was that had entered.

Michael Volkenoff stood there looking down angrily at Olga.

"Send her away," he said, and walked over to the window, where he stood looking sullenly out at the sea and the twinkling lights of the ships in the harbour.

"Olga, child, the master is here; thou must go."

Olga didn't heed the words,—she hadn't heard them; she raised her streaming eyes, asking,—

"Why, then, are we so cruel to the Jews?"

Michael Volkenoff turned sharply round from the window and made a passionate gesture to Marya to take Olga away. Marya rose and grasped the girl by the arm, lifting her almost forcibly from the floor.

"The master is here; come, child, thou must go."

"The Jews!" muttered Michael Volkenoff. He hated the word, and had forbidden it to be spoken in his house.

Marya drew Olga quickly away and into the girl's own room.

"Rest there, Olga, in thy chair, and I will bring thee a cup of tea."

"But the master will be angry to see thee waiting upon me."

"Not so angry as he will be to see the tears on thy face, and to know what thou wert talking of."

Olga shrank up close to Marya. "I do not understand," she whispered; "master says he loves Christ, and yet he is more cruel to the Jews than any one I know of."

It was Marya's turn to shrink now. All her love, all her pleading had not been able to abate one jot of his hate to the unhappy people.

"Art thou sure that Christ was a Jew?" asked Olga. "Because how can he be a Jew and our God?"

"Marya! Marya!" shouted Michael Volkenoff from the end of the hall.

"I will answer thee another time, child. Rest there now, and I will bring thee some tea. I am coming, husband," she called, and hurried away into the room, straight to the samovar, and poured out a cup of tea for Olga.

"I shall be back again in a moment," she smiled to Michael, going to the door.

"Who is that for?" he asked.

"For Olga;" and before he could stay her she had flitted away and was back before he had realised her smiling defiance of him. He was still standing staring at the door.

"What was that talk of Jews?" he asked, beginning to walk restlessly up and down the room, sipping his tea.

"Something that Olga was asking me," she replied.

"Yes, but what was it?" He waited for an answer,

and receiving none, put down his cup and flung himself in the window-seat, with his back to her.

Marya began to look hopeless; she wanted to speak out and tell him everything that had happened since the morning, but the old dread of his anger, all the years she had been his wife had not had power to lessen, came over her: she seemed as weak now as on the day she first felt the full force of it; and the bitter part was in knowing that if she had but the courage to calmly set her will against his for the things which she knew it was but right and just to fight for, she could conquer. Once she had opposed him and conquered, and though the fight, for it was a tough one, shattered her in heart and brain for days after, she gained a knowledge of the strength which was latent in her, and which she knew she was letting run to waste for want of healthy resistance to each selfish whim of his.

"Am I to be a coward all my life?" she now asked herself.

Old Wolf crept out from under the settee and licked her hand. "Thank you, dear old friend," she whispered to him. "Do you remember that my fear of his anger once got you beaten and kicked till I feared that you would die? Go under, boy; I will be strong this time, God helping me."

There was a little nervous catch of her breath at the end, very like a sob, and Michael turned fiercely round, exclaiming,—

"In the name of Heaven, what is the matter with you women?"

Something in the utter disproportion of his anger to the small sound she had made so tickled Marya's sense of humour that she burst out into one of her rare, merry peals of laughter, and stood shaking and laughing, unable to speak, while Wolf's tail made sympathetic taps under the settee.

"What's the matter now?" asked Michael, between his teeth.

"I will tell you," answered Marya, going over to the window and standing in front of him, "if you will listen patiently."

He looked up, pleasantly surprised. She was on the defensive, and was eyeing him resolutely. How he loved to have this slight, pale wife of his defying him! There was nothing he loved more, only she did it so seldom. If she had but known all the power she possessed and how to use the power, he mused.

"Well, it was this," she began: "when you came in just now Olga was talking about the Jews——"

"I have forbidden you to mention that word," he said, already beginning to lose control of himself.

"I know you have, but I must disobey you."

"You must disobey me?" he cried.

"Because you are wrong," she answered, calmly.

He looked up at her, scarce able to believe his ears; this was defying him indeed.

"You are wrong, and I can no longer obey you in neither helping these people nor in speaking for them when I can," said Marya.

The young moon was shining through the window on her face, and Michael felt a sudden, superstitious quaking of the heart at the luminous light it made about her.

"Well, well," he muttered, uneasily, "what has this to do with Olga? You said that she was talking of the—the Jews," he ground out at last, as though biting at the word.

"Yes, a strange thing happened to-day, and you must listen to me quietly and help me."

Marya sat down on the window-seat with her face turned towards him. "Olga loves David Rheba, the Jew."

"My dear Mimouchka, what nonsense have you got now in your little head?"

"It is true, Michael."

"No, no, you are just seeing how far my patience will carry me. If it were true, I would——" He breathed quickly for a moment or two, and Marya could see that his lips were drawn tight and hard over his teeth, and her heart grew sick for Olga.

"Go on," he said, quietly, after a while, "go on; finish your fairy tale."

Marya knew the tone; it had the power to quell her spirit and make her meanly submit her will to his; but the remembrance of the meeting in David's room, his face, Olga's love for him, the certain knowledge that a power greater than a man's had brought these two people together, steeled her to it now. Feeling the happiness of these two dependent upon her alone, it lost its potency to wound or silence. She began in a firm, calm voice, saying,—

"You remember that I wanted a crucifix for my

sister Catherine, do you not, and that I could not find any silversmith here to make it for me? Well, this morning, while I was dressing, I suddenly thought of David Rheba, who made that wonderful rose-water dish for Princess Czartoryski. I sent for his address, and called on him to-day to ask him to undertake the work for me. Olga was with me——"

"Stay, one moment," interrupted Michael. "You asked a Jew to make a crucifix?"

"Yes. I hesitated a long time, because I feared it might pain him, but——"

Again Michael interrupted her, but this time with harsh laugh after laugh. At last, wiping his eyes with his handkerchief, he said,—

"Well, that's the grimmest joke I've ever heard! Why, even I should not have thought of that."

"You do not understand," she said. "I went to David Rheba as to a skilled workman, and not because I wished to insult him. Indeed, I did not realise that he was a Jew until I saw that my request pained him."

"Oh! So he was pained, was he, the dog?"

"How cruelly you wrong these poor people!"

"Well! well! go on! What about Olga?"

"She loves the man."

"Was that why she was sobbing?"

"No; she was sobbing because she learned for the first time to-day that Christ was a Jew."

"Who told you that?" he cried.

"No one in the convent, Michael; I found it out for myself."

"You found it out for yourself? How?"

"By reading, thinking, reasoning of things."

"You mean it is your sister who has poisoned your mind since she abjured the Holy Orthodox Church."

Marya smiled. "She has not spoken of it; indeed, I think that, like yourself, she has never questioned what she has been told."

"And you, my wife, believe that the God you worship was a Jew?"

"Yes, I believe it."

"Now, at last, I understand!" he cried. "This is the thing which has come between us; this is the thing which has been growing in your mind, making you shrink from my friends, from what I consider your duties as a wife, while I imagined it was your love of a quiet, simple life."

"I do not understand you," she exclaimed.

"Ah, no," he sneered; "it does not suit you to understand; and now that your own mind is poisoned and defiled with this horrible sophistry, you seek to poison others, but I say you shall not!" He sprang to his feet, towering over her, his face ghastly pale, his hands twitching.

Marya thought that he was going to strike her, and sat looking at him without a word. Wolf whimpered and crept close to her feet.

"My God! and I loved you," he whispered, and sank down with his head bowed almost to his knees. Presently he started up again and stood over her, saying,—

"Have you not told Olga that Christ was a Jew?"

"Yes; I thought it best that she should know the truth."

"But you shall tell her it is a lie! Christ was God! How, then, could he be a Jew?"

"I cannot agree with you that Christ was God. I believe that Christ was a Jew, that he was filled full of the Spirit of God, as we may be filled full if we choose. It was God speaking that Truth through him, and inspiring him to teach it, that for a time made paradise of one corner of the earth." Marya raised her face; it was very pale; it seemed almost that a white light was shining throught it.

"A heretic!" he cried, his voice rising almost to a shriek. "You, my wife, a heretic!" In a sudden fit of frenzy he seized both her wrists in one hand, while with the other he forced her head back by the hair till her long white throat lay upwards in the moonlight, strained and curved like a bent bow. He peered into her face. No sign there of the beast which he felt had taken possession of her and destroyed for ever her purity and sweetness. Marya closed her eyes; she became silent as stone. Michael looked down on her, his breath coming in quick, panting gasps. He let his eyes travel from her smooth brow, pale, trembling little mouth, to her perfect throat. He thought of the many happy times he had kissed it rosy red for very love of its loveliness, thinking it only one of the outward signs of her beautiful soul. His knees began to tremble; his rage ebbed for a moment, then it welled up again, overwhelming all the better part of his nature, stripping away in its course every scrap of the veneer of civilization, leaving him frankly the savage he was under his fine manners and cultured speech.

He stooped over her, his face distorted, his eyes like a wild beast's.

"Hypocrite, liar, heretic!" he tried to hiss in her face, but instead he mouthed and stuttered, gnashing his teeth madly in his fury, that speech would not come to him, till at last, with a wild cry, he snatched her up fiercely in his arms, then flung her down again upon the seat and rushed from the room, cursing and muttering under his breath, gesticulating like a madman, and so into his own rooms. Up and down he raged, setting his nails deep into his flesh to restrain with actual physical pain the strong craving to tear, and rend, and lay waste everything within the house. He raved, bit at his hands, now and again howling like a wild beast. Not one of the serfs heeded the sounds: they knew the master's moods and the danger to themselves of trying to stem them. Thus through the night he fought with the brute that was in him. By sunrise he had subdued himself, then he sent for his confessor, and sat with him till his steward came with the message that the secretaries were waiting for work.

For five weeks neither he nor Marya saw each other until one evening he suddenly appeared at the supper-table. Marya was sitting there pale and thin-looking, but she met his eyes without shrinking. She knew his fanaticism and the horror the discovery of her belief would be to him. She had tried to regard his act as the act of a madman, but the shock to her love and trust had been too great to be reasoned away.

During supper he was polite, slightly contemptuous, coldly tolerant of her. The spiritual bond between them was broken. To him now she was simply an animal who by her own will had cast away her better part, but who was still useful to him in many ways: ways which, somehow, had grown to be part of his life, and which he had been asking himself for the past five weeks whether he were strong enough to put aside and all the sweetness and joy they made for him, and the answer had been a definite and decided "No." He had discovered that he drew inspiration from her very presence. That no one could create for him such dreams of future greatness as she when reading aloud or singing; no one give such impetus or strength to his every thought as she by the atmosphere which radiated from her to him. And so while hating himself for his dependence, which he could neither fathom nor master, he came back to her, expecting, even though regarding her as a thing without a soul, to draw the same bounty from her love.

The very thought he brought with him made this impossible,—made Marya insensibly shrink from his eyes and from his touch, and at the end of the evening he went back to his rooms dissatisfied and irritable, and Marya went to her bed and wept with a subtle sense of degradation that he no longer regarded her as his wife, but merely as a useful little plaything he could not get on very well without, because it helped to make the wheels of his life go round smoothly.

CHAPTER V.

MORNING TIME.

David was up before sunrise the morning following his meeting with Olga. First he plunged his face and arms into a vessel of cold water which stood by the stove, then he towelled himself down, dressed, and after having prayed fervently, with his face to the east, he stood thinking for a moment, silent, then presently saying,—

"Yes, I will go; it may be that she is stirring, though it is hardly light." He started off and out to the west side of the town, where Michael Volkenoff's house stood, a good mile away. No one had told him the house lay west; instinct led him, and he obeyed, being still so young at heart that to feel was to act. So on he went, drawing in eagerly the keen, fresh air, lifting now and again his face to the vast space of sky and to the stars that were by now losing their light in the flush from the rising sun.

On he went, never doubting he should see Olga. David with a song in his heart, his soul aglow; David going to meet the sweet, mild-eyed maiden who held all his life, his future, in her two small hands.

And Olga! she too wakened before dawn and lay wondering awhile whether she might venture out so early with Wolf for his morning run. And trembling, scarce confessing to herself why, she sprang up, and in a short space of time she was dressed and muffled in her sleeved fur-lined cloak and hood, and was stealing along the hall to where the dog lay on the rug outside Marya's door. He sniffed at the cloak and frisked about; it meant a race in the free air and fun and frolic with Olga; but she whispered "Hush!" and, taking him by the collar, she crept down to the Little Mother's door and slipped out, closing it softly behind her. She let Wolf go the moment they were outside the court-yard, with an inward laugh at Ivan, who slept in the lodge, and who boasted of his quick ears, and who for all his quickness had not heard the bar which had fallen from her hand with a crash on the stones when she lifted it from the holdfasts of the gate.

"Now, boy, now!" she said to the dog, when they were some little distance from the house, and away they flew side by side over the hard, white, frozen road. And so on she ran, lessening the distance every moment between herself and David. Never had the air been so full of the scent of the sea, the sky so deep and blue, the stars so wonderful to her as now, though growing pale and dim in the light from the east.

Suddenly she stopped. A man had turned the corner of the opposite side of the street and was coming towards her with swinging stride and head erect.

It was David.

Her first impulse was to run away, and she darted into the porch of an old wooden house near by and huddled up close to the door, Wolf after her, regarding her curiously.

A SON OF ISRAEL

On came David, swift and firm of foot, on, past the house, to the end of the street where the houses became scattered into twos and threes with spaces between.

Olga craned forth her head and watched him, with her heart leaping up into her throat.

He stopped and looked about, seemingly uncertain which way to go, and, turning, crossed the road and came back down the street on Olga's side.

Olga set her hands hard against her heart to still its leaping. Her blood surged and flowed so swiftly through her veins and made such a drumming in her ears she couldn't hear his steps, and Wolf, amazed at her hurried breathing, sat down on the step with his back to the street and looked up at her, making rapid little taps on the steps with his tail to express his desire to help. On came David, more slowly now, wondering what had attracted him from the sun to the shady side of the road. He was now close upon the house where Olga was hiding in the porch. She trembled and grew cold with fear. Suppose he should pass not knowing she was there and they two never meet again. With a sudden, impulsive movement she thrust forth her right hand, with the little thimble shining brightly upon her second finger, beyond the lintel of the doorway, and then covered her rosy face with a corner of her cloak, half laughing, trembling, longing, dreading to see him; hungry for his voice, his eyes on hers, and yet fearing them, and waited. Presently she felt David's warm, strong hands take possession of her hand. He came up the wooden steps to her side, when suddenly down slipped the cloak from her face, and she looked shyly at him; smiles dimpling her face, tears in her eyes. Back and forth from each to each sped the full, pure rush of soul to soul. Earth, sky, and air seemed to flush rosy-red, wonderful music to peal around them, and they two the only beings in all the world.

A sleepy, dull-eyed old servant with a broom in his hand to sweep away the snow opened the door behind them. They heard him not. He softly closed the door again, and, smiling, went to other work, saying, "I, too, once was young."

"Thou hast come," she whispered at last.

"And thou," he replied.

No more was said; it was enough that they were together. They walked slowly on, hand in hand, towards the road which led to Michael's house, the dog following after.

At the entrance to the court-yard Olga raised her eyes frankly to David's and said, simply,—

"Thou wilt come again to-morrow?"

"Surely! And thou?" he asked.

"Surely!" she smiled, repeating his own word; then she ran in, and David stood with bared head, watching her until she disappeared round an angle of the house; then he put on his cap and strode off home to work.

Olga went straight to Marya's room, without waiting to remove her cloak and hood. Marya was in a restless, troubled sleep, her face white, her eyelids red and swollen from the tears she had shed. Wolf whined and snuggled his nose against her shoulder, standing up on his hind legs to reach her.

"Down, boy, down!" whispered Olga. But Marya wakened at the old dog's touch, and her hand went out instinctively to his head, fondling it. Then she looked at Olga.

"Well, Olga," she said. Suddenly, remembering how bitterly she had wept during the night, she turned away her face to hide it from the girl.

"Thou art in trouble," said Olga, brokenly, kneeling down by the bed.

"Trouble!" Marya gave a little sobbing laugh. "Nay,"—she turned her face again and laid her cheek on Olga's hands,—"there is no trouble where thou art. Why, how sweet thy cloak doth smell! It is full of the scent of the sea. Hast thou been out already?"

"Yes, mistress, and—— I have come to see whether thou art ready for thy bath."

"Not yet; I will take my coffee first. What has happened this morning?" Marya raised herself on her elbow and looked in Olga's face.

"Mistress! ... I have seen him ... David Rheba." Olga began to straighten out the lace on Marya's nightgown, her voice faltering, her face aglow. "And—and it was that which I came to tell thee, not to ask about thy bath."

Marya lay back on her pillow, sighing to herself,—

"God help thee, child." Then, seeing that Olga was anxiously watching her, she smiled,—

"That was right not to keep it from me. Come

now, sit here on my bed and tell me how it happened that thou didst see David Rheba so early."

Olga, nothing loath, told Marya the whole, from the time she awoke to the time she returned and left David at the gate; and such was the girl's fervent delight that she had seen her lover, such her serene faith and trust that God had given her to David and so no man could put them asunder, that Marya's misgivings were swept away and she was beguiled into forgetting her own pain and sorrow, and for a while lived only in Olga's joy.

Michael Volkenoff had seen Olga and David part at the gate. During the afternoon he stopped her as she was crossing the court-yard with some money for a poor Jewess who was sick and who had often, unknown to Michael, done fine needle-work for Marya.

"Who was the man you were speaking to at the gate this morning?" he asked, sternly.

"David Rheba, Excellency," answered Olga.

"And who is David Rheba?" he sneered.

"A Jew," she answered, proudly lifting her head.

He looked at her sharply from under his brows.

"You may go," he said, abruptly.

Olga left him with a slight inclination of her head and went on to the gate.

"Curse her!" he muttered; "in her soul, I believe, she is a Jewess, else how could she love this vermin, this rat? Oh, that I had the power to sweep the whole race into the sea like the swine they are kindred to!" he muttered, and turned, muttering, into the house and called for Nicolas.

"Is your son still in the town?"

"No, Excellency; the steward gave him permission to go to the Crimea; he can make more money there in winter-time than in Odessa."

"He wished to marry the girl Olga. Take this note to the steward. Let someone be despatched to bring your son back without delay."

"He cannot be here in less than four or five weeks, Excellency," said Nicolas. He, too, had seen the parting between Olga and David.

"The master of this house is a Christian," said Michael Volkenoff, and went without more words into his room.

Olga ran to the gate. She was troubled; she had been insolent to the master; she knew the serfs were often whipped for less than that, but how could she help it? His tone, his eyes, had made something hard and fierce, something she had never felt before, burn in her heart and beat up in her throat, and it would out.

Near the gate, some few steps away, she found Miriam Ludolfino, the sister of the sick Jewess, waiting. Olga called to her and gave her the money Marya had sent and a warm, woollen kerchief of her own, saying,—

"May this be of comfort to your sister."

Miriam clutched the shawl, scarce able to believe her ears. Olga had always thrust whatever she might have to give from Marya into her hand, and then had shrunk away as though she feared some contagion. What miracle had happened?

"You are to come again to-morrow," said Olga; then she smiled: almost the same words she had used at parting from David.

"I will remember," said Miriam, gratefully, then she sped away.

"One of his people," murmured Olga; "one of his people, and one of Christ's."

CHAPTER VI.

IN BONDAGE.

David walked on, feeling that all the world was coloured golden and rose, the air full of music and sunshine. Everyone he met seemed to wear a smiling face. So on he went swiftly, till at last he realised that every step took him farther from Olga; then he paused, and began to count the hours until the next morning.

"From now to sunrise to-morrow, twenty-three hours," he muttered, ruefully. "Twenty-three; it is a lifetime!" He turned back in the direction of Michael Volkenoff's house. When nearly half-way there he said, resolutely,—

"No, no, I must home to work for her, for her!" he smiled, already regarding Olga as his wife. He walked back again homewards, walking slowly, deep in a pleasant dream. He saw Olga flitting about his room, now sewing, then again preparing the meals or helping with his work, as his mother had been wont to do for his father. He stood still at last in a street not far from the Jews' Quarter and saw himself bending over Olga, showing her how to polish the finished work with the palm of her hand.

"The little tender hand," he smiled, shaking his head. "I doubt but the work will be too rough for it."

"Is that how you finish my bowl and ewer?" said some one, laughingly, in his ear.

David looked round half dreamily. It was John Pemberton.

"And yet I was thinking of it. Of that and *Olga*," smiled David.

"Got so far as thinking of the work?" asked John Pemberton, hopefully.

"Yes. Yesterday after you were gone from me God spoke, and I have the whole here and here;" and David touched his head and his heart. "Come now back with me and you shall see."

"Well, I will, though I haven't eaten breakfast yet."

"We'll buy some rolls as we go along," laughed David, "and you shall make the coffee. It won't be the first time you've done that for me when I have been full of work."

The two walked on briskly side by side, talking and laughing on the way.

David went into the first baker's he came to within the Jewish quarter, bought some rolls, and then on again to his room. While John Pemberton put out the cups David took off his coat, put on his leathern apron, then going to his forge, he puffed away at the embers with the bellows, and soon the charcoal was glowing bright red.

"Set the water here," he said, then he sat down on his stool and took the convex side of the bowl on his lap and began to tap away at it with a small hammer sheathed in leather.

"Well, you have made progress!" cried John Pemberton, pausing by him with the coffee-pot in his hand. "It will be ready before the time you named."

David shook his head.

"There is the concave side yet," he said.

"You intend to chase both the concave and the convex?"

"Yes; there is the design." He gave the sketch which he had made to John Pemberton.

"Perfect! Perfect!" cried John, his face beaming. "And the ewer?"

"That," and David gave him another smaller sketch.

John Pemberton looked critically at it for a while, then he gave a long satisfied "Ah!" and stood smiling at David, with the coffee-pot in one hand, the sketch in the other.

"Rheba," he cried, "I had nearly given up all hope of getting this ewer and basin! I had, on my faith; but this is worth waiting twenty years for."

"Wait until it is finished," said David; "it may not turn out all you expect."

"I know, David Rheba," nodded John Pemberton, laying down the sketch and proceeding to make the coffee. While it was simmering he sat down on David's bed and said,—

"By the way, Rheba, who is the Olga you spoke of when I met you this morning?"

"I? I spoke to you of her?" said David, amazed.

"You certainly did. You said you were thinking of the ewer and basin, and *Olga*."

"I did so?" asked David.

John Pemberton smiled. "Well, if it wasn't Olga, it was a name very like it."

"I was thinking of her, I know," said David, frankly, "but——" He looked wistfully at John Pemberton. Should he tell this matter-of-fact Englishman that he had found his mate? At that moment there was just a softening of his friend's keen eyes, so he said,—

"Well, then, I will tell you. Olga——" David paused, his breath came quickly; he had spoken the name, the beloved name, for the first time to another. A mist seemed to swim before his eyes, and in it was her face. His strong brown hands gripped hard at the bowl for a moment, then he said, quickly, fervently,—

"That which I told you of has revealed itself. It was for her that I waited,—the other half of my soul, the purer and diviner part of me, the woman God hath given unto me,—Olga." He sprang up and seized John Pemberton's hands. "How shall I make you understand? Ah! if I might but speak Hebrew to you! You should know then all that I have here of joy, and delight, and delicious pain."

John Pemberton shook David's hands heartily in silence for a second or two; then he coughed. Thorough Englishman that he was, it was his only way of expressing what he felt. He was sincerely happy to find that David was in love, but David's intensity made him feel bashful as a girl.

"Who is she?" he managed to say after a while.

"She is a Russian girl."

"Not one of your own people, then?"

David shook his head.

John Pemberton raised his eyebrows, got up, drew the coffee-pot away from the fire in the forge, then sat down again and looked anxiously at David.

"Where did you meet her?" he asked.

"She came here yesterday with her mistress," said David.

"You don't mean to say that she is a serf?"

"A serf!" David repeated after him. "What is that?"

"Surely you haven't lived all these years in Russia without knowing that nearly all the servants here are serfs?"

"Yes, yes, I know; but she—I had not thought of her as a serf——"

"Or that her mistress might sell her any day if she so please."

"Sell her!" David sprang up again to his feet. "She is not a slave!"

"No; but some of these Russians treat their serfs as though they were slaves."

"Slaves! No, no!" exclaimed David.

"No? Then listen here to this advertisement in the *Moscow Gazette;*" and John Pemberton pulled a newspaper out of his coat-pocket and began to read,—

"TO BE SOLD—Three coachmen, well trained and handsome, and two girls, the one eighteen and the other fifteen years of age, both of them good-looking and well acquainted with various kinds of handiwork. In the same house there are for sale two hair-dressers: the one, twenty-one years of age, can read, write, play on a musical instrument, and act as huntsman, besides dressing hair in any fashion or style."

"An extremely versatile young man," laughed John Pemberton; then he added, again reading from the *Gazette,* "'the other can also dress ladies' and gentlemen's hair. In the same house are sold pianos and organs.' And here, a little farther on, I see a first-class clerk, a carver, and a lackey offered for sale, and the reason given for their being disposed of is a superabundance of the 'articles.' I intend to cut this out and send it to some Russian friends of mine in England, who declare there are no slaves in their country."

David sat silent, with his brows bent, thinking.

"It seems to me, Rheba," said John Pemberton, "that you'll make a big muddle of your life if you don't give this up."

David didn't reply; he began working again at the bowl in his lap.

"Here are you, a Jew, in love with a Russian girl who is not even free. She is a serf, and, of course," cried John, "she is a Christian!"

"That is very likely," said David, quietly.

"Then how can you marry her? Would your rabbi marry you to a Christian? or would her priest marry her to an infidel, as he would call you?" said John, excitedly.

David looked up, smiled, and said,—

"All that you say seems so little, so small, beside the fact that she is to me what Rachel was to Jacob. I would serve three times seven years for her, and three times seven years again, if at the end I might but live one day in the light of her eyes."

"Ah! that's like a lover," said John, grimly, getting

up and straining the coffee into a jug he had stood by the forge fire to warm. "You forget that at the end of the twice three times seven years your Olga would be a middle-aged woman, with not much light in her eyes to speak of."

David laughed, an infectious, ringing laugh, at the idea of Olga's eyes ever growing dull, and his friend laughed, too, as he set the jug of coffee on the table.

"Come!" he said, "the coffee is ready."

"Bring mine hitherward!" cried David; "I'll eat and work at the same time."

"Oh, very well. There! isn't that a cup of coffee fit for a king?" he cried, pouring out a cupful for David and waiting, with his eyes twinkling full of pride in his office of coffee-maker.

"Or for a workman," cried David.

"Well, I might have said that with truth," answered John, bringing his own coffee and roll and sitting down opposite David.

"Seriously, now, Rheba," he said, "this matter of the serf girl may be a bad thing for you. Who is her master?"

David winced at the word master. "Michael Volkenoff," he answered.

"Don't know him."

"Nor do I. But there is one thing you have thought not of, John Pemberton: that if he be her master and have power to sell her, why should not I——"

"Buy her?" asked John.

David nodded; he didn't care to use the words himself.

"Well, why not?" said John Pemberton, in reply to the nod.

"So we will work! work! work!" cried David, tapping away at the bowl. "Your basin and ewer shall be finished before perhaps you have the money ready for them. Ha! ha! how we will work!" he laughed between his bites at the roll and his draughts of hot coffee, and then working away again excitedly at the bowl in his lap.

"Where shall I put the cups?" asked John, when they had finished.

"Stand them there on the top of the stove; Judith shall see to them for me; and if there is some coffee left, leave it on the forge in the jug."

"Now I'll be off, Rheba; I have to see Princess Czartoryski before twelve. Farewell for the present; I'll look in directly I return from Petersburg."

"Farewell!" cried David.

"I'm half sorry I have never been in love myself," John sighed, as he went down the stairs, "real, genuine, overwhelming love like this. It is amazing what an effect it has had on David Rheba. I've never seen him so much alive. It must have its discomforts, though," he mused, stopping in the middle of the narrow street. "Perhaps it would be rather risky for me at my time of life, even if I had the capacity. That's just it! Has any Englishman the capacity of being absorbingly, madly in love, to the exclusion of everything else, even of himself? If there is, I've never met him," he growled, going on his way.

CHAPTER VII.

JUDITH MANUELLI.

About noon, Judith, wife of Ezra Manuelli and Salome's mother, tapped at David's door.

"I am here!" he cried; "enter. Is it thee, Judith?" he said, seeing her. "I shall need thee for four or five weeks to keep my room clean. See, I have begun."

"So!" Judith said, with a faint smile, and she sat down listlessly on the foot of his bed. "I see thou hast begun." She was thin, almost emaciated; her face and hands bloodless and grey in their unhealthy pallor; she had deep-set, sorrowful dark eyes and a mass of thick, tangled black hair, half pinned up, half straggling down her neck.

David looked sharply at her, then he said,—

"There is some coffee in the jug there and two rolls."

Judith darted upon them and was going.

"Come back!" cried David. "Now close the door and sit there." He pointed to his bed.

Judith obeyed him, looking at him with feverish, hungry impatience. He took the jug, poured out a cup of coffee and gave it to her.

"Now eat and drink," he said, sternly, going back to his work, "and tell me what it is thou hast come to say."

"But the children are hungry, David, and Ezra——" she pleaded.

"Shall have the roll and coffee that is left. I've just awakened to the fact that thou art starving thyself for those children of thine;" again he looked sharply at her with eyes which seemed to be newly opened.

Judith watched him, dipping her bread in the coffee and eating it slowly, hoping that he would presently relapse into his old engrossed way, deaf and blind to everything around him when fired with a fresh idea for his work, so that then she might slip part of the roll into her pocket. But not so to-day. He worked on as usual, as though he were being burnt up with the fervour of his inspiration, but now and again lifting his eyes to her, so she had no chance. With a sigh she finished the last crumb.

"Now, what is it thou hast come to say?" he said, and smiled at her.

"Well, it is this——" and her wan face flushed a little, for Judith Manuelli was proud, and, though it was David who kept her children from starvation, she could not endure to ask him for help. "It is this——" She hesitated.

"Well?" asked David.

"Daniel Pereira, the great *impresario*,—indeed, he is the most celebrated and greatest *impresario* in all Europe, Kezia told me,—is coming to-night to see Salome dance, and Ezra said if we could eat our evening meal with thee and receive him here afterwards in thy room—— It is the Sabbath——"

David nodded impatiently. "I know, I know; it is the Sabbath."

"Thou couldst not work to-night."

"No, thou art right; though, if thou but knew the need I have to work! . . . But come, then, all of ye," he said, pencilling out the design on a fresh section of the bowl; "but before thou goest make my bed and prepare the table. Thou wilt find a white linen cloth in the chest."

"Kezia, the Meldola, will be with us," said Judith, nervously, shaking the bedclothes and looking at David from under her eyelids.

"The dancing-woman," he said, frowning.

"She is old now, David, and she hath taught Salome and never asked for payment."

"But she is one of those who bring reproach upon our race by turning to harlotry. I cannot eat with her. She is unclean."

"But it is so many years since she sinned, and she hath wept such tears to me——"

"I cannot eat with her. My mother hath sat at that table. And Olga! . . . No, she shall not enter my door."

"Then I know not what we shall do, for there are things which only she can explain to Daniel Pereira."

"Take him, then, to her room," said David.

"She is poor as we are, and she wants not Daniel Pereira to see her poverty."

"It is useless, Judith, I have said."

Judith sighed heavily.

"Come!" cried David; "I can explain to him. Salome hath often practised here."

"Oh, if thou canst!"

"Well, I will endeavour. Now, what of supper?"

"Alas! Ezra hath been running about since sunrise, and he hath not earned that." She swept one hand across the other with an expressive gesture, signifying "nothing."

"Take this." He gave her a silver coin. "It is the last I have till this work is finished, so bring me the change, and buy as much bread and as much else as thou canst for as little as thou canst."

"A rouble, David!"

"As I told thee, it is my last. Now go, and do bring a smile on that pale face of thine when thou comest with Ezra and the children."

"Ah, David, how good thou art!" she cried; and before he could stay her she had clasped his head, had kissed him twice upon the cheek, and was gone.

CHAPTER VIII.

"LA MELDOLA."

DANIEL PEREIRA was, as Judith had told David, the greatest *impresario* of his day. He had never been known to make a mistake. His judgment was infallible, and, added to his grand, intellectual qualities, he had the rarer qualities of sympathy, and an intuition which was almost divination. He knew instantly whether the people he "discovered" were those who would simply use him as a ladder to climb by when they had secured the *cachet* of his name, or whether he would be to them always the kind master who had found them and set them on the path to fame and honour, and they his devoted friends. To the first kind he was hard, exacting to the uttermost farthing the terms of his contract, but to the other kind, the loyal, the poorer they were the greater his pleasure in helping them. If it happened that they possessed genius for either acting or dancing, or that God's gift, a voice, he would have them educated, trained, fed, and clothed at his own expense, and in some cases paying a small salary from the very commencement of their apprenticeship, when their relations were very poor, for the simple love and delight of giving yet another great artist to the stage. And as a man's good qualities are seldom heard of, his bad trumpeted in every street, so Daniel Pereira was more chiefly known as a grasping, sharp-dealing man, who knew how to make a good bargain for his own profit, than as the generous, great-hearted man that he really was.

He was always looking out for genius. Talented people he could have found by the dozens, but he was content to leave them if he found but one black swan in a year. Sometimes it happened he was lucky enough to find two. He trusted no agents. He would travel over the whole of the known world to get what he sought, and thus it was that the winter of 184- found him in Odessa, and there, strolling into the theatre one morning, he saw a ballet mistress, dressed in a shabby black silk and a dirty woollen shawl over her shoulders, rehearsing some dozen girls or so on the stage in a dance for the opera which was to be given on the Sunday night. She was a tall woman, and so thin that she seemed literally but skin and bone.

He looked on for a moment or two from the back of a box at the girls' heavy one, two, three; one, two, three steps to the right, a swing round of the body, then three steps to the left, and smiled, thinking, "Nothing here, at all events." Suddenly the ballet mistress lifted up her hands with a quick, passionate gesture and shook them at her pupils, screaming,—

"God of my fathers! what is this? What are your legs made of, eh? wood, or putty, or what? Am I to teach! teach! teach! and this to be the result?" And she mimicked the girls' stiff, wooden movements.

"Dance with your heads, your hearts, with every

vein of your stupid, sleepy, Russian bodies,—like this."
And she swept them to right and left of the stage,
flung her shawl contemptuously at the girl nearest to
her, twisted her old black silk skirt up round her waist,
fastening it with a hair-pin which she tore out of her
hair, gave a nod to a solitary fiddler sitting in the orchestra, and began to dance. Ah, the difference! the
perfect, wonderful grace!

Daniel Pereira leaned forward, a mist clouding his
keen eyes for a moment. Something in the woman's
style was familiar to him.

"It is Kezia! La Meldola!" he murmured; "and
come to this."

Yes, it was Kezia, his first great discovery. He had
found her one sunny day in old Rome, dancing in the
Ghetto, wild and unfettered as the wind, and beautiful
and golden as the sun itself, which was shining down
on her ruddy hair, and wonderful deep grey eyes and
straight black brows. And this was she! This! This
old, haggard, hollow-eyed woman, with scanty, discoloured hair, streaked with grey; fierce, hungry face,
and hands like the claws of a bird of prey.

She ended her dance and swept down to the footlights, unpinning her skirt as she went.

"Now, let me see you do something like that, if you
can!" she said, scornfully.

The girls formed again into two rows and went
through their steps once more.

"Did you ever see the like?" cried Kezia, turning
in despair to the fiddler.

"They are better than they were," said the man,

lifting a pair of patient, dim old eyes to her face. "But why do not you yourself dance to-night?"

"I?" she cried. "Look at that!" and she bared her arms and flourished them at him, "and that!" and she lifted her skirt and thrust out a slender foot in an old slipper and a leg that the stocking hung on like a loose, dun-coloured bag. "Why, the audience would throw the seats at me. No, no; I am not intending to lose the glory of my name by appearing now. I am— ugh! You can see that which I am." She spread out her hands in derision of herself, and went on once more with the rehearsal. In about half an hour she dismissed the girls, telling them they were only fit for kitchen-maids. Some went away crestfallen, while the others muttered they'd rather be that than have her legs.

Kezia sat down on a stool in the wings, changed her slippers for thick boots, and then began to pin up her hair. The fiddler leisurely put his violin in the case before going to his noonday meal. Daniel Pereira made his way behind the scenes and met Kezia just as she was rolling a thick, heavy shawl over her head and shoulders to go home.

"Pereira!" she gasped. Then she stood with her eyelids lowered, her thin breast heaving with shame and anger that he, of all men, should see her now.

"You are going home?" he said in Italian, raising his hat; "may I walk with you?"

"With me!" Kezia looked at him and laughed bitterly.

"Why did you not let me know that you were

come to this?" His voice trembled; he had loved the woman.

"No," she muttered, twisting herself away from the light, that he might not see the wrinkles in her face. "If I was too proud to be your wife when you wanted me thirty years ago, I was too vain to let you know I was past work and take what would have been charity."

"But you are so thin. . . . You look half starved."

"Oh, no; I am only taking care of the money I earn. I am hoarding, hoarding every penny," she said, passionately. "I, La Meldola, who used to throw away her thousands every year, am hoarding. Ha! ha! ha!" she laughed, "because I have known what it is to want bread, and do not mean to suffer that pain again."

Daniel shivered and looked at her. Some of the old, subtle fascination clung to her, in the movements of her lithe body, in the flashes of her great hollow eyes, which were filled with a world of remorse and regret that seemed to be drying up the life in her blood.

"After my illness in Petersburg I found I was ruined," she said, leaning against a side scene, her back to the light. "I thought my beauty would last for ever; that too went, so, rather than linger on till I was hissed off the stage, I disappeared, came here, and here you see me."

The fiddler had been a long time putting his violin in its case. He had been listening dreamily to the beautiful, liquid Italian, though he could not understand a syllable of it; anything with music in it filling his soul with rapture. And besides, he had another reason for lingering. Kezia had once or twice given him an engagement to play at the private lessons she gave to one of her pupils, a daughter of one of the actors. So he waited, hoping she might require him again soon.

"And have you no friends?" asked Daniel.

"One or two," she answered. "Not the old sort!" she flashed out. "They went with my money, and it was a pity they didn't go before," she muttered, wearily, with a shrug of her shoulders. "But those I have now—— Ah!" she cried out, suddenly grasping his arm and looking eagerly into his face, her voice shaking, becoming husky in the excitement which rushed upon her.

"You are the man I want. God of my people, why have I not thought of you before? Karl Helfmann! Karl Helfmann!" she screamed, breaking off in the midst of her words and darting down to the foot-lights. "Ah, you are there!" she panted; "come to-night, to my room, I shall want you. Be there by seven." Pereira had followed her.

"It is of Salome! Salome that I want to tell you," she said, vehemently, turning to him.

"Oh, that I could pour it all out like old Tiber at flood-tide when it dashes against the houses in the Ghetto! She! she! Oh, how can I describe her to you! She is music, dance, poetry, colour, sunlight! She was created to dance, from her little, curly head to her wonderful, slender feet. If she hears music her blood is all one glorious rhythm of movement with it; there is not an action that is out of tune. She is a genius. You shall see her. Ah, Salome, my pearl, thou shalt be what I was, yet not like me, for there is good in thy soul, not evil, as was in mine. Kings shall bow down to thee! Thy mother shall never wail for bread again."

"Is she your daughter?"

"My daughter!" She drew herself to her full height and looked at him with a strange expression of woe, yearning, and defiance in her face. "Have you ever known God give children to such women as I?" She shrugged her shoulders. "She is a child of one of our own people, Judith Manuelli. Wait till you see her. Wait till she moves to the music light as the morning mist on the face of the waters. Till to-night!" she cried, and started off to the stage door.

"But you have not told me where I am to see her," said Daniel Pereira, following her and smiling.

"Oh, my head!" she cried, clutching it with both hands and shaking it. "It is as stupid as it always was. Why, in my room to-night at seven."

"Let me walk with you and talk over the old days," said Daniel, interrupting her, "before you were famous."

"Haven't you forgotten?"

He shook his head.

"You are not married?"

"There was only one woman I wished to make my wife."

"And that was——"

"Yes—yourself."

"It was a fortunate thing I didn't let you. I should have fallen just as madly in love with that man, and"—giving a half-comic, side-long glance at Daniel—"with all the others. And the only thing I regret about it is that my youth is gone and the loss of my people's love. They loathe me. It consumes me as with fire when I think of it. Oh, God! if I might but creep back to the old, sunny room in the Ghetto and die there!" she cried, passionately, no tears in her eyes, only the hunger and undying regret.

"Come," she said, "you shall walk with me. Tell me, are my sisters and brothers still alive?"

So they walked out of the theatre, and slowly on to the Jews' Quarter, where Daniel left her at the door of the house, promising to come again at seven.

CHAPTER IX.

FINE FEATHERS.

DAVID worked on till it was close upon sunset; then when he found the light growing dim within his room he jumped up from his work, laid down his tools, covered up the embers on the forge, and, after he had lighted a fire in the stove and the candles in the two tall candlesticks placed ready on the table by Judith, stood with his arms folded, leaning by the window and thinking of Olga. What was she doing? What thinking? What saying? He pictured her with her frank, tender, fearless eyes looking out eastwards; looking towards his home.

"Oh, if I could but draw thee to me!" he cried; "make thee free! give thee liberty! And I will! I will! I will toil for thee! Thou shalt be free as the birds of the air, bondwoman though thou art! I will sell myself to Michael Volkenoff. He shall be master of me and of my work. I will be his slave if he will but give thee thy freedom."

Then he was silent and fell a-dreaming again, while the sun dropped down in the west a great red ball of fire, and the twilight thickened in the street below.

"David! David! David!" screamed Salome. David could hear her flying up the stairs. "Open thy door, and open thine eyes! Something is coming, something so wonderful! something so beautiful!"

She stood on the threshold holding the door half open in her hand, shrouded from head to feet in an old sheet.

"Look not at me yet, or all my effect will be spoilt."

"But I can see thee," said David. "What hast thou on?" He pulled her into the middle of the room and turned her round.

"Close thine eyes," she cried, springing away from him, "and wait now till I say 'Look!'" David obeyed.

She threw off the sheet she was wrapped in, and when she had done that she carefully placed herself so that the light from the candles fell full upon her, then, with her great eyes sparkling with joyous expectation of the surprise she had in store for him, she cried,—

"Look!"

David opened his eyes and could not speak for a moment for wonder, Salome enjoying his amazement immensely.

She was dressed in a quaint, short-waisted frock of purple velvet with slashed sleeves, and soft hanging ruffles of lace at the neck and wrists, and velvet shoes and silk stockings of the same colour as the velvet frock, her wonderful dark curls hanging round her pale face and neck in the wildest confusion. She kept making him dainty little curtsies with her frock delicately lifted by the very tips of her thumbs and forefingers, till she finally broke into a wild, whirling dance, ending with a joyous, ringing laugh and a spring into his arms.

"There! did I not say it was something beautiful? wonderful?" she asked, panting.

"Yes, indeed!"

"Now put me down and look at me again. There!" she murmured, when she was once more on her feet and turning round and round like a tetotum. "Now tell me what I am most like."

David looked at her, almost expecting to wake and find that he was dreaming.

"Well, what am I like?" she cried, impatiently; "tell me, quick!"

"Well, thou art like—like a bunch of purple grapes from a vineyard on Lebanon, or like the violet mist which steals over the hills at eventide."

"The violet mist is most rare, so thou shalt tell mother that. She hath said to everyone, 'Tell me, what is my little Salome like?' Belah said I was like a great poppy."

"But how didst thou come by all this finery?" asked David, touching her frock.

"Kezia coaxed Marfa Ivanavan, the woman who buys cast-off clothes for the theatre, to lend it to us that I may look well before Daniel Pereira."

David was silent.

"But thou hast not said how good my frock is. See! it is the finest Lyons velvet, mother says. Look! it is lined with yellow silk. And my petticoat, see!" She caught up her skirt and twirled round, displaying a soft, white lawn petticoat with lace on the edge. "There! Márfa Ivanavan said while she was about it she might as well make the outfit complete."

"But thy father and mother, child, will be in—— Well, well, I need not say what! Daniel Pereira will know from them that these fine feathers art not thine own."

"That is so," cried Salome, gaily; "but if he doth not see my own ragged plumage, what matter? Besides, mother is to wear Kezia's black silk. There are some holes in it, but they'll not be seen if mother doth not lift her arms, and father wants thee to lend him thy old summer caftan, then we shall all be so magnificent! Oh!" she clapped her hands and twirled round on her toes; "Daniel Pereira will be so dazzled that he will at once sign my contract, and we shall never be hungry again."

"But thou hast forgotten Belah; is he to remain down-stairs?" asked David.

"No; we thought"—Salome nestled her head against David's arm—"that he might lie in thy bed, if thou wilt not mind, and only show his head, he doth so much want to see me dance."

"He shall come. Run, now, down with the caftan for thy father," he said, taking it out of the chest, "and tell thy mother to bring supper."

"It was nigh upon ready when I came up to show thee my dress, and the fish doth smell so good; but thou hast not taken off thine apron nor brushed thine hair," she said, anxiously.

David laughingly took off his leathern apron and threw it over his stool, and run his fingers through his hair, saying, "There, doth that please thee?"

"No!" she stamped her foot at him; "I want thee

A SON OF ISRAEL

to look best of all. Let me do it for thee. Sit down on thy bed so I canst reach thee." She knew where he kept his hair-brush; it was in a little drawer in the side of the chest. She got it out and brushed away vigorously at his thick hair, David wrinkling up his brow when in her ardour she stuck the bristles in his forehead and almost blinded him.

"There!" she cried, triumphantly, looking at him from all sides. "Now thou art almost as smooth as mother. I was close on half an hour getting her hair out of tangle."

"Wert thou? Poor Judith! But come, the sun is set," said David, giving his head a shake to set his hair free again, and, looking at his watch; "away now with the caftan, or thy Daniel Pereira will be here before we have eaten our meal."

Salome ran to the door; she looked back. "David," she cried, "am I not more beautiful than the Christian woman who came hither yesterday?" Then she flew laughing down the stairs, and David's heart beat fast and hard for a moment.

"After all, she is a Christian," he murmured; "suppose her creed should come between. No, that cannot be. God hath sealed her mine. He doth not take back his word. He hath wedded us together for all eternity. Ha! ha!" he laughed, joyously; "doubt? not I; we are one, one for ever. . . . Where is that Belah?" he called down the stairs; "send him hither and he shall wear the little woollen shirt I used to wear in Nazareth in winter-time. We'll have no boys hiding in bed to-night."

All the house heard the joy in his voice. Up flew Belah in his rags, and by now David had dragged out the coarse, woollen garment from the bottom of the chest, where it had been treasured because it was the last his beloved mother had woven for him with her tender hands. Soon Belah was dressed in it, David touching it reverently. He kissed the hem, while he told Belah why it had been hidden, and that it must return to its place when the evening was over.

By now Salome was come back with a bowl of haricot bean salad in her hands.

"Look at thine head!" she wailed to David. His fine, smooth hair that she had taken such pains with was tangled and rumpled as though it had not seen a brush for days.

"I have been thinking," he said, guiltily.

"Let me smooth it again for thee."

"No, no, no; nor Belah's," as she was darting on Belah, brush in hand. "We look best uncombed. Come, boy, we'll bathe our hands, and then we shall be ready for the feast."

While they were washing their hands Judith came in with a dish of fish stewed with rice and salted cucumber, and Ezra followed her with a large loaf of white bread.

Ezra Manuelli was a tall, lean man, with a haggard, anxious face, sunken, fiery eyes, and a great head thrust out at the end of a thin, wiry, brown neck and covered with bushy, thick black hair. He was a broker, and would have run about Odessa all day for sixpence; but, somehow, luck nearly always went against him, and many were the days he could not earn half that sum. It was a constant fight between him and starvation, and but for David it is hard to tell what would have become of him and his family. He was a silent, seemingly cold-hearted man; but Judith knew him. In sickness he would wear himself nigh to death, whether for friend or enemy, and all the while without a word or smile.

When David turned and nodded, smiling, to him, Ezra touched the caftan and said,—

"I thank thee," and spoke no more till the meal was finished.

CHAPTER X.

THE DANCE.

NEVER had Judith, the children, and Ezra eaten such a joyous meal, though they had often supped with David on the Sabbath; but he sometimes was silent, thinking out a fresh design for his work, and Ezra and Judith, too, would be silent, thinking of the hunger which always stood at their elbows. But this night there was the hope of the good fortune Daniel Pereira might bring, and David was like a boy. He kept the children and Judith in one delightful twitter of merry, innocent laughter, Belah once nearly falling off his stool, shrieking with delight at a bread elephant which David made and stood up on his hind legs, with his trunk stretched out for the salad the boy was making disappear so rapidly. Even Ezra chuckled more than once, and Judith quite forgot that she was wearing Kezia's old black silk dress, with the cracks under the arms and the frayed sleeves; and Salome, too, forgot the holes and the promise to nudge her mother whenever she lifted her arms too high.

When the meal was finished, they all rose and stood round the table, while David, with his hands held out, said, in his fine, full voice,—

"Let us say grace."

And Ezra, Judith, and the children replied,—

"'Blessed be the name of the Eternal from now unto Eternity.

"'Blessed be he of whose gifts we have eaten.

"'Blessed be he of whose gifts we have eaten and by whose goodness we exist.

"'Blessed be he, and blessed be his name, who feedeth the whole world with his goodness; with grace, kindness, and compassion he giveth food to all flesh, for his mercy endureth for ever. And through his abundant goodness food hath not yet failed us, nor will fail us for evermore, for it is because of his own great name that he feedeth and sustaineth all and doeth good unto all, and provideth for all his creatures which he hath created. Blessed art thou, O Eternal, who feedeth all.'"

When he had spoken the whole of the beautifully worded blessing, Judith helped him to clear away the plates and dishes, while Ezra stood the coffee in the stove to keep hot, and afterwards he walked about the room with his great head thrust forward, examining into everything. Presently he came upon the sketch of the crucifix, which David had elaborated and finished.

Ezra's face went ashen grey with wrath and resentment, and he turned and looked at David with the sketch shaking in his clenched hand. But David was moving the table to leave the centre of the room clear, and so did not see him. But now Ezra looked again closely at the face of the Christ, and gave a deep sigh. It was haggard, and the eyes were full of agonised appeal, almost 'reproach, and over the head was written on a scroll, in Hebrew,—

"My God, my God, why hast thou forsaken me?"

Ezra pointed his long, lean finger at the words and said,—

"Would God call upon God? . . . Ought we to blame this man for the sufferings we endure, and not the blindness of these Christians?"

Just at that moment came a light rapping from some one's knuckles at the door. Salome flew to it and opened it, and there stood Karl Helfmann with his violin-case under his arm, his dim blue eyes blinking and watery from the keen wind.

"Is this David Rheba's?" he asked, smiling at Salome's eager face. "Madam Meldola directed me here. I am come to play for the little lady who is to dance to-night."

"I am the little lady!" exclaimed Salome, highly pleased. "And oh, thou hast thy violin! . . . I ought not to have said 'thou,'" she quickly corrected herself, "because you are a stranger; but you are to make the music, and I so love music with all my soul that I couldn't help it."

"Who is it, Salome?" asked David, coming to the door.

"It's—— Oh, I know not thy name!"

"The fiddler," smiled Karl, longing to get inside the clean, cheery room: "Helfmann by name."

"Then come in, man, and take off your coat, or your legs will be frozen if you stand there much longer," said David.

Karl Helfmann entered, and Salome held the violin-case, hugging it with both arms, while he took off his cap and coat. Afterwards she stood close by him while he tuned it and twanged the strings.

Kezia was watching for Daniel Pereira by the light of a candle which she had stood on the stairs, and which flared and guttered down the candlestick, and threw flickering fantastic shadows over her face and old red dressing-gown.

"Up there," she said when he arrived, pointing in the direction of David's room; "the second door on the left."

"But are not you coming?" he asked, quickly.

She shrugged her shoulders. "David Rhoba is the master there, and has not invited me."

"Yet you wish to go." He eyed her keenly.

"Wish! when the sight of Salome dancing brings back all my lost youth! I hunger to go," she answered, fiercely; then added, brusquely, "They'll be waiting for you." She held up the candle, and waited until she heard him rap at the door; then she went into her own room and flung herself down on her narrow bed, with her eyes staring rebelliously at the ceiling.

David opened the door to Pereira's knock.

"Daniel Pereira?" he asked. Daniel bowed. "Please enter."

David helped him to take off his coat; then he said,—

"Ezra, Judith Manuelli," introducing them. "Salome and Belah, their children; and this, Karl Helfmann."

"My fiddler," whispered Salome to Karl, after she had made a little curtsy to Daniel Pereira.

Judith's heart was beating quickly; she feared Salome was too careless of the great man; but he was well pleased, and watched the girl's beautiful pale face and great eyes, and the charming simplicity of her whole manner. She was natural and graceful as a wild bird fresh from the woods, he told himself.

"You are fond of music?" he said.

"Yes," fervently, from Salome.

He smiled and signed to Karl Helfmann.

David sat on the edge of his bed, Belah on the floor at his feet, Ezra and Judith by the stove, and Pereira with his back to the forge, so that the whole space of room was clear to the door.

Karl drew his bow over the strings, uncertain what to play; then he set down his violin and fumbled in his pockets, looking dismayed and troubled.

Daniel Pereira guessed his difficulty.

"You have no music," he said.

"Gott in himmel!" gasped the poor man; "I did forget!"

"Improvisare?"

"When I am in the mood," whispered the old man, a light coming into his face. He looked at Salome, who was standing by his side watching him. He smiled, nodded, closed his eyes, and played. . . . Salome gave a little cry and clasped her young hands hard against her breast,—she had never heard such music. It was like a soft, murmurous summer wind playing hide-and-seek with elves and fairies in a sunny wood. Daniel listened in amazement. Was he to discover two people in one night? And now a second wonder, for Salome began to dance with a gliding, swaying motion, her arms and feet moving in a rhythmic measure, her face filled with innocent delight and joy of the dance, and yet serious with it all. Karl Helfmann opened his eyes and watched her awhile, then slowly there crept into the music another theme, as though a wicked sprite were hiding behind the trees and sowing mischief and discord among the happy, careless fairies. Salome gave a wild burst of laughter and instantly her face changed; it became elfish and sharp in outline, and full of mischief and cunning. She sprang hither and thither, now stooping, as though creeping under ferns, now pointing upward with her hands, and leaping in a wild, whirling dance. Faster and faster played Karl Helfmann, wilder grew the dance; the wicked sprite was driving all the fairies and elves out of the wood with shrieks and cries and trills of laughter. The flowers began to droop with sadness, the trees moaned and sighed; tears dripped from their leaves. The birds flew fluttering and frightened to their nests; the whole wood seemed filled with moans and sighs and bitter sobs; desolation and despair seized every green thing and lowly flower, and all seemed on the point of death, when suddenly the wind came sweeping through with a scream of rage, whistling and shrill and cold, bowing the great limbs of the trees down to the ground and making them crack and groan in pain and agony of heart. The sprite shivered and shrunk away, striving in vain to hide himself, to battle with its piercing, icy breath, and flew on, on, in terror and dismay, till the wind caught him, and bore him away weeping and wailing to the nethermost recesses of the wood, and the music ended with a faint chuckling of delight, as the elves and fairies came creeping back to their nests in the flower bells and the fragrant, mossy dells in the deep green wood.

The little audience sat speechless and spellbound, looking alternately at Karl Helfmann then at Salome, who was putting back her tangled hair from her eyes and wondering why they were so silent.

"Ha! ha! ha!" laughed someone wildly from the stairs; "look upon her! Is she not a true daughter of our race? Art thou not proud of her?" It was Kezia speaking. She had crept up the stairs and opened the door inch by inch to feast her eyes upon the dance. She now thrust it wide open, and stood pointing at Salome, with the tears streaming down her hollow cheeks, a laugh on her lips, and her old red dressing-gown twisted tightly round her lean body to keep her from the freezing draught that came through from the street up the narrow stairs.

CHAPTER XI.

BELAH'S DREAM COMES TRUE.

The music and her intense desire to see Salome dancing had drawn Kezia, spite of her pride and resentment, up to David's door.

"Have I pleased thee?" cried Salome, running to her and looking up into her withered face.

"Greatly, greatly," she murmured, stroking the girl's head and kissing her; then she sat down on the landing with her arms clasped round her knees and looking defiantly at David, as much as to say, "This is as much mine as thine;" while aloud she said, "Well, Daniel Pereira, have I not shown you a treasure great as Solomon's?"

Daniel smiled at her, nodding, "Yes, yes."

"And the contract! Come, now, what terms will you make?"

Even the fear of offending the man who would perhaps keep them from semi-starvation could not prevent Judith saying, "It is the Sabbath, Kezia; we have already transgressed."

"How, in dancing? Dancing is worship! Remember Miriam. I never felt so near to our God as when I lifted up my soul in the dance. Would it had been always so with me!" She looked straight at David as she spoke; then she quelled, and something hard seemed to mount into her throat. He was looking straight at her, his face stern and his eyes bent coldly on her. After sitting there awhile longer she rose and went away slowly down the stairs to her room, no longer able to endure the scorn in his eyes.

"Stiff-necked and hateful!" she hissed when she had closed the door. "Wait; some day you may need help of me."

Daniel Pereira had been watching David sharply from under his bent brows. He rose when Kezia left, and said to Judith,—

"The contract shall be drawn up to-morrow." She clasped Ezra's hands fervently, both having much ado to keep from falling on their knees in praise of God. "And sleep in peace to-night," he added, softly, knowing from their wan faces and sunken eyes how often hunger had gripped them. "This little maiden will keep the cupboard filled till you bring her to Milan next autumn. In the mean time she will be Kezia's pupil, and her salary, a small one at first,"—he smiled,—"shall commence from the signing of the contract."

Salome threw her arms round Belah in a transport of joy, crying,—

"There, I told thee thy dream should come true!"

"What dream was that?" asked David, drawing the children to him.

"Why! why!" stammered Belah, excitedly, "I dreamed I saw Salome—— Thou tell it," he said, pulling her by the sleeve.

"No, thou," she answered, giving him a little push.

"Well, I dreamed I saw Salome dancing in a field

of ripe wheat and holding out a big slice of bread to me; and she had her lap full of purple grapes," he said, in answer to another push, his eyes solemn and round as an owl's that he had been such a seer.

"And that's what I will do, too, soon as the corn is ripe!" cried Salome; "only thou shalt have two slices of bread instead of one, and some fish."

Belah pulled her away into a corner of the room after that to ask her whether she really meant two slices of bread. He thought the fish entirely too good to be true, so he wouldn't put her to the sin of saying "yes" to that.

Karl Helfmann had been sitting quietly behind Ezra and Judith looking on. He was a lonely old man, and was loath to leave the pleasant place for his own cheerless, grimy room, with a stove which smoked in all weathers. He was so quiet that, except Daniel Pereira and Salome, the others thought he had slipped away.

"I must not intrude any longer upon you," said Daniel Pereira, rising; "but if you will permit me, I should wish to speak to Karl Helfmann before I go."

Old Karl's face flushed nervously, knowing well the name of Pereira, and Ezra and Judith looked round, seeing Daniel Pereira's eyes were turned their way.

"Ah, sir!" said Karl, rising before anything further could be said; "you think that what I did just now was clever, eh?"

"Why, yes," said Pereira, smiling; "it was something more than clever. It was genius!"

"So it has been said before!" exclaimed Karl, spreading out his hands and shaking his head. "A great man like yourself once heard me play when I thought no one was listening. He said he would make my fortune. But what was the use? The music will not come always when I say, Come! So what good? You would be ashamed to have me on a platform and then I stare, stupid, so, with my eyes and my mouth wide open because my soul will not speak unless she do please."

"That is strange," said David. "So you cannot always play as you played just now."

" No; it sometimes happens my hands are dumb, and then I can play, not at all—no more," answered the old man, sadly.

"As with my work," thought David. "The ways of the Eternal are strange."

"Wilt thou never play again for me?" asked Salome, who had stolen over to his side with her eyes full of tears.

"I know not," whispered Karl Helfmann, his dim eyes gathering fire from hers. "But it seems now that I could always play with thee before me."

"Then let us make a bargain," cried Pereira. "Your daughter"—turning to Ezra and Judith—"will need someone to play for her while she is practising; who better than Herr Helfmann? And when you are not in the mood"—addressing Karl—"you can play from notes. I will send you some dance music which will be suitable. What say you?"

"It is beautiful!" exclaimed the old man.

"Then I will bid you all good-night," said Daniel Pereira, taking his overcoat over his arm. "Madame,"

—he bowed to Judith,—"I will bring the contract tomorrow evening—to bind you to me for ten years," he smiled to Salome.

"She is young," sighed David, "for a dancer's life."

"But she will not dance in public until she is sixteen," said Pereira. "She will spend the first five years studying languages, music, painting, and acting, as well as her own art. That is my way of work with the young people I have the good fortune to discover. To be great in their one particular art they must have a close friendship with other arts; it keeps the mind healthy. For, look you at singers, actors, painters, composers, anyone whose work comes solely of the imagination; if they have no other work to turn to when the soul is weary, how often they sink into a loose, sensuous life till the holy fire burns again within them. To be wedded to one idea is dangerous; it saps the vigour of the soul. Good-night, good-night," he said, abruptly, remembering an engagement, and was gone, and Ezra and Judith feared they would wake and find it all a dream.

"And I, too, must get to my home," said Karl Helfmann, reluctantly putting on his coat.

"But thou art to come again," called Salome. "When wilt thou come?"

"To-morrow after sunset," answered Judith for him.

"And so thou wilt sing to me every day," laughed Salome to the violin, with her cheek pressed against it; then she gave it up to Karl and its case, and to Belah, as the old man went slowly away, she said, "And thou shalt come and listen if thou art good."

"No more rags after to-morrow! eh, boy?" said David to Belah. "This"—touching the little woollen garment—"thou canst wear until Monday, when Salome shall buy a new one for thee for thy very own."

"Yes, something all purple colour, and something for myself that will rustle,—I love to rustle,—and something for mother that will rustle, only I fear she is not of a rustling character," said Salome, looking doubtfully at Judith.

Judith smiled and took the children by the hands, saying, "Thou shalt buy rustling garments for me when we have a good store of bread in the house. Come, now, to bed. Good-night, David; the angel of peace watch by thee."

So they went down to their cellar, the last night they would sleep there, Salome vowed, Ezra pressing David's hands, saying not a word and darting after them.

Then David, he too went to his bed after calling in a long-headed German boy who happened to be near the house, and giving him a kopeck to extinguish the candles, for it was the Sabbath, and it is a sin for a Jew to touch fire on the holy day.

CHAPTER XII.

BETWEEN JEW AND CHRISTIAN.

Five weeks after Salome signed the contract binding her to Daniel Pereira, David was out one Sabbath morning before it was light, as indeed he had been up and out every morning since the first morning he had met Olga; and just as the sun was rising he came in sight of Michael Volkenoff's house. The shutters were still shut fast; no one seemed stirring. He tried the gate on the eastern side. It was locked, and not a sound came from behind it. He waited some time; then, thinking perhaps Olga had come out by some other way, and was now waiting in the porch of the old house, he sped back, only to find the dull-eyed old servant busily scouring the little flight of wooden steps, and no sight of Olga. Heart-sick, he turned again westward. Then he beheld her coming towards him, Wolf with her, his tail down, his ears depressed. She was panting and breathless, her face as pale as the snow under her feet, and her eyes dim with weeping. David took her cold hands and warmed them in the breast of his furred pelisse.

"What is the trouble, heart of mine?" he said, and tried to smile.

"I was called into the master's room last night; he has commanded me to marry Foka, the son of Nicolas

Saviska, on Thursday, six days from now," she said, in a dull, toneless voice.

"Marry—thou——"

"To save me from thee, because thou art a Jew," she went on in the same dull voice, as though all feeling had been swept out of her.

"But thou lovest me," said David, through white lips.

Her hands tightened on the front of his blouse; she swayed sideways a moment; then, stifling a cry, she said,—

"With all my soul."

"My beloved, what have we, then, to fear?"

"But I am a serf. He says that if I refuse he will have me whipped. David!"

"Hush!" David laid his hand tenderly over her piteous, staring eyes. "I will see him to-day; I will plead with him to give thee to me. I will toil for him in return every hour, every moment of my life. I will give him all the work of my brain, of my hands. When he hears us, he cannot, if he be human, refuse; he dare not oppose the will of God." He smiled at her. He felt it must be so.

"Art thou sure?" The natural tone was back now in her voice.

"Come thou with me and see. But first let me give thee some hot coffee. We'll face the enemy as well braced as he." He took her hand and hurried her along; once she faltered and nearly slipped on the snowy ground.

"Shall I carry thee?" he asked, and before she could

protest he had her in his strong arms, and she was being borne along as though but a feather's weight, old Wolf panting after. At the end of the road they came to a workmen's café. David set Olga on her feet and led her inside.

"Peace be with you," he said to a bright young woman who was serving some men seated at the tables.

"And with you," she smiled. "Peter Petroff," nudging a big yellow-haired fellow who was sitting by the stove, "jump up and give thy seat to the lady."

Peter Petroff rose with a smile and a duck of his head and gave his seat to Olga; then the young woman brought hot milk, coffee, and bread. "There, eat and drink," she said, heartily, "and good Saint Nicholas watch over your digestion, for what is food without it?"

David and Olga ate and drank the simple breakfast even with relish, for Hope was whispering to them, and were not they together for at least the time? Very sweet it was, too, to Olga to break bread with her beloved and hear his softly murmured petition to God to bless the meal. Old Wolf got his share, and then they rose and prepared to start. The bright-faced young woman sprang forward to help fasten Olga's cloak.

"Is this white pigeon your sweetheart?" she asked slyly of David.

"Yes," he answered, fervently and simply, and Olga's face shone.

"The blessed Mother of Christ watch over her and give her joy," said the woman as she held the door open for them.

David shivered; he took Olga's arm and hurried her away.

"I am right; he is a Jew," the young woman muttered, looking after them. "God in heaven help her, for she comes from the house of Michael Volkenoff."

David and Olga walked on quickly. Arrived at the house, they passed through the court yard to the "Little Mother's door."

"Wait," whispered Olga, "while I tell my mistress thou art here and wish to see the master."

"Say to her that I must see him," said David. Then, seeing Olga's eyes grow faint with fear under the lids, he drew her close to him, saying, "In the Book of the Prophets it is written, 'Love is stronger than death.' Shall, then, Michael Volkenoff have power to divide thee from me?"

Olga held her hands to her face for a moment, then with a brave, resolute "No!" she entered the house.

She found Marya sitting in the cedar room, sipping her chocolate and making out a list of things to be given that day to certain of her pensioners, among them a parcel of clothing specially marked for Judith Manuelli. Marya held out her hands, smiling, as Olga ran to her, and saying,—

"No need to ask where thou hast been and whom thou hast seen; thine eyes tell that." She drew the girl down to her side.

"Mistress, he is here, waiting at thy door, and says that he must see the master."

"But that is foolish. Patience is best."

"Hath not the master told thee that he sent for me

last night, after thou hadst bidden me good-night, and commanded me to marry Foka six days from now?" asked Olga, rapidly, answering the question in Marya's eyes.

"He has not breathed one word of it to me. Is that why David Rheba is here?"

Olga nodded "Yes."

"Bid him enter," Marya said, "and let him wait here while I go to thy master and beg that he will see him. And, child,"—Marya turned at the door—"pray that ——No, no; he could not be so cruel," she whispered to herself, turning and walking quickly through the long corridors to the eastern side of the great house, to the room where Michael Volkenoff received nigh upon a hundred people every day. She waited in a small room adjoining, where he took his midday meal, and sent in a servant to say that she desired to see him, and at once.

Michael guessed why she was come to him; only things of the most vital importance brought her to that part of the house.

His steward was there, and two clerks, receiving instructions. He made a gesture with his hand to the servant to wait after he had delivered the message, saying to the steward,—

"Tell Fedor Ikonin five thousand roubles is my price, not a kopeck less. And you may tell Ivan Valahins and Kolpikoff the wheat in the north granary is worth three thousand roubles, that I want four thousand for it, and if they haggle tell them I know that in three weeks' time it will be worth double in the

European markets. I won't bate a jot of my price. Take these papers,"—turning to the secretaries,—"copy them, and send them at once to the governor." The secretaries bowed and went out through a closely curtained door into a room beyond.

"Fedor Ikonin has had heavy losses lately, your Excellency," said the steward.

"Tell your mistress I am waiting to receive her," said Michael Volkenoff to the servant. Then to the steward, "Fedor Ikonin's losses are his concern, and not mine. Why should I pay his gambling debts? I do not ask him to pay for my ships when they are lost."

The steward was about to speak again. "I have said. See that I am not disturbed while your mistress is here." Without another word the steward bowed and left him.

"So she is come to plead for the Jew," thought Michael, rising and bowing coldly when Marya entered the room. He placed a chair for her by the stove, but she remained standing just a little beyond the door she had left open behind her.

"Is it true, Michael, that you desire Olga to marry Foka Saviska in six days from now?" asked Marya, quietly.

"That was my command to her last night," with a significant emphasis on the command.

"Why?"

"To save her from the Jew, David Rheba."

"But they love each other."

Michael Volkenoff laughed.

"Yet I say she is to marry Foka Saviska."

"You do not ask whether I will consent to part with a servant I love so dearly as I love Olga?"

"No, because I consider you incapable of judging what is best for her salvation." Marya came farther into the room and looked at him as though she thought her ears had deceived her. "Foka is a good, industrious, hard-working boy. He will not beat Olga nor spend his wages at the dram-shop, and on the day they are married I will give him his freedom."

"Michael, you do not know him; you take all that Nicolas says for the whole truth. Foka is industrious, but he thinks only of saving money. He stints himself of food, even of wood for his stove in the winter, to save money; Olga's life with him would be one of privation, of misery, and of loathing."

He laughed. "Shut her up with him for a week, nay, for three days, and you will find her perched on his knee, her arms round his neck."

"Your words are an insult to Olga's womanhood," exclaimed Marya, hotly.

"I know her breed," he answered, bitterly.

"You do not or you could not commit this sin against nature. Olga is pure and sweet and womanly, and she loves David Rheba with all her heart and soul. See her; see him; he is here waiting to speak with you. Let them plead, and if you are, as I think, a man, you cannot deny them."

"So, then, would you say I am less than man if I refuse? Yet how could you judge? woman that you are without a soul."

"Without a soul!" faltered Marya.

"Have you not denied your God?"

"Not as thou meanest!" she cried.

He waved his hand towards the door.

"Send your Jew hither, I will see him, though I have said no infidel's foot should cross the threshold of my house."

Marya went to the door of the room and said to the servant waiting there, "Bid my woman Olga and David Rheba come here." Then she returned and seated herself by the table, while Michael stepped up into the window and stood looking out over the courtyard to the dark forests beyond the vast stretches of snow-covered meadow-land. Marya watched him, her heart feeling bruised and sick, yet she had determined what to do should he refuse David Rheba.

David and Olga entered hand in hand. David had thrown aside his heavy coat in the hall. In his workman's blouse he looked lithe and strong as his namesake when he faced the giant with the sling in his hand. Marya pointed with her hand towards the window, and the two moved to within a few paces of it, David measuring Michael from top to toe.

"David Rheba is here, Excellency," said the servant; then he went out and closed the door.

Michael Volkenoff turned, started, and changed colour. He had not expected this sunny-hued man, with his clear, fine face and resolute eyes. He had expected the type of Jew common in Russia, with the hideous side curls and close-cropped head, and instead, David's hair was the colour some artists give to the hair of Christ.

"I have come, Excellency," said David, in a voice deeply stirred, "to ask this woman of you for wife."

Something in David's voice moved Michael Volkenoff to the very depths. It swept away the last human objection that he sought to hold fast to; it convinced him of the utter goodness of the man facing him and of the nakedness of the sin he would commit in parting him from the woman Olga, but atop of his conviction his fanaticism cried aloud,—

"He is a Jew! one of the accursed race!" so he hardened himself, whispering to his soul that it was deceived, and he sneered,—

"So you, a dog of a Jew, wish to marry this Christian woman, my serf!"

David looked him full in the eyes and replied, quietly, "Yes, follower of the man named Christ. I, a dog of a Jew, wish to marry this Christian woman, your serf."

A cold, crafty light crept into Michael Volkenoff's eyes.

"Do you, then," he said, softly, "intend to renounce your creed and enter the Holy Christian Church?"

"No," answered David.

"Perhaps you hope that this woman may be induced to forswear her God, the Lord Christ, and embrace your belief?"

Again David answered, "No."

"How else, then, can a marriage come about between you?" asked Michael Volkenoff almost tenderly, as though solicitous for the two facing him.

Marya drew in her breath sharply; she had heard the tone once before, and knew what it foretold.

"By your consent," said David. "This woman"—he put his arm round Olga and drew her to him, for she was trembling—"is your serf; you are her master, with power"—he set his teeth hard at the words—"to sell her. Why not, then—give her to me? Give her to me, and every hour of my life shall be yours. I will work for you as man never yet worked for man, I pledge you my word."

"And you are a clever workman; one of the finest in the whole of Russia, I am told; so it would be a good bargain on my side," muttered Michael Volkenoff; and he paused, as though considering the advantage of such an offer; then he went on again in the same solicitous, caressing voice, "Would you also pledge me your word that you would not tamper with this woman's faith? that you would not, in time, wheedle her into taking up your creed and denying her own?"

David smiled. "There is but one God," he said, "and that God is the same that is worshipped in your church as in the synagogue, else why do your priests make our book of law theirs? Why, then, should I seek to turn Olga from her way of worship to my own, if that her way seemeth good to her?"

"Ah! now, Jew, I have you!" cried Michael, passionately. "You say if that her way seemeth good to her. You, with the craft of your race, would make it seem other than good. You would so work upon her that she would grow to think it evil, and thus lose her soul, which I, her master, must answer for."

"By the faith of my fathers, I would not act thus!" exclaimed David.

"And by your fathers which hung Him upon the tree, I say that you would, and this woman shall be saved from you! Have you thought that I was in earnest! Nay, I wanted to gauge you; to trap you; to watch the sly devil leap to your eyes when you imagined that you had pinned me! Oh, I know your race! A race of usurers, thieves, spawn of the Evil One, with God's curse tacked to it for evermore."

"And you are a Christian," said David, coldly; "doubtless with the book in your house which tells you to love your enemies. I know the law of the man named Christ."

"His law is not for you!" cried Michael Volkenoff, with upraised fist.

"His law was for all men," continued David, warmly; "and if you, his followers, obeyed it, peace would follow in your footsteps, songs of joy and gladness would fill the air, there would be no more striving, all would live in brotherly love, each man his neighbour's friend, and between us two anger could not be."

Michael Volkenoff's face turned white; the Jew hit hard. Marya rose from her seat and made a gesture of entreaty; his soul strove to wrestle with the stubbornness of his heart, but he conquered and threw it, and he turned to David with a bitter laugh, saying,—

"Nevertheless, the woman Olga shall marry Foka

Saviska six days from now." Then he strode heavily past him without once looking back, through the curtained door into the room where the secretaries were writing, and Marya heard the key turn in the lock.

CHAPTER XIII.

THE MARRIAGE.

Marya laid her hand on David's arm when he would have followed.

"It is useless," she said; "he would not yield though the Czar were to plead to him."

Olga clung about David's neck and looked at him with despairing eyes and ashen cheeks.

"Canst thou not save me?" she cried.

"Yea, when I leave this house thou shalt go with me," he answered.

"If I consent to that," said Marya, "will you promise me not to tempt her from her religion? else you will place yourself in the power of the law."

"Have I not said?" replied David.

"Then come, child," whispered Marya, "come."

She took Olga's hand and led her swiftly away to the cedar room, David following. Marya rung a little silver bell. It was answered by the laughing-faced boy Dimitri.

"Send Father John to me." The boy sped away, and soon returned followed by a priest, a tall, pale, sad-eyed man, with a refined, delicate face. He was a member of the White Clergy, but differing in almost every particular from the greater number of that class, which is filled with low, coarse men, drunkards, swindlers, who defile and degrade the Greek Church in Russia with their abominable mode of life, their dirty habits, and godlessness.

"Dimitri!" called Marya, as the boy was closing the door, "saddle Turka and carry a basket of flowers to the hospital of St. Barbara. Ivan will cut them for you. He is working in the conservatory."

Dimitri clutched the piece of money she gave him and ran as fast as his young legs could carry him down the corridor.

Marya smiled. The hospital was nearly two miles off, and the delight of a ride on Turka's back would speedily put all lesser things out of Dimitri's head.

"Father John!" She motioned the priest into the window and spoke to him in a low voice. The priest at first shook his head. Then Marya spoke to him more earnestly, pointed to Olga and David, the priest's gaze following her hand and fixing it on David's face.

"But what if he should tempt her to deny her God?" he said, deeply moved.

"And what if she were to make a Christian of him?" urged Marya.

The priest's face changed as though a white light flashed across it; he breathed quickly; his sunken eyes burned with some of the fire which had filled them when he left all to enter the Church. "It shall be done, and I will keep it secret. Maiden,"—he lifted his hand to Olga,—"come hither, and thou," to David. He placed them one on each side of him, then, taking their right hands, he joined them, saying,—

"By the law of Christ and of our most Holy Church,

A SON OF ISRAEL

I declare ye to be man and wife, and may the curse of the Almighty God rest upon him who shall cause this woman to swerve from the Christian faith."

"I cry amen to that with all my soul!" said David, lifting his glowing face and eyes to the priest's face. Then he clasped Olga in his arms, saying, "The God of my fathers bless thee, dear one."

Marya stood aside and watched them with wet eyes. Presently Olga went to her, drawing David by the hand; and all Olga could say was "Mistress! Mistress!" with little sobs and smiles, finally casting herself on Marya's neck and weeping there like a child.

"I know not whether this marriage is valid according to present Russian law, for I know little now of worldly things; but I, a servant of God, hath joined your hands, and no earthly power, do what it may, can put you asunder," said the old priest, earnestly. Then he saluted Marya and went out of the room.

Marya held out her hand to David over Olga's head, and said to him, "You will cherish and guard her?" David bowed his forehead to her hand in token. "In two days hope for your passport to carry you both to England. Now, my Olga, get thy cloak and hood; time is speeding fast to noon. I will keep the knowledge of this from the master till thou art safe on the sea."

She hurried Olga, who was dazed and bewildered with the rapidity of her actions, to the girl's room, and muffled her up in her cloak, the old dog running after them thinking there was a walk in store.

"Now thou art ready," said Marya, kissing her on the eyes and lips and cheeks. "Thank God it has been mine to prevent the crime my husband would have committed in giving you to Foka."

"Shall I see thee again, mistress?" asked Olga, suddenly grown calm.

"Ay, most surely thou shalt. I will bring the passport, and I will bring some of thy clothing to thee this very day."

"But when, mistress, when shall we meet again?" Olga's lip began to shake. "Will it be when we have crossed the sea?"—she was calm now; "because, if not——"

"If not?" questioned Marya.

"Answer thou what I have asked," she entreated.

"I shall see thee every year, for each winter from now I shall spend in France, so it will be easy to go to thee. The cold here has grown to be too great for me, and, moreover, a great change has come——" She broke off suddenly. "Art thou now content?"

"Yes, now," answered Olga, smiling like April through her tears. "Had it not been that I should see thee again I could not leave thee."

"Not even for thy beloved?" smiled Marya.

"Oh, it is hard to say! Thou each art dragging at me; one this side of my heart, one this, and I know not which tugs the harder."

"Thou wouldst soon have discovered had thy David left thee here. Now go, my sweet Olga, it is not safe for thee to stay longer. Go by the western door, and keep in close under the wall while thou art passing the house. I will send David Rheba out by the eastern door."

Olga snatched up Wolf by the forepaws and kissed his old black nose; then she darted away to the "Little Mother's door," Marya following with David.

"Bless thee, dear one," said Marya to her. "Run thee out through the gate, then walk slowly on till thy David overtakes thee."

Michael Volkenoff stood at the window of the secretaries' room watching the people who went to and fro from the house through the great gates. An ugly look came into his face when the moments passed and David didn't appear.

"She is letting them bid each other good-bye," he thought, and watched, growing impatient. After some little time he saw David cross the court-yard and go out. He caught a glimpse of David's radiant face and noted his buoyant step.

"What has she promised him?" he wondered. Presently he smiled, and, turning, asked what ships sailed within the next few days. One of the secretaries gave the names of several freight vessels, and among them the name of the "Wanda," a passenger and freight ship which was to sail for England on the following day, the Sunday.

"That is it," he guessed. Then he went into his own room and sent for Anton, Marya's coachman.

When the man came he asked,—

"At what hour does your mistress drive out to-day?"

"At the usual hour, Excellency."

"If the time is altered bring me word at once."

The man nodded and backed out of the room.

Olga ran lightly across the court-yard and out through the servants' gate, no one seeing her, and a little time after David caught her up on the road. With a joyous laugh he tucked her arm under his, she clinging close, and now and again rubbing her cheek against his shoulder, and so through the crisp snow they went, the great sky over them like a deep, blue bowl, the sun sparkling and shining as though rejoicing in the joy of his children, the sharp, frosty air feeling as soft and kind to their faces as the air in June. When they were near the porch of the old wooden house Olga saw Nicolas across the road some little way ahead.

"It is Nicolas, the father of Foka," she whispered, hurriedly, and dragged David into the porch, making him stand in front of her while she squeezed herself close to the door and peeped over his shoulder at the old man, who went by swinging his arms and talking excitedly to himself.

When he was gone a good way up the road, the two came out and walked on as before in the direction of the town.

"What was he saying?" asked Olga.

"'Now Foka will have a girl to wash and cook for him and nothing to pay,'" answered David, repeating Nicolas's words; then they looked into each other's eyes and laughed, saying no more till they came to the house where David lived, and, passing in, mounted the stairs to his room.

A SON OF ISRAEL

Salome had seen them; she was coming with her father from the house where the prayers had been read that morning, for at that time there were no synagogues in Odessa.

"Look, father, look! There is our David with the Christian woman!" she cried, and she wanted to run after him, but Ezra held her and wouldn't let her go.

CHAPTER XIV.

HOUSEMATES.

DAVID unlocked the door, and, taking Olga's hand, he led her into the middle of the room, and, placing his hands one on each side of her face, he said, in a voice that trembled with very love of her,—

"Welcome to your home, my beloved, my wife."

Olga blushed rose-colour, and all at once a strange, unaccountable shyness came over her. She dropped her eyes, feeling she dare not look at him, and stood there shamefaced and wondering at herself. Then David unclasped her cloak, and folding it up put it in the chest, smiling to himself, and still Olga stood with head down, her fingers gripping one another, and feeling there she must stand to all eternity, for she hadn't courage to move. David turned and looked at her, with the lid of the chest held up in his hand. In a moment he understood it all. She was grown suddenly shy, this sweet wife of his; it was the first time they had ever been really alone. What should he do to take her out of herself? He looked at the stove: the fire was dying. Ah, now he knew; so, stepping up to her, and laying his cheek against hers from over her shoulder, he said, softly,—

"Housemate, the sweetest God ever gave to man, wilt thou not help me out of my trouble? See, the stove is growing cold, and, as I am a Jew, I may not touch fire on the Sabbath; but thou canst tend it for me, wilt thou? or I fear we shall be nigh frozen."

"Surely I will tend it for thee," cried Olga, forgetting all her fear in a moment and springing over to the stove. "Where shall I find wood?"

"There, stacked up by the side of my forge; but first let me take off thy snow-shoes."

Olga grew rose-coloured again, but she sat down on a stool, and, though David had much ado to keep from touching the little slipper which covered her foot under the shoe, and from clasping her in his arms to make her dear face more rosy still by kissing it from the forehead to the round, dimpled chin, he did not, wisdom whispering,—

"The maid is shy; wait till the place hath lost its strangeness." Nevertheless, he was a long time untying the second shoe; and when at last it was untied and in his hand, one glance of his hungering eyes made Olga jump up with a distant, demure little "I thank thee," and a dart over to the wood-stack, where she made a great bustle collecting a few pieces into her apron.

David remained on his knees by the stool: he was mightily puzzled at this fresh glimpse into woman-nature. That this maid, who had been so sweet and frank, should now be, as it were, miles away from him. Olga was passing him by this on her way to the stove. One shy look at his troubled eyes, and down rolled the wood from her apron, and she was on her knees beside him, her arms around his neck, her face half hidden in his hair; and she was saying, with catches of laughter and tears in her voice,—

"David, I don't know myself. One moment it seems that I am with thee now for the first time; another that I have known thee all my life; then, again, that I want to run away from thee and hide. I know not what is come to me; it is all so strange, so solemn, so dear. But bear with me, for I love thee. Ah, dear God, how I love thee! though I could not look thee in the eyes and say it. See now how foolish I am. Oh, it must be that I am a woman,"—she sat back on her heels with a merry laugh, and shaking her head at him,—"and women are queer things, the books say."

Then David sat back on his heels and laughed merrily with her, but with a lump in his throat for very love of her sweetness; and suddenly he clasped and kissed her, and seemed as though he would never tire, till Olga sprang out of his arms, declaring it sinful to waste so much time, and that the stove was cold.

While she was making the wood burn David watched her, saying, when the fire was roaring behind the stove door,—

"To-morrow, thy Sabbath, I will tend the fire for thee."

"But the Christians do not trouble about these things. Week-day or Sabbath-day, they tend the fire; and indeed I have not seen much difference in anything else, except that we eat and drink more on Sunday."

"And we must have some food, too," said David;

"it is close on two o'clock. Art thou not famished, sweetheart?"

With a laugh, Olga sprang away from his outstretched arms. "Nigh to starvation!" she exclaimed.

"Canst thou cook eggs?" asked David.

"Yes," she nodded.

"There are some in the cupboard yonder, and coffee and rolls; and, yes, some honey," he cried, looking into the cupboard over her shoulder.

"But thou must sit and not look at me, or I shall not be able to do anything," pleaded Olga.

"Very well, wife of mine," he laughed, seating himself by the stove, with a small leather-bound book in his hand, and watching all her movements. She seemed to know by instinct where to find everything she wanted, and she flitted about in a dainty, lightsome way that was enchanting to him. It was a new and wonderful delight to watch her make the coffee and set it inside the stove to simmer,—to watch her deft, quick fingers breaking the eggs against the edge of a basin, and turning the yolk into one place, the whites into another, with a pinch of salt to each; then whisking them up with a fork till they seemed to be nothing but froth, and then mixing both together and whisking them up again before turning them into a buttered earthenware dish to cook while she set the table. Twice or thrice she began singing a song, her voice as sweet as a linnet's. Once she caught the look of joy in his eyes as they followed her, and, as she seemed in danger of becoming shy and strange again, David had to pretend he was reading until the meal was ready. Then they washed their hands, and he, standing by the table, asked a blessing on the food, the music of the beautiful Hebrew words charming Olga of the sudden desire to run away, now that her hands had no more housewifery to fill them. After that they sat down and ate heartily, for they both discovered they were exceedingly hungry, and they laughed merrily at the fact. Never had David tasted such coffee and such an omelette, and he rejoiced to know that Judith and her children and the silent Ezra were eating a meal as good, for Daniel Pereira, who was still in Odessa, had sent a basket stocked full and brimming over with food ready cooked; so Salome, running up, had called to him through the door about an hour before midnight, after he was in bed.

Olga's eyes danced with delight of his praise, and when grace was said and the table cleared David showed her his work, explaining how the silver was broken up, put into the crucibe to melt, then poured out, and, when cool, beaten into a flat sheet, thence again into whatever shape he desired.

Olga wondered whether she might ever hope to help, and she asked whether it was possible for a woman to do such things. And David told her his mother had often helped with the polishing when his father was hard pressed for time, and that she might, in time, with her nimble fingers, learn to do even the delicate chasing, such as was on her thimble.

"And then we can work together like man and man," said Olga, gladly.

"Nay, beloved, like man and wife; but that only for

a little time each day. I could not have thee stooping and toiling hour in and hour out as I must for our bread; you must be the sunshine of our home, I the roof-tree."

"It must be sweet to be a man," sighed Olga, "to fend and work for what one loves."

"Sweeter still to be a woman, to be the crown and joy of her mate, to give of the very spirit and soul, while the man but gives of his strength and love in humble thankfulness for the haven that she makes for him."

"David,"—Olga's cheeks were glowing,—"shall I be that to thee?" For the first time since her coming she looked unfalteringly in his eyes and let him see all the love in hers. Involuntarily he held out his arms and gathered her into them. There was a long spell of silence in the room, broken only at last by their drawing a little apart and clasping each other by the hands and laughing low out of sheer happiness and very gladness of heart for the love which filled them.

CHAPTER XV.

ACCORDING TO JEWISH LAW.

About four o'clock Salome flew up the stairs to David's room. She felt she must satisfy the curiosity that was burning her heart out or die. No one had seen the Christian woman go from the house, for she had asked every one likely to know; what, then, could she be wanting of David all this time? Perhaps she had cast some charm upon him. Her little bosom was panting with excitement and fear for David, and when she came to the door her fingers trembled so her tapping was too light for the sound to reach within. She waited awhile, then, all on fire to succour David, if need be, she pushed the door wide open, and there stood David in the window with his back to her, his arm round Olga, and pressing his lips now and again to her hair and eyes as he talked.

Salome gave a queer, half-inarticulate "O-h!" the two letters lengthened out to six, and then stared at them till her great eyes seemed to absorb all her face.

"Come in, my pigeon!" cried David, turning and seeing who it was. "Come in; here is a new friend for thee."

She went slowly forward to Olga, who stooped and kissed her, then she darted over to David and snuggled her hand in his, watching Olga suspiciously from that vantage. Yes, the Christian woman was very beautiful; far more beautiful than when she came the first day. Perhaps it was because her soft dark hair was loosened and hung about her neck in thick waves and curls, or because of that wonderful light in her eyes. Then Salome turned and looked up at David, and in his eyes, too, that wonderful light was shining. She swung about to go; there was something here beyond her understanding; she would run and ask her mother what it meant.

"Nay, thou art not going like that!" cried David, catching her up in his arms and seating himself by the stove, Salome between his knees. "Thou hast not told me of all the good things Daniel Pereira brought thee."

Salome looked up at Olga, who was leaning over the back of his chair smiling at her, then at David, as though to ask, Was she to expose their poverty to her, the Christian woman?

"Thou canst speak," said David, reaching up to take Olga's hand; "she is my housemate, my wife."

Salome's passionate little breast rose high, then as suddenly sunk, and she felt strange, forlorn, and as though David were divided into two beings, the husband of the Christian and her own old playfellow.

"May I fetch Belah,—he can tell thee best?" she said, without a trace of her usual spirit; and at David's "Yes, and thy father and mother too," she darted away, keeping as far as possible from Olga, and so down the first four or five stairs. There she sat down to think, a great wofulness upon her. She felt inclined to scream and tug fiercely at her hair, but instead she wept, and weeping she slid, sitting, from stair to stair till she came to the flight of broken steps which led to the cellar; then down those she sprang with one bound from top to bottom, and flung herself into her mother's arms, sobbing bitterly,—

"David has taken the Christian woman to wife."

Ezra looked up from the book he was reading to Belah and muttered, "The child is crazy!"

"Come thou, then, and see!" cried Salome. "He calls her his wife, his housemate, and—and he did not even see this beautiful frock Daniel Pereira sent me."

"Art sure of what thou art saying?" asked Judith.

Salome nodded vehemently, her tears as suddenly gone as they had come.

"Shall we go, Ezra?" asked Judith.

"What did he say to thee?" enquired Ezra, cautiously.

"He wanted to know what Daniel Pereira had sent us, and I asked whether I might fetch Belah to tell him, because I—I felt so full here," and Salome pressed her hand over her heart, "and he nodded 'Yes,' and said, 'And thy father and mother too.'"

"Then, wife, we will go," said Ezra, rising.

So the four went up to David, the children first, Judith last, carrying a dish of the fruit Pereira had sent, and very proud was the woman's tender heart that she could now take some small gift to David.

David heard them coming, and he was standing hand

in hand with Olga in the centre of the room, facing the open door, as they entered.

"This is my dear wife, Olga," he said.

Judith stood the dish down on the first thing that was nearest, which happened to be the bed, ran and kissed and blessed Olga; for whatever David loved was most dear to her. Then she stood smiling at Olga's blushing face and radiant eyes. Suddenly remembering the fruit, she presented it to her, saying in Hebrew,—

"May the Lord of Israel bless thy womb and give thee a son for thy first-born."

"Thou seest I was right," whispered Salome to Belah, whose eyes were wide with curiosity and a hundred questions.

Ezra had taken David into the window and was asking question after question, a grave look on his face.

"Hast thou a ring?" at last the others heard him say.

"Only this," answered David, taking a finely chased iron ring from his finger, which his father had made and given him years before.

"That will do," nodded Ezra.

"Olga," said David, going to her, "nothing will pacify Ezra but that we should be wedded again here, for, as thou dost not know, our marriage this morning is not valid according to Jewish law."

"Take her hand," said Ezra, "put the ring upon her finger, and say, 'Behold, thou art consecrated unto me by this ring, according to the law of Moses and of Israel.'"

David repeated the words in Hebrew, Ezra and Judith adding,—

"And we are the witnesses thereunto."

Then each in turn kissed Olga, Salome springing at her and clasping her round the neck, after regarding her steadfastly for a moment. Presently she snuggled close and said,—

"I think I shall love thee. I am not yet quite sure, but I think I shall love thee dearly."

"I am sure that I shall love thee," smiled Olga. "Indeed, I have felt some affection for thee since that first day I came, when thou didst stand over there and gaze at me so intently with thy two big eyes."

Now Judith, Belah, and Salome all began talking at once, telling David of the fine things Daniel Pereira had sent,—not only food, but clothes; this fine, warm caftan and shoes and stockings for Ezra; these garments for Belah, clothing for Judith, and these warm, good things for Salome. They all crowded round David, making him feel the quality of the material; Ezra, now silent as usual, submitting to be turned round and round while he was extolled by Judith alike for his sweet nature and the fine appearance he made, and pushed and pummelled by the children.

And it being by now sunset, Ezra was for starting out to see what work he could find to do, but David would not hear of it; he said it must be a holiday and feast-day for all. So coffee was made, Belah and Salome despatched to bring up some of the cakes and rolls which had been sent, and, when a jug of hot coffee had been carried down to Kezia with a plate heaped with cakes and fruit, they all gathered round the stove, sang songs, told stories, between whiles sitting in deep silence, just so long as a bird might be in passing, until Daniel Pereira came in to say good-bye, it being his last day in Russia.

CHAPTER XVI.

A MAN'S WIT AGAINST A WOMAN'S.

For about an hour after Olga left the house Marya sat writing letters. Some were to friends in London asking them to do all that lay in their power for David Rheba and his wife, and a few others to friends in Moscow. When these were finished she went into Olga's room and commenced putting out what clothing she thought the girl would require until safe in England. When that was done she tied it up in just such a bundle as the others lying on the window seat in the cedar room which she was going to give away that afternoon, and then she sat down by Olga's bed to think of all she had to do. She had no time to grieve for the loss of her sweet companion; there were more important things to be done; the sorrowing could come after Olga and David were safe in England. First she must tell Nicolas that Olga was ill and was not to be disturbed, or he might be curious at seeing her drive out alone and go peeping into Olga's room. It would be best to go from the Jews' Quarter straight to the Princess Czartoryski, the governor's wife. The princess was a broad-minded woman, and if her sympathy could be aroused, Marya knew that she could be depended upon for arranging the whole matter, from the obtaining of the passports to securing a cabin in the "Wanda," the freight and passenger ship which was to sail early on the following morning, and Marya's hand not be seen in the matter.

From Olga's room Marya went into her own, and put all the gold and notes which were in her desk into her pocket. She knew her country well and the number of bribes which would be required to compass what she wished to do in so short a time; then she ate some soup and bread, and told Nicolas the carriage was to be at the door by two o'clock, adding, carelessly,—

"Olga is not well, see that no one disturbs her."

When Marya stepped out from the "Little Mother's door," she found Michael standing by the carriage, muffled up, dressed for driving. There was a peculiar light dancing in his eyes; a kind of devilish humour, a Mephistophelian silent laughter that would out in spite of him. In a voice which belied his face he said, tenderly,—

"I have given myself a holiday purposely to drive out with you to-day and to obtain forgiveness for my refusal of the Jew this morning. What! no smile! that's ungrateful!" He opened the door of the carriage as he spoke, and helped Marya in, wrapping her round carefully with the great fur rug, and then he jumped in after her.

"What are these?" he asked, sharply, as Nicolas began to stow away the bundles on the front seat.

"The clothing I have arranged to give away this afternoon. I thought you knew that every Saturday——" Marya got thus far, when he said, quickly,—

"Yes, yes, I had forgotten. Where shall we drive

to first?" He looked sideways at her, the devil laughing again in his eyes.

"To the Jews' Quarter," she said, firmly, giving Nicolas a list of the numbers for the coachman. "Natalie Nicolaevna has given me a long list of poor creatures that I can help there."

"The Jews' Quarter!" he laughed lightly. "I must look after you, little wife, or they will be converting you to their godless creed." He pulled off his thick gloves and rubbed his hands together in a jovial, boyish way; he seemed to be enjoying some huge joke. "It is cold; I was greatly minded to call out Dimitri for a game of snowballs while I was waiting for you, but I learned that he was gone to the hospital of St. Barbara with a basket of flowers from you." He put his arm round her and drew her tenderly towards him. "After all, I think I need have no fear of your being made a convert. There are not many women who would send a boy flying off on a horse's back with an offering of flowers to a poor little place two miles away." She felt him shake with inward laughter. "No, no; other women would have sent the flowers to the town hospital, that all Odessa might see their bounty. What a fool I've been," he exclaimed, "to let your odd idea that our God was a Jew darken my sky for a moment!" He laughed outright now, and continued talking carelessly of every kind of trivial thing until they came to the Jews' Quarter.

"Lord in heaven, how it smells!" he cried, when Mikej, one of the men-servants, opened the carriage door. Marya rose. "No, I will not permit you to get out." He laid his hand heavliy on her arm. There was no resisting that grip; she had perforce to sit down. "Which bundle shall I give him?" he asked, blandly.

"That." She pointed to the topmost one. "They nearly all contain the same kind of things with the exception of two or three, and those have the names of the women upon them. This one is for Mirzah Pogosski; she lives on the second floor," she said to the servant.

"Delightful place for an afternoon drive," smiled Michael, while Mikej was gone. "Odessa has not much to offer, but the public gardens are surely better than this."

"Then why did you come?" asked Marya, smiling in her turn. There were lies and strategems to be thought of for the safe delivery of Olga's bundle. She knew she must play her part well or give up the game.

"To be with you, little wife," he whispered, peeping under her eyelids to try to discover the meaning of the quiet smile that was still playing about her lips, and which at his glance broke into a merry one; but he learned nothing by that.

The servant returned, saying that "Mirzah Pogosski sent a blessing to her Excellency."

"Stop!" called Michael, as the man was mounting to his seat. "Take the rest of these bundles and deliver them according to the names and numbers on the list."

"Not those two," said Marya, taking possession of Olga's bundle and the one she had intended to ask Olga to give to Salome's mother.

"Why not?" asked Michael, sharply.

"Because," said Marya, simply, "I do not know the woman's name. You see they are not labelled as the others were. I only know her face, so I must see her and give them to her myself."

"Drive on, then," said Michael; "and when you come to the last number on the list——"

"The last but one,—I visit the governor's wife last."

"Do you?" He pretended to yawn.

"You need not go in," said Marya, quickly, "if you are tired."

"No, no; of course not. "But"—with an air of great resignation—"I'll go in with you. After all, the Princess Czartoryski is charming and exceedingly useful. Drive quickly," he called to Anton, the coachman.

Away went the carriage on the smooth runners, Marya's heart beating hard and fast. Suppose Michael should insist upon carrying the bundles? Did he suspect? No, he could not, or he would at once have set about bringing Olga back. So far they were safe; but it was best to be prepared for all things.

She commenced drawing off her left glove under cover of her muff. On that hand, on the forefinger, she wore a big, oblong signet ring of red onyx which Olga knew as well as she knew Marya's face. Marya's idea was to open the door of David Rheba's room a little way, just far enough for the bundles to go through, and to place them inside with her left hand, then quickly close the door. Olga would see the ring and would understand there was danger afoot or Marya would have entered.

Marya drew in a deep breath, praying that her

scheme might prosper. She had counted the number of bundles; Mikej had delivered them all. Only the two on the seat facing her now remained. The carriage stopped. Michael jumped out the moment the door was opened, and gave his arm to Marya. Without a protest she took it, smiling,—

"This is very good of you;" and so on up to David's room she climbed leaning on his arm, Mikej following with the bundles. When only about five stairs from David's door she stopped and, holding up her hand, said, "Oh! I had forgotten. The poor woman is very ill with small-pox——"

Away went the bundles flying out of the servant's hand on to the landing above and he going at headlong speed down to the carriage, while Michael Volkenoff leaned back against the wall with a face as white as chalk. Before he could recover himself Marya sprang up the few remaining stairs, softly opened the door, and placed the bundles inside. All was quiet within the room; it happened to be one of those moments of deep silence which settled down now and again on the little party sitting round the stove, between song and song or story. Marya closed the door again as softly as she had opened it, and followed Michael, with a laugh in her heart, to the carriage.

"The woman was sitting by the stove," she said, reassuringly, when they were again gliding along, "so I may have been misinformed about her illness."

"Nevertheless, you have made me feel sick. There is nothing I have so insane a fear of as small-pox."

A moment after they were rushing on once more.

He lighted a cigarette and leaned back, watching Marya.

There was a sweet, serene look on her face, not at all the look of a woman who had just outwitted a clever, crafty man; and there were tears in her eyes when she turned presently to say to him,—

"I am so sorry I frightened you." Being a true woman, she was genuinely sorry that she had been compelled to hurt him. He thought her either the most consummate actress, or that his instinct for the first time in his life was leading him astray. He decided, however, to trust to his instinct.

About fifteen minutes later they stopped at the house of Princess Czartoryski. Prince Vladimir Ogareff was governor of Odessa, but it was his wife who governed the province. He was big, good-natured, and indolent, and when the office was conferred on him people lifted their hands and said, "Poor Odessa!" But the Princess Czartoryski smiled in her pretty sleeve and ruled behind him. She chose the officials, suggested reforms, set many things straight which had been crooked, and fully justified the choice of the prince as governor of Odessa. She was a woman of indomitable spirit, courage, and charm, besides of ever-varying impulse. No one, once in her presence, could resist her; she pervaded them with a sense of rest and sunshine, of repose and strength. If she found a scheme impossible, she quietly put it away without fume or regret and took up another. She must always be doing something, either for herself or for Russia, but chiefly, in justice to her let it be said, for Russia. In winter she was content to be idle, simply to be charming, entertain, and reserve her force for the sunny days. Smilingly she would sometimes say that her forefathers must have been of the hibernating species. Directly the great thaw set in, she would shut herself in her rooms, for ten days or a fortnight, taking alternate baths of warm milk and perfumed oil, and a diet of white fish, milk, honey, and rye bread, with perfect rest between each bath and meal; only listening occasionally to one of her women, possessed of a beautiful mellow voice, who read to her or sang. At the end of her beatification, as she named the beautifying process,—and it was an apt term, for she came forth happy and in a state of perfect felicity,—her body was rounded out, and she was beautiful both to look upon and to be with. Then there was no stint in the harmony she let flow out from herself to others, and that was the secret of her power; she rejoiced in herself and made others rejoice with her, and, being neither angel nor devil, but a delightful combination of the two, a very woman from her small tawny head to the soles of her slender feet, life was like a garden of roses, and she the queen.

She was chatting with two visitors when Marya and Michael entered. She rose from her chair to greet them, and made Marya sit close by her side; but not a moment did Michael give Marya to whisper a few words to her, or even to scribble a message on a card. He sat close by her elbow, enchanting the princess with his wonderful flow of conversation, for no man could be more fascinating than Michael Volkenoff when he chose, and taking all the attention to himself. At the end of an hour he took Marya away, telling the princess, in spite of Marya's protest, that she was tired and must be taken home to rest. So away down to the carriage he led her, and when they were seated and flying homeward he leaned back and closed his eyes with a soft little laugh, while Marya sat heartsick and bewildered that the day was gone and the passports as far away as they were when she first started out.

CHAPTER XVII.

CONCERNING MICHAEL AND MARYA.

"Do not dismiss the carriage," Marya said to Nicolas, on arriving at home; "I may need it again. Has Dimitri returned?"

"Yes, mistress."

"Bring in the samovar."

Michael followed Nicolas.

"Take my coat, remove my snow-shoes." He sat down in a chair in the corridor within sight of Marya's dressing-room while Nicolas pulled off the shoes. Presently Marya came from her room and went into the cedar room. He followed her.

"Come and look at the lights in the harbour," he said, cheerfully. He put his arm round her shoulders and drew her into the window. "That big ship, you can just see her outline," he said, carelessly, "is one of our gun-boats; that with the red and blue lights is the 'Wanda,' the passenger and freight vessel: she sails to-morrow, I believe."

He felt a little convulsive movement of Marya's heart under his hand. He smiled and went on, "She carries a fine cargo—some of our grain—to England, and Volodja tells me that everyone of her berths is filled up. She has only twenty, and more than half of them are taken by English merchants. Sharp fellows, those English; they know that in a few years Odessa will be one of the greatest export stations in Russia. Ah! here is the samovar. Now, sit here in your cosy little chair, I here in mine, and let us take our tea as we used to take it. . . . Why, how pale you are!" He smiled quietly, turned to Nicolas, and said, "You can dismiss the carriage; your mistress will not need it again to-day."

Nicolas bowed and left the room.

"Still so pale and silent," said Michael, looking at her, sorrow in his voice, the look of a conqueror in his eyes and the carriage of his head.

"I am tired," she answered, in a broken voice, "very tired." She leaned back in her chair and sighed wearily.

Michael smiled and hummed a little folk-song that he was fond of hearing her sing, and poured out the tea. Something in the melody started a fresh thought in Marya's mind. She had forgotten that Olga belonged to her. Olga was, in Russian parlance, her soul,—hers to give away, to sell, or to keep. Olga was hers! Why had she not remembered that before? Her whole being was cheered; the thought came like sunshine.

Michael carried a cup of tea round to her left side, because her face was turned that way, and he wanted to see what she was thinking of. He went down on one knee and put his finger under her chin, tilting back her head. Marya opened her eyes full on his. They were filled with bright, merry, mischievous laughter.

His eyebrows went up, then he frowned.

"You said——" he began.

"That I was tired. So I was; now I am not. Come, now; pull your chair up to the fire and I'll sing you the song you were humming. It has cured me of my fatigue, and I must repay you for it." So she sat and sang, thinking of Olga's freedom, the ring of joy in her sweet voice, feeling sure that all would be well.

She sang and talked till it was time to dress for supper. When she left him, he watched her go down the corridor and turn into the lobby leading to Olga's room. He stole on tiptoe up to the door. It was closed. She was talking soothingly to someone within, —the woman Olga, he thought. Presently he heard Marya moving towards the door. He passed hurriedly into her dressing-room, and was standing absorbed in a book when she entered, followed by Wolf. She had unknowingly shut the old dog in Olga's room, and thus in talking to him had set Michael thinking that the girl was there, possibly preparing for her flight with the Jew. He sat talking to Marya while she dressed, smiling when her woman, having asked which gown she would wear, was answered,—

"The white silk with sable and lace." It was the gown he used to love best to see her in. He watched with intense interest the woman arrange the soft, straight, heavy folds of the skirt and the delicate, filmy lace at the wrists. The neck was cut round, in the fashion of those days, coming up nearly to her perfect throat, with a narrow band of sable, which made her skin look rosy white above. Her thick hair was coiled in a loose knot on the nape of her neck, and a fichu of rare old lace, with ends that nearly touched the floor, covered her shoulders. She smiled at him with sparkling eyes as she fastened it, asking, "Are you satisfied?" She felt that she held all the ends of the tangled coil in her two hands, and with one tug could set the whole straight, so she could afford to be sweet and gracious.

"More than satisfied," he smiled.

She turned again to the dressing-table. Suddenly her gaiety ebbed. She had caught the reflection of his smile in her glass; there was something in it she could neither understand nor read, yet it made her face flush with a strange sense of insult and degradation. She finished dressing in silence.

He watched her into the cedar room, saying before dashing into his own room,—

"We will eat our supper here to-night."

He sent his man for Nicolas. When Nicolas came he said, "No one is to leave the house to-night, either to carry letters or messages. Give the order to the porters and the gate-keepers and bring the keys to me." Nicolas bowed and left. The order went round; the gates were barred, the doors bolted and locked. When Michael locked up the great keys in a cabinet in his dressing-room, he nodded,—

"Now if her visit to Princess Czartoryski meant a passport for David Rheba and Olga to leave by the 'Wanda,' there is no need to watch her farther to-night. Anyway, for the present I can let things slide, and amuse myself up to the hilt with her. Who would have dreamed she could be so cunning?"

Supper passed; Marya was again as gay and merry as a child, while he seemed to be lightly, carelessly amused, as one might be by a performing dog hired to help one escape a tedious hour. His words were courteous, almost caressing, but the tone, the manner, the very expression of his face, was a covert insult.

Marya didn't pause to ask herself why this remarkable change in him. Only once or twice her heart was shaken with the thought that he seemed to have lost all his reverence for her, but she would not entertain the idea; she put it away. She was happy; she could afford to be happy. To-morrow, the Sabbath, he must discover that Olga was gone, for on that day all the serfs on the estate assembled in the chapel for service, then she could say to him,—

"She is gone. She was mine, and I have given her to David Rheba to be his for wife, for I felt it a sin to stand between them and their love."

Why trouble now for a passport? Olga could still live in Odessa, and they might see each other every day. And so the evening passed till it was close on midnight.

At the door of her dressing-room Marya held out her hand, saying, "God guard you, Michael."

"No, no," he said, "we have made up our quarrel; let us end our evening in our old way. I am coming to read Alcman to you."

"Not to-night, Michael, please."

"But I say yes," he smiled.

"And I say no; I am not in the humour," she pleaded.

"Not in the humour! Well, may the saints then help me to understand a woman! You have been singing like a linnet nearly the whole evening long, and now, suddenly, you say you are not in the humour for Alcman."

"Well, whether you can understand me or not, let me have my way in this; I want to think—to pray——"

"Pray! You!" His shoulders shook with suppressed laughter; he pinched her ear in a patronizing, half-tolerant, wholly-amused way, then, turning lightly on his heel, he said, "I am going for Alcman," and Marya walked slowly into her boudoir, and stood looking blankly into the fire.

She felt that she could not listen to the poetry that had once been one of her greatest delights to hear. She felt that she must run shrieking away from it; from the house, from all association with a love that seemed as dead as a tree that had been smitten by lightning, and had no more sap or life in it from root to top. . . . Yet, as he said, she had laughed—had sung——

She sighed, bitterly contemptuous of herself, remembering that her joy and light-heartedness the whole evening through had been at the prospect of Olga's freedom. Not once, under all her gaiety, had there been the smallest touch of the sweet, old, accustomed tenderness when her heart would go out to him more as a mother's than a wife's. Why had she not been frank with him? What terrible change had come over her love for him? She shook her head and sighed aloud,—

"I cannot fathom it."

Her woman came forward from the dressing-room, asking,—

"Did you call, mistress?"

"No, Natalia, but you may unfasten my gown."

Then the questions began again while the woman brushed out her hair, and in and out, weaving themselves between like a glittering golden thread, went some lines of Alcman's, keeping time with her thoughts,—

"Would that I were a sea-bird with limbs that could never tire,
Over the foam-flowers flying with halcyons ever on wing,
Keeping a careless heart, a sea-blue bird of the spring."

"A sea-bird! a sea-bird!" she said, aloud, then she thrust her fingers in her ears, thinking to shut out the rhythm of the lovely words, but the song held on its way, while the questions held fast to theirs. Had he himself utterly killed the wife's love in her with his brutality on the evening she had told him of Olga's love for David, and by his cruelty that morning? and yet it was not the first time he had been cruel. Perhaps the change had been slowly growing, and this last outburst had culminated it. She sighed again wearily, and put her arms listlessly into the sleeves of the warm robe that her woman held out for her. Then she seated herself in a chair by the fire, her thoughts travelling on again. Or was it some subtle reflection of the change in his love, for it was changed, that had altered hers? He had that morning said she was a woman without a soul. . . .

"Come, come, little wife. Here is Alcman."

Michael was standing beside her chair; he had been there some moments observing her. She looked up appealingly, and a slight shiver passed over her.

"This is not your usual welcome to our poet of poets," he smiled.

"No," she answered in a dull voice, and, rising, she sat down upon a cushion with her head resting against the arm of the chair she had just left. Michael seated himself in her place and brushed his hand lightly over her hair, looking down on her with the devil's laugh back in his eyes, his lips twitching to hold back a smile.

* * * * * * * *

When he left the room, two hours later, he left her with her face thrust in among the pillows of her bed, silent, still as stone, degraded, her womanhood outraged, her love for him slain, the light of her spirit seemingly gone out for ever.

He walked up and down the corridor outside her room twice or thrice before going to his bed. He was smiling; satisfaction glowed upon his face. He had taken his revenge; he had been five weeks thinking out the way to it. At last the way suggested itself, and he had obeyed it. He turned and looked in the direction of her room. He thought he heard a sob. He laughed softly to himself. He had punished her. He had made her bite the dust. She had destroyed for him the ideal he had set up as his wife, and he had destroyed for her her ideal of the sanctity of married life, of the perfect, holy love which should be between man and wife. Where now was her self-reverence? He shrugged his shoulders at his want of logic. Was she not a heretic? No more to him henceforth than any wretched wanton of the streets. Self-reverence! He laughed again softly to himself. What, now, of her fine, poetic theories? Let her weep over the ashes of them, as she had left him to weep over the idol he had set up in her, and that she had shattered.

He had walked this time as far as the passage that led to Olga's room. He stood looking down it for a while, then he walked noiselessly to the door and stood there awhile, considering whether he should enter, and if she were awake, tell her that she would be kept a prisoner in her room until the Thursday when she would be married to Foka, or, if she were asleep, lock the door and take possession of the key.

He turned the handle and went into the room. It was one large room divided in two by an archway, and curtains slung from it on a brass pole. The part nearest the door was furnished as a little sitting-room, the other as a bedroom. The light from the snow shone through the windows and made things visible.

He paused by the door listening. There was not a breath, not a movement in the place. He strode heavily over to the bed and thrust aside the curtain. He pulled in his breath as though he had been struck when he saw the bed was empty, the clothes tossed down to the foot as though someone had just thrown them off.

Had Olga, hearing the door open, in fear hidden

herself somewhere in the room, or was she gone? He put his hand on the bottom sheet; it was cold.

He walked out of the room and into his wife's, entering without knocking, and seating himself by the bed. The candles were still burning on the table. Marya was lying all her length along the bed, her face still hidden.

"Are you asleep?" he asked.

There was no answer.

Then a little creeping feeling of horror crept over his right cheek; she was so still, so motionless. Had she killed herself? He rose, and, lifting her up bodily, laid her with her face upwards. She moaned and turned it away from him. So she was alive.

"Where is Olga?" he asked, coldly.

Marya was silent.

"Where is Olga?"

"I will not tell you." Slowly and with pain came her reply.

"I will compel you."

"You cannot."

There was a pause, then Marya spoke again,—

"Olga is mine, my slave, as you would say; you gave her to me, and I have done what I pleased with my own."

"Yours!" He stood looking down at her, the power of his will breathing out of him, pervading the room as though an evil being full of anger, domination, and craft had suddenly entered.

Marya felt it in all its force; it seemed to beat against her, making her heart shake and her limbs rigid as she set her will hard against his in the silent fight for mastery.

"Did you say yours?" he asked.

"That was my meaning," she answered, in a steady voice.

His will had been wrestled with and conquered. He considered within himself for a moment. What stuff could this woman be made of, she so seeming soft, so fragile? She was beginning to interest him anew.

"Please to understand in what way she belongs to you," he said. "She is yours for your use as is anything I possess, but that does not give you the right of disposing of any one thing without my consent. You had no deed of gift with her; she is mine, and unless she returns to-morrow of her own will she shall be whipped in the yard in the presence of her fellow-serfs, as other runaways are punished."

It was final; he waited yet awhile longer, but she spoke no more. Then he rose and went straight to his own room, sat down at his desk, and wrote to the head of the police department.

"David Rheba, a Jew, by trade a silversmith, living in the Jews' Quarter, has kidnapped a female serf named Olga with intent to pervert her to the Jewish creed.

(Signed) "MICHAEL VOLKENOFF."

This he closed and sealed; then he looked at his watch: it was nearly three. Should he send it at once? No; Marya might hear and guess and set on foot some counter-plan. Best that he should carry it himself in the morning.

The Jew should have this one night; it would incriminate him the more. So Michael undressed, bathed his face and hands, prayed fervently for protection and mercy, in consideration of his having saved the soul of a Christian from one of the accursed race, went to bed, and slept soundly, no dreams disturbing his rest; all was peace with him.

CHAPTER XVIII.

THE ARREST.

OLGA was singing like a bird as she flitted about David's room,—her room now, he told her, and made her blush and laugh for happy pride of his words. She swept and dusted the place and polished the tall silver candlesticks. It was about nine in the morning, and David had been working since eight,—since the time they had eaten breakfast. Suddenly he threw down the smelting-pot and set his mouth against the ball of his left hand. Olga flew over to him.

"Thou hast hurt thyself."

"The tray slipped, that's all, sweetheart, and some of the molten silver dropped on my hand." A piece of the hot metal was sticking to the ball of his thumb. He pulled it away, the flesh coming with it, leaving a deep triangular-shaped red mark in the ball of his thumb. Olga caught his hand and wiped away some blood that oozed out with her apron.

"I was looking at thee or it wouldn't have happened," he smiled.

"Well, now, how can I heal it?" she asked, kissing the wound, the blood oozing out again and dabbling her lips.

David shuddered and snatched his hand away.

"Thou wilt find some tarred twine in that tool-box;

ravel a little of it out and then bind it to the place over a band of linen dipped in oil; that will heal it. But wipe the blood from thy lips first; the sight fills me with pain. I seem to have seen them like that before——"

He put his hand to his brow. Why should the sight of his blood upon her lips so fill his heart with foreboding? Was it the recollection of some horrible dream or a foretelling of some trouble?

Olga knelt down by him with the ravelled twine in her hand. First she staunched the blood with her apron, looking closely at the wound to see there were no specks of dirt in it; then she bound the linen and twine firmly upon it with strips torn from one of her handkerchiefs.

"It is an oddly shaped cut," she said, sewing the ends of the pieces of linen together.

"Yes; it is like a triangle, a mystic sign of the ancients. Let us look upon it as a good omen, housemate."

"David!" cried someone outside the door. It was Salome. She came in like a gust of wind, and stood with her little body against the door; her face white, her eyes staring.

"What's the trouble, my pigeon?" asked David, gravely.

"Some men have been enquiring for thee. Mother says they are the police."

David looked at Olga.

"They are coming!" whispered Salome. "Oh, canst thou not get away?"

She was suddenly thrust from the door by someone pushing it roughly open, and two men entered, others crowding upon the landing.

"You must go with us," said the foremost one sharply to David.

"What have I done?"

"My orders are to arrest you. You must ask someone else what for."

They took him by the shoulders and pushed him towards the door.

David wrenched his shoulders from their hands and went back to Olga, who was speechless and white as death. He caught her in his arms.

"I shall soon be back, sweetheart." He kissed her cheeks, her lips; then the police gripped hold of him again and dragged him away. "Don't lose heart," he smiled.

"David," shrieked Salome, "thou wilt be frozen!" She was at the door fronting the men, her eyes blazing at them like a Fury's, her slight body staggering under the weight of his fur-lined pelisse.

The men swore at the delay while David put on his pelisse. Olga gave him his cap without power to utter a word,—without a tear. He kissed her cheek, like ice under his lips, and was about to take her in his arms to comfort her when the officers thrust rudely between them and pushed him out of the room and down the stairs, three of the police going in front, three behind, leaving no chance of escape, and so out and along the streets to the police barracks. No explanation was given him; he was put into a cell with some other prisoners and the door locked upon him.

After he was gone, Salome threw herself down on the floor and screamed in impotent rage and anger.

"Oh, I could kill them! I could kill them! Dost not thou want to kill them?" she asked Olga, looking up.

Olga was sitting on David's work-stool staring at the spots of blood on her apron.

"I have a strange weight here," she said, in a heavy, lifeless voice, lifting her hands to her head. "Why have they taken him away?"

"It is because thou art a Christian, mother says."

"I? No!" Her speech came slowly. "I hurt him!" She looked round helplessly; then without a sound she rolled off the stool on to the floor, and lay there with pale, upturned face and staring eyes.

"Oh, she is dead!" wailed Salome. "Mother! mother!" she sobbed, almost falling down the stairs in her terror and haste.

"What is the trouble, child?" asked Kezia. She was standing at the door of her room, and stopped Salome as she was passing.

"The Christian woman, David's wife, hath fallen dead."

Kezia asked no questions, saying, merely, "Fetch thy mother," and went up to David's room. She paused a moment on the threshold, thinking of the night she had crouched there, watching Salome dancing. She went forward slowly to Olga, and leant over her.

"She has fainted," she said, calmly; then she sat

upon the floor by Olga's side and waited for Judith. Judith came hurrying up with tears in her eyes. She rapidly explained things to Kezia, so far as she had been able to gather what had happened from the men who guarded the door of the house.

Kezia was still sitting cross-legged on the floor by the side of Olga. She regarded her a long time in silence after Judith entered, her chin on her hand.

"This will be a bad thing for thy friend David," she said at last; "it may be hanging; at the best, exile."

Judith made a movement with her hand to Olga. Kezia said, "Lift up her eyelids." Judith obeyed. Kezia peeped under them, saying, "No, she is not coming out of it; she cannot hear. What wilt thou do with the things here?"

"She is David's wife," said Judith, sitting on the floor facing Kezia from the other side of Olga. "She will have care of them."

Kezia regarded Judith with a queer, contemptuous little smile. "How long hast thou lived in Russia, Judith Manuelli?" she asked.

"Since I was betrothed to Ezra, fifteen years ago."

"And thou canst suppose this woman's master will let her remain here! He will have her dragged back, and most likely flogged for running away."

"Then I hope she is dead," said Salome, passionately.

"Don't crowd upon her," said Kezia, pulling Salome away from Olga's head.

"Why dost thou not give her some water?" asked Judith, who had offered some to Kezia in a cup.

"Best let Nature have her way; why bring her poor sense back to suffer? I know."

"Verily, I believe thou knowest everything, Kezia."

"And in everything there is knowledge. What is the name of the woman's master?"

"That I cannot tell thee; David did not say."

"Well, her master knows where she is; the arrest proves that."

Olga moaned and moved a little. Kezia told Judith to sprinkle a few drops of water in her face.

"The pillow," said Kezia. Salome flew to fetch it from the bed. "Put it under her head, so. Now a little more water. No, you give it," to Judith, who offered the cup to her.

Olga opened her eyes and stared at them awhile; then she shivered and closed her lids again with a moaning sigh and lay motionless.

"She has fainted again," said Judith.

Kezia shook her head and rose from the floor.

"She is not one of the crying sort; that is all. Try to get her on to the bed. Salome, help your mother."

The two raised Olga partly up, then on to her feet.

"I think I can walk," she whispered. Between them she walked to the bed and sat down upon it. "I don't know why I am like this," she said, faintly. "Something happened——" She shivered violently. Salome darted for her cloak, that was lying in the chest. "What was it?"

Kezia shook her head and turned away.

"There, now, thou art warmer," said Judith, tucking the cloak about her and trying to smile.

"Thou, thou——" Olga caught her hand and looked hard at her; then around the room at David's stool, his bench; then at the stove, where he had stacked the wood ready to her hand. At that she gave a sharp, bitter cry, and sat huddled upon the bed, staring at them with despair in her eyes, her lips white and dropping apart.

Judith wept and wiped away her tears on the skirt of her dress; Salome tugged at her hair in a tempest of anger in a corner of the room, trying hard not to scream aloud; Kezia stared, dry-eyed and silent, out of the window.

Someone knocked softly at the door; then it opened, and Marya Volkenoff entered. Olga saw her and held out her arms, like a tired, lost child, at sight of the mother's breast, crying, "Little Mother! little Mother!" and as Marya ran to her she slipped off the bed and on to the floor, clasping Marya's knees, crying bitterly; the flood-tide of her grief at last bearing all down in its course and gushing out over her cheeks in big, round drops, and falling, a drenching shower, into her bosom.

Marya raised her, and together they sat upon the bed clasping each other, Marya gripping her tight, as though she feared Michael would come and snatch her away.

"They have taken him," sobbed Olga, "they have taken him."

Marya nodded, "I know."

"Canst thou not help him?"

"I cannot help even thee, my poor Olga, except to

take thee back with me, and that is what I have come to do."

"The master——"

"Commands it."

"Was it he, then, who——"

"Yes."

"But I am David's wife."

"That does not make thee a free woman; thou art still a serf." Marya said it sharply and quickly after a struggle. It was best after all to speak it out; the whole painful thing had to be done, the more speedily the better.

"But he cannot force me to marry Foka."

"No, he dare not," said Marya, quietly. Kezia turned for the first time and looked at her. Judith and Salome turned too; they had been trying in vain to fix their attention on the street below.

Marya turned to Kezia. "Are you one of David Rheba's friends?" she asked.

"No; these two are his friends. I only came to see what I could do for her," answered Kezia, pointing to Olga.

"Then will you, as his friend," said Marya, turning now to Judith, and attracted by the tender, womanly expression of her face which not all the hunger and privation had had power to destroy, "take this money and buy food for him until he is released. For he will be released," she smiled, trying to cheer Olga with a hope she herself was hopeless of. She gave Judith several roubles; then she muffled Olga in the big cloak that had been lying on the bed and turned towards the door.

A SON OF ISRAEL

"But, mistress," said Olga, drawing back, "this is David's room; these his treasures, this his work, his tools. I must not leave them. He will need them again."

Just then someone tapped on the landing; it was a nervous, hurried noise as from some one in deadly fear. Salome opened the door. No one was visible; but on a level with the threshold was the butt end of a whip with a leaf from a note-book stuck on it, and away down the stairs, as far off as he could get from the room, was Mikej, the servant, trembling violently, and the colour of a plucked goose.

"For her Excellency," he said. Salome took the note from the whip, and he seemed to vanish, so quickly he went.

"It is for me," said Marya. She smiled as she read what was written upon it. It was from Michael.

"I give you another five minutes," it began; then, underlined, "I trust the small-pox patient is better."

"Come, child," she said to Olga.

Olga hung back. "I cannot go unless I know that my David's home will be safe."

Kezia gave Judith a look.

"Wilt thou trust it to me?" asked Judith, taking her hand. "David loves me, and I will be faithful in the smallest thing."

"Yes," said Olga; "I will leave them in thy hands." She looked round the room. David's gloves were lying on the top of the chest where she had left them because they needed mending. She snatched them up and hugged them under her cloak, following Marya, who could hear an impatient tapping at the foot of the stairs. It was the scared Mikej, who had been ordered to stay there to wait her coming or be soundly flogged. Michael was tramping up and down outside the carriage.

"Well, is the small pox patient better?" he asked.

"She is quite recovered," said Marya, gravely, without looking at him. "Mikej, call a drosky for your master; Olga will ride with me." She put the girl into the carriage as she spoke and got in after her. Michael bowed proudly to her, saying,—

"I thank you, madam; it is what I would desire."

When Olga was gone Kezia turned to Judith, saying,—

"When thou seest thy friend David, tell him my hands have not touched his wife; he will understand."

CHAPTER XIX.

RUSSIAN JUSTICE.

DAVID was put into the common cell of the prison,—among thieves, swindlers, men suspected of murder, footpads, and two poor, demented, nameless wretches waiting to be conveyed to the asylum. At the end of two days he was put into another cell about seven feet long by six broad; this he had to himself. He then learned the crime he was arrested for. He was accused of perverting a Christian woman to the Jewish creed, and he was removed from the common cell for fear he might corrupt the religious morals of his fellow-prisoners. David was glad of the quiet; he could now think of Olga. In the other place it had seemed pollution to her purity to let his thoughts dwell on her among the riot, the foul words, the obscene talk and games, gambling and libertinism that possessed all there save the two madmen, and these David protected from tortures the others would have inflicted on them, giving them the chief part of the food that was brought to him twice a day by Ezra. Judith, sometimes Salome and Belah, would go with Ezra, and would wait at the prison door, greedy for news of their friend. When David was removed the warder let Ezra see him for a few moments; but all the silent man could say in answer to the questions David showered upon him was,—

"God hold thee in his hand."

Two days after that Judith and Salome came, the prudent, careful Ezra having said,—

"Best those go that can talk and give our David comfort for all the roubles we are wasting on the officials."

So they went to David, and at first all they could do was to weep, because his face had grown so wan; then they poured out in a stream all that had occurred: first, that Olga was gone back with her mistress; that no word had come from her since because she was sick with a low fever, but the mistress had sent a messenger to Judith, bidding her tell David that she would be surety for his wife, and that she also sent a kerchief of Olga's. Judith took the kerchief from her bosom and gave it to him.

It was of silk, the threads of many colours, mellow green, and pink, and blue, with a deep shade of purple, like a lustrous grape, shimmering predominant above them all. It caught a ray of light from the grating above his head, and shone in the gloomy place like a shell just cast up on a sunny beach and glistening with a thousand drops of spray. He turned away with the precious thing held fast in his hands and gazed at it with luminous eyes, murmuring some soft, inaudible words; then tenderly, with reverent touch, he folded it and lay it in his blouse, over his heart, and it seemed to him that his girl's own dear hands were resting there, warm and light, and he felt as sure as though he had been witness to it that Marya Volkenoff had pressed the kerchief to Olga's face, her lips, her bosom, for it was full of her sweet self, and made his spirit leap up and fly out past all the bolts and bars, the thick prison walls, and hold converse with hers. At the same hour the fever left Olga. She turned with dewy eyes to Marya, smiled at her, and said, "David," then fell into a sweet, deep sleep.

All the rest of the time David stood like a man in a dream, not heeding Judith's talk of how she had stored away all his tools in the big chest, and how she and Ezra and the children were living in his room to keep it for him, for, she said, now that Daniel Pereira gave Salome a salary, they could afford to pay the rent for an upper room, and why not take David's and thus keep it safe until he was at home again? And also what a strange being Kezia was; for, though she had sat watching all they did, yet she would not touch one thing of his. No, she would not even give Olga some water when she fainted,—David roused at this,—Kezia had made Judith give the drink, and afterwards said,—

"So tell him, if thou likest, the Meldola hath not touched one thing of his. Let him sleep in peace; they have not been defiled."

"Then didst thou tell her, Judith, that I said she was unclean?"

"No; but on that day when Pereira was coming to see our Salome I said thou couldst not bid her welcome, —no more."

"Her wit told her why," murmured David. "So she was with Olga?"

"Salome told her of the trouble, and when I went to your room she was sitting by Olga's side, but she would not touch her. She said, 'Tell thy friend David my hands have not touched his wife.'"

"I am glad," was all he said.

"She said that you would understand."

"Aye, I understand. And so thou art living in my room?"

"Aye. Thy wife would not go, though her master had commanded, till she knew your things would be in good hands."

"The brave, loving heart!" he smiled. Then with a glad, ringing voice and a lift of his head he said, "I thank thee, Judith, with all my soul. Thou hast brought me great comfort."

Someone could be heard talking in the passage outside the cell.

"The officer is coming," whispered Salome.

"Well, come say, 'God be with thee,'" said David, cheerily, and held out his arms to her. She sprang up to his neck, clasping it passionately.

"God be with thee," she cried. "Oh, if I could die for thee and thy Olga, for I love her, but thee greatest of all!"

"Die! Nay, thou shalt dance for us when I am free. Such hope is come into my heart that I feel our God hath set his hand to my cause, so it falter not. Carry my love to Ezra, and come again to-morrow if they will permit."

He kissed Judith on the cheeks and brow and sent her happy and smiling away. And Salome, glowing through her tears like a cluster of ripe peach-blossoms after an April shower, went swinging her mother's hand and dancing lightly on her toes down the foul, dark passage-way. Such infection had there been in the great wave of love and hope which had swept through David's heart it had carried all mistrust, all doubt away; it had borne down for them the stern, cruel illusions of the visible world. A veil was lifted, and they lived for a few short hours with the Real, the Infinite.

* * * * * * * *

Michael Volkenoff knew his country; he knew that from the highest to the lowest in office bribery and corruption seem to be Russian second nature, and, having full use of his knowledge many times before, he found it mere child's play to have David, a Jew, convicted as a man highly dangerous to the moral and religious welfare of the Holy Orthodox Church. David's trial lasted about five minutes. When he tried to speak he was shouted down, baited, and at last thrust out of the court like a dog, with "Twenty years in the mines" grunted at him by a vodka-sodden, greasy official.

But he went to his cell with his head held high; hope strong in his heart. His cause was in the hands of God, and could not fail.

The next morning before daybreak he was chained to a fellow-prisoner, guilty of some slight political offence, and the long terrible march to the mines commenced. It was over two thousand miles as the crow flies; it would be months before the journey could be at an end.

CHAPTER XX.

THE LITTLE MANNIKIN.

EZRA carried home the news, for Judith had been refused admittance that day. She stood up and wailed, her arms cast about her head. Salome and Belah clung to her, weeping; Ezra stood grim and silent, the great tears rolling down from his eyes and dropping into his beard, from thence to his caftan.

"I left some money for him with the officer, but the Lord of our race only knows whether he will receive it," he muttered after a while.

"Twenty years! twenty years!" wailed Judith, "and many drop dying on the road. Max Helfmann's wife hath told me of the terrible hardships. If the prisoners have no money they have to beg food from the people they pass on the road. Cold and disease cut them off as the first frost cuts down the flowers, and they are left by the roadside for the wolves to eat or for the first man who comes along to bury, if he will."

"No, no, no!" screamed Salome, "not our David! Oh, no!" She covered her shaking lips with her mother's gown, and looked out over it with her great eyes wild and wide, staring at something beyond. Her vivid imagination had conjured up a picture of David dying of cold and hunger by the roadside;

great wounds in his body from the blows of the whip; the wolves crouching in the forest waiting to tear him limb from limb as soon as the darkness had settled down.

"Cease, wife," said Ezra, sternly, picking up the child and comforting her. "David is strong, he will come through safely; he hath warm clothes—his fur pelisse——"

"Yes, I made him take it," sobbed Salome, greatly cheered at heart.

"And I will go enquire what time the prisoners leave. So look round and put together what thou canst for him, and the money Daniel Pereira left yesterday I will carry and put into his own hand myself." Ezra muffled himself up in his caftan and fur cap and went out.

"Now the Lord be praised for that man!" said Judith, fervently; "he speaketh little, but when he doth, it is to the purpose. Come, children, let's work for our beloved David."

They stuffed two thick pairs of stockings which they found in the chest into David's high boots; found a pair of ragged old fur gloves that with much patching and darning would protect his hands; and his two blankets they tied up with string ready to sling on his back. They also tucked what bread they had between the blankets, and Belah, with supreme self-sacrifice, put in his one toy, a little mannikin of wood, with movable arms and legs, that had comforted him exceedingly many a cold night, and he thought it must comfort David too.

A SON OF ISRAEL

The next morning Ezra was at the prison two hours before daybreak with the precious things. The soldiers wouldn't allow David to stop to speak to him, but Ezra, dodging their buffets and fists, ran by his side, giving him the things piece by piece, David slinging the boots round his neck ready for changing at the first halting-place they came to. Ezra wept when he was at last compelled to leave, but David, looking brightly at the rising sun that set his hair and beard aglow, said,—

"The God of our fathers is with me; tell thy beloved ones that. And tell my Olga. Nay, she knows. Though they can chain my body they cannot bar up my spirit. The universe is fluid, and the soul of man hath power to flow through and commune with whatsoever it will, so it be done in love."

David kissed Ezra heartily on the cheek as they moved on side by side, then waved him good-bye, and marched forward, his stout heart not once quailing; Olga's face before him like a star, the strength of God in his soul.

At night he found Belah's little mannikin. He had often seen the boy cuddling it up to his cheek as he lay asleep, and knew what store he set by it; so with a kiss to the queer odd thing for Rachel's sake, and a lump rising in his throat for the sweet thoughtfulness of the boy, he slung it round his neck by a piece of string and let it hang there close by Olga's kerchief. And many a time on the march when his fellow-prisoner drooped he would bring out the little mannikin, and would tell such marvellous tales of him that the man would be charmed of his fatigue, and would jog along more hopeful. At last the little mannikin became known to the other prisoners, and its appearance in David's hand at the end of the day, when they were halting for the night, was the signal to them to draw round and listen.

Some sitting on the floor, some lying, others curled up upon the sloping bare wooden shelves that served for beds, and are fastened one above the other to the walls of the Ostrog like bunks in a ship; all the men alike, whether rough, gentle, or vile, with their faces turned to David, listening, entranced. And with his back to the wall, the little mannikin standing on his knee, sat David, his vivid face glowing, his eyes flashing in the light of the tallow candle one of the prisoners would hold while he told some wondrous story And what stories they were! Belah's doll the hero of them all; the grave and gay, whimsical, fantastical, tragic, homely; of lovers, soldiers, children, goblins, fairies; into them David put all the fine imaginings that had made his work the rarest in the world. The subtle thoughts, the originality, the energy of the man having no other vent, found an outlet in beguiling these poor wretches of their misery for a short hour or so, and was himself beguiled of his own, for while he talked Olga seemed to be by his side; her sweet fragrance about him; her hand encircling his neck. To her as well as to them he poured out all his brilliant fancy, his poetry, his fire. He made her weep and laugh, even as he made the ragged, unkempt men, all with their eyes intent on his, weep and laugh, clap their hands, then tucking their chins in their folded arms again, listen once more, greedily fearful of losing a word; forgetful of the filthy floor, of the loathsome odour of the place, of the hunger which would often be gnawing at them, in the charm that was cast upon them by David's voice. And it was hard to tell which had the greater influence over the minds of the men, David's strong dramatic grip, his magnetism, the constant changes of his face and voice, or the superstitious awe each man felt for the little mannikin, for it grew at last to be a sentient thing, and would sometimes tell extraordinary tales of each one there. "Little Father," they called him, and Little Father kept them from the cruel games and foul jokes which had made David's heart sicken until there came into his mind this simple way to stay them.

Not once did David's heart sag or his strong hope faint, neither doubt nor misgiving that his liberty would be given back. When his soul would have veiled her face and drooped in sheer despair as the days lengthened into weeks, the weeks to months, and still the weary march went on and no sign of pardon, he said,—

"My soul, what of her if we thus sink into lamentation and grief and grow faint under the load? Nay, let us gird ourselves with cheerfulness and send out our spirit to her, filled full of solace and of comfort, that she may laugh and show men there is no bar to love; that it can speed along on the wings of thought swifter than flight of wind, than light itself can travel, to the heart of the chosen one, and, resting in peace, fill her with all the gladness of its being."

A SON OF ISRAEL

Thus he would commune with himself, putting away with resolute hand the despondency that strove to drag him down. The warmth of the sun that shines on the cedars of Lebanon was too deep in his blood to be driven hence by the chill, leaden apathy that settles on nearly all exiles on the march to the mines; he conquered, and by the conquest helped himself and others.

CHAPTER XXI.

COMPENSATION.

DURING the few days David lay waiting his trial, and for three weeks after he was sentenced, Marya found that she was a prisoner in her own house. When she wished to go to the governor to lay David's case before him, she found the "Little Mother's door" locked and the key in Michael's possession; the same with the great door leading to the chief entrance, and with the door to the garden. She understood and asked no questions, but sat down at her writing-table and wrote a letter to the Princess Czartoryski, begging her to call. She gave the letter to Nicolas with instructions to carry it at once to the governor's house. The old man hesitated and stood shamefaced before her, twisting the letter between his fingers. At last he said,—

"Mistress, if I speak, will you be silent of what I shall say? otherwise I may be flogged."

Marya winced, and said, "You may speak."

"I have orders from the master to carry all the letters you may give me at once to him. So, mistress, it is useless giving this to me; I must obey."

"Obey, then, Nicolas; carry that letter to your master, or, if I send out no letters, he will guess that you have told me his commands, and may punish you for it."

Nicolas bowed and left her, and, going straight to his master, laid the letter on the table close to his hand. Michael looked at the address, then tore open the envelope.

"She begs the princess to intercede for David Rheba." He read it through, not a line in his face softening, then he lighted a taper and burnt up the letter, blowing the charred pieces on to the floor before he went calmly on again with his work.

Marya made one appeal to him, then tried no more; she might as hopefully have appealed to stone. She went about heartsick and full of dread for David. She feared he might be flogged, perhaps hanged; she could not tell how shamelessly his case might be misrepresented. She knew that no opportunity would be given him to state the truth, and if it were, that no one would believe him, a Jew. She could only pray that the Princess Czartoryski might hear of the charge against him and use her influence to get him a fair hearing, but the chances were against the case coming to her ears, it would only be one among so many. And then suppose she did hear, what interest would she feel in a man perhaps unknown to her, and that man a Jew?

Olga had mended rapidly. From the time she woke from the long, deep sleep which followed immediately upon her return to consciousness, she had been cheerful, hopeful, her sunny temper unclouded, unflagging. It was she now; with numberless little artifices and plans, that kept Marya from the utter despondency which threatened to seize her.

After Marya's appeal to Michael, he had kept his own rooms. He refused to listen to any message from her, to look at any of the notes she sent begging to be allowed to go out into the air. He stopped her work for the poor people in the town, and kept all the letters that came for her. But for Olga, Marya would have broken down under the cruel isolation and restraint. She wondered what was to be the end of it. Had she been told that a man could keep his wife a prisoner in his house and no one seem the wiser, she would not have believed the tale. What had he told her friends? That she was sick, no doubt. But what was his intention? He could not keep her imprisoned for life.

At last one morning, three weeks after David was on the march to the mines, she found the key of the "Little Mother's door" lying upon her writing-table, and at one o'clock old Nicolas, with a beaming face, for his office of jailer had pressed heavily upon him, asked her at what hour she would wish the carriage to be ready.

"What for, Nicolas?"

"For your drive, mistress."

"So I am to be released," she said to herself; then to Nicolas, without any change in her face, she said, aloud, "At two. And, Nicolas, the open carriage, so I can feel the fresh keen wind upon my face. Ah, God, the wind! the sweet, free, glad, wild wind!" she whispered, with her face pressed to the window-panes.

At two she started, with Olga by her side, both rejoicing like girls at their sudden freedom, and their thoughts turned to one common point, the town prison for news of David. But when Nicolas asked where the coachman should drive, Marya said the road by the sea until three.

"But, Little Mother," whispered Olga, her eyes piteous to look upon, "David!"

"By and by," said Marya, smiling at her. "This is a bad hour for calling at the prison. Trust me, I know. We will stop for news on our way home."

That was only half a truth. Marya felt, if it should happen to be bad news, it was best to put off the learning of it as long as she could; at least it was best they should get all the sunshine possible at that time of year; it would make Olga better able to bear ill news. So they drove along westward, the pure, sweet air blowing on their faces.

"Oh, the sun! the sun!" cried Olga, with her head thrust forward, the hood falling from her hair. Marya was leaning back, taking in deep, big breaths.

"Ah! it is good," she cried, "God, how good, to be out once more in the air." Then she said no more till, at three, she ordered the man to drive to the town prison. To within three minutes of the place she had hesitated whether to let Olga go in with her or wait in the carriage. One last, quick look at the girl's eager face decided the question. It would be cruel to compel her to wait one moment; they should go in and make the enquiry together. Marya sent in her card to the chief official, and in a short time an officer came out and conducted her into an office on the right-hand side of the chief entrance. Olga followed, giving a tight little grip to Marya's arm while she put her question.

"David Rheba?" said the official. "David Rheba?" He drummed with the tips of his fingers on the desk awhile, thinking. "A Jew?" he asked, suddenly.

"Yes, a Jew," answered Marya.

He went to a pile of papers held together with a nail against the wall and turned them over one by one. "How long since he was arrested?" he asked.

"Four weeks," said Olga, breathlessly.

The man walked to another pile of papers.

"Sentenced to the mines. Twenty years. He is three weeks on the road now," he said, turning to them.

Olga rose, standing straight up, staring at him. Marya gave a bitter sob and caught the girl's hand.

"Twenty years?" asked Olga in a steady voice.

"Yes,"—referring again to the paper,—"twenty years."

"Thank you," she said, without one falter in her voice. Then she turned to Marya, who was heart-broken for the moment, as much at thought of Michael's relentless nature as of David's unjust sentence.

"Come, Little Mother; we'll go home," said Olga. She put her arm round Marya and led her out to the carriage, Marya wondering at the girl and at herself. As soon as they were seated, Olga said,—

"Now, mistress, don't grieve. David is happy, else why have I been so light-hearted these three weeks? Nay, three weeks and two days! It is either that I shall go to the mines and live with him there or that he will return to Odessa. He has some great hope in his heart, and has sent it to me. I'll not grieve, nor shalt thou, either." Some heavy tears dropped down her cloak. "I am weeping, I know, but that is only because I did not see him before he set out on the march, not because I have lost hope."

Michael supped with Marya that night. It was a silent meal, he watching her closely, she avoiding his eyes. At the end he said,—

"It is useless thinking of a pardon for that Jew. The machinery you would have to set in motion to get your appeal brought before the Czar is so complicated that any attempt of yours to move it must come to my knowledge."

"I know that, and how utterly hopeless it is to think of moving either you or that machinery," she said, bitterly, passing him and going to her boudoir, where she sat sewing and reading, talking between whiles with Olga until it was time for rest.

So the days came and went, and spring was near at hand; the snow was disappearing from the low cliffs above the sea and soon would melt away from the meadows, and still the barrier between Marya and Michael remained fixed, hard, unyielding, unsurmountable. They met, were coldly polite to each other before the servants, silent when alone. Marya gave up visiting or receiving; she allowed her friends to think that she was ill. Down in her heart she feared to meet them; she felt they must guess all that had befallen her, for she could not sit and smile and talk of simple, homely things with her soul struggling to cry aloud,—

"I have been outraged and degraded! Will no man put forth his hand to help me?" So she lived alone with her grief, even to her beloved Olga speaking no word of it.

Slowly a change crept over her; insensibly she became conscious that she was bearing another life besides her own. Her heart leaped into her throat at the thought. It was not possible! It was not, —no, it could not be that a child should be given to them!

She fancied for a time that her brain was giving way under the strain and was deceiving her. But days passed on, and with the beginning of spring she knew. Then—strange that it should be so!—Olga went to her one day with eyes overflowing, with tender, tremulous mouth, and, standing before her with loose clasped hands, happiness breathing out of every breath she took, said,—

"Little Mother, I have a wonderful thing to tell thee. I am with child to David——"

Before she had finished speaking she was down on her knees by Marya's side, kissing her hands, her face, saying how David would leap for gladness could he know, and that she was the most joyful woman in the whole world.

"My dear Olga, my dear," said Marya, trembling; then she bent her head and whispered, "I, too, am with child."

Olga sat back on the floor and looked at her. There

was no joy in Marya's voice, only her eyes looking out wistfully as she said again, "I, too, am with child."

Then Olga clasped Marya tight in her arms and could not speak one word of comfort. for the face above her was so wan.

CHAPTER XXII.

WHAT WILL IT BE?

Some few nights later in the week, while Marya was reading in the cedar room and listening to a storm of wind that was shrieking and tearing over the cliffs, and shuddering at thought of the wrecks they would hear of in the morning, Michael came in and stood looking at her, then he seated himself beside her, saying,—

"Will you close your book and listen to me for a few minutes?"

Marya closed her book, and, giving him one brief glance, said, "Yes."

"It is about Olga," he began. Marya's heart began to shake; she knew what was coming. "Inhuman as you think me——" he paused, hoping that she would contradict what he had said. Marya made no sign, so he continued, with a deep sense of injury, "I have behaved with the uttermost kindness to Olga; I have given her more than two months to recover from the loss of her Jew lover, now she must consider my wishes. I expect her to be prepared to marry Foka Saviska to-morrow morning. Foka has my orders and will be here at ten."

"You should have consulted me before sending out

your commands. Olga is the wife of David Rheba, the Jew."

"There can be no marriage bond between a Jew and a Christian."

"My confessor made them man and wife here in this room on the morning you refused to listen to David Rheba."

"Here in this room!" He laughed. "That was no marriage; the law will declare it void. To-morrow morning at ten I expect Olga to be here; aye, in this very room she shall be given to Foka Saviska." He was moving angrily to the door. Marya put out her hand, saying,—

"One moment." He turned impatiently. She rose and faced him. "Olga is the wife of David Rheba; she will be the mother of his child. You may sin against yourself, against me, against your God, but you shall not sin against Olga. She is in my hands; I am surety for her to her husband."

He made a disdainful gesture and moved again to the door.

"If you do this thing," cried Marya, shrilly, losing control of herself, "then I will leave your house, and you shall never see the face of your child, for I will take such means to hide myself that though you search to all the ends of the earth you shall not find me."

"My child?" He was dazed, and thought she was suddenly gone mad, or that he was.

"Your child; for I, too, am with child." Her heart choked her for very grief. Was this what she had dreamed in their first days of marriage? Where was now the joy, the tender feeling of shy, happy pride she had imagined would be hers when God blessed her with the crown of motherhood? Grief shook her, seized her with a strong desire to rush weeping from the place. But she conquered her sorrow; she took pity on his amazement and said again, with her face turned from him, "I, too, am with child."

"You mean——"

She turned her face to him, and in her eyes there was an expression of such profound pity for him, together with the memory of the great wrong which he had done, that he turned and walked abruptly to the door, unable to meet her gaze. Half-way down the corridor he went, then his lips tightened. What if it were only a trick to save Olga? Back he turned and into the room again.

She was sitting in her chair, her eyes closed. Big tears were forcing their way out at the corners of her eyelids and falling slowly, one by one, down her cheeks. For the first time for many weeks he allowed himself to look at her. Before, he had merely let his eyes glance at her, seeming to see but not seeing, then wander to something else; now they took in every line, every shadow of her girlish face.

How pale she was grown and thin! what a piteous droop of her small child-like mouth! what lines of suffering around it! Even her hair had lost its gloss and looked lifeless and dry. He half stooped towards her. What if it were true! A child, heir to his name, heir to the vast lands of Anton Volkenoff, which would pass from his house for ever if he had no issue. What if it were true! He rose again to his full height. She shall tell him again, but he must find some test to try her by.

He touched her sharply on the shoulder. She sighed wearily and rose.

"What now?" she asked.

"Will you swear to this?"

"Why? By what could I swear to satisfy you? You say I have no soul."

"Swear——" He hesitated, casting about in his mind the surest way to pin her,—the surest way to leave no loophole for a lie. He had found one. He put his face close to hers, saying,—

"Swear by the child you say you bear that it may die before it see the light if what you say be true."

For a moment she could not grasp the full meaning of what he had said, but presently it burst upon her in all its cruelty and cunning. She put out her hands to thrust him away, but he caught them and held them strongly gripped in his while he watched the red chase the white from her face, then again the white the red.

"That would be to slay my child," she cried, wildly, "if God heard me."

"Then it is true!" he said, his hands trembling with the vehemence of the feelings which swept over him, and shaking hers till the whole of her slight body swayed and shook like a young hazel-tree in a strong wind.

"Have I not told you it is true? Please let me go; you hurt me," she said, with a sob of pain.

He released her hands, and went suddenly from the

room and away into the east side of the house, and tramped fiercely up and down the wide, silent corridors, and in and out the great state-rooms, muttering to himself. Half through the night he wandered there, questioning, doubting, believing, doubting again, then exulting with,—

"A child! a child! Heir to the vast lands of Anton Volkenoff! Heir to his name, his house!"

But while he cried thus, once, there came into his mind the memory of the night, and the shame of what he had done was brought home to him at last. He stood trembling and afraid, asking himself what manner of child would it be?—the child for which he had longed, had prayed, what would it be?

The wind came sweeping along the low cliffs from over the Black Sea. It ravened at the windows and answered him with shrieking, and shrill, witch-like laughter, and then went thundering away over the roof with gusty bursts and cries, driving the ragged clouds across the white face of the moon that flooded the place with light, then screaming again at the windows, lashing him into fury.

"A child! No, I'll not believe it," he cried. "It is a lie to keep Olga. Perhaps she thinks to soften me with this, and send the girl to her Jew. A child! She knows it is my heart's desire; she knows I would almost forego my hope of kneeling at the feet of Christ when my time is come to die for a child to bear my name, to perpetuate my house. She knows, and now has used this, the strongest weapon, to force me into doing her will, but it shall fail."

He began to mutter under his breath, striding up and down the great room. Why had he taken such a revenge? Why had he not obeyed the strong racial desire, which had filled him on that night, to punish her by whipping her after the fashion of his grim ancestor, Dimitri Donskoi, with his rebellious womenkind? He paused; why had he not done so? He thought of the whip in his strong hands, of Marya's white limbs, of her tender throat. He saw her there before him in the moonlight, crouching at his feet, half dead with grief and agony. Why had he not obeyed the instinct? The wind moaned at the windows. His throat began to work with an impulse to cry out; his knees shook, and he stood staring blankly before him.

"Because I love her," he said, in a strange, toneless voice; "that was why. I love her, and yet I hate her, too, for that part of her which eludes me; for this strange, unholy belief that our Lord Christ was a Jew. Oh, if I could but seize it and tear it out of her soul for the sake of my child! Child! Ha, ha, ha! Child! Nay, devil rather, as it must be if it be true, begotten as it was in such a way."

His voice went ringing through the great room, and was taken up by a rising shriek of the wind, which hurled itself at the windows, then sank sobbing and wailing, breaking into faint, piteous sighs, and broken, almost articulate speech, like the voice of a shipwrecked man going down under the stress of great waves, and striving to cry against the force of the mighty sea that gushed through his open throat, quenching his shrieks to little helpless moans and gasps and stifled cries.

Sudden terror of the spirit which seemed to be abroad in the storm that night took possession of him.

Threatening, unseen things seemed crowding around him; he fancied he heard them moving nearer to him in the shadows made by the moon, and as though in propitiation of them, he said,—

"Nay, nay! The sin was not mine. It was her unnatural belief which forced me to it. The sin was hers."

Swift upon his words the wind rose again, crashing among the trees, and screaming with a thousand laughs and yells in seeming derision of him, and he, casting fear behind, flung up his arms and cried with it,—

"Nay, I lie! it was hate and sudden lust of revenge which forced me to it. Raven at me! shriek! wreck me as you wreck strong ships and hurl drowning men to death and hell, Old Wind! I did sin against my own soul and against her. I sinned! I sinned! Do you hear me? I sinned!"

He stumbled forward and flung open the windows, crying fiercely, with the wind sweeping round him,—

"I sinned then, but she is the sinner now; go shriek at her for her lies. Oh, that I could pluck the truth from her! God that I worship, why canst not thou give me the power to see into her soul, if she have one," he mocked, "as thou seest into mine?" He thrust forward his face, dark and defiant, into the piercing wind and the white blinding light from the moon, and cried again, "As thou, God, that I worship and pray to, seest into mine!"

A savage gust of wind drove him backward from the window, then it dropped moaning and wailing round him, and on it was borne a sound like a faint, sweet voice sighing in his ear,—

"Because her soul is white and clean, and thine is stained with sin."

He turned slowly round, a creeping feeling of superstitious awe making the flesh of his cheeks shiver and crinkle up. He listened with suspended breath. Had something spoken to him, or was it only his imagination? As he turned he faced a picture of the Madonna with the Child in her arms. The Virgin's eyes seemed to be gazing intently into his. He stood fixed as though he were rooted to the spot, and again he heard the faint, sweet voice sigh in his ear,—

"Because her soul is white and clean, and thine is stained with sin."

A cloud passed over the moon, the room and the picture were shrouded in darkness for a moment. When the moon sailed out again the Virgin's eyes were looking down at the Child with the rapt, absorbed expression of utter love they always wore.

"Her soul!" he cried. "Thou didst say her soul?"

The lips that he was gazing at seemed to smile, and between his eyes and the Virgin's face his wife's face seemed to float still and pale. He saw again the red chase the white from her cheeks, then the white the red, and he heard again her moan,—

"That would be to slay my child if God heard me!"

A flood of light seemed suddenly let in upon him; the bonds of self were loosened; something sharp and piercing clave through his heart, and he saw himself there revealed, cruel, intolerant, hateful to himself and God. He cried out and covered up his face with his clasped, shaking hands, praying through them with stammering, choking voice and trembling lips, humbled to the dust.

"Holy Virgin, Blessed Mother of our Lord Christ, cleanse my soul of its sin, cleanse it of the foul stuff that clogs it, cleanse it of my sin." He fell weeping, and crouched prostrate before the picture, praying silently for a long time. At last he rose and crept away down to Marya's door. It was locked, as it had been every night. Before, the knowledge had only filled him with fresh rage and hate, but now it cut him to the quick; he bent his head against the panel and said, brokenly,—

"Marya, Marya, my wife!"

Utter silence answered him, yet he felt that she lay there awake listening.

Again he said,—

"Marya, my wife," and strained his ears hungering for the smallest sound. He thought he heard one; his voice rose on it entreatingly,—

"Speak to me, let me in; I will not hurt thee, as God is my witness!"

He heard the sound of a light being struck; a moment passed and Marya opened the door, her soul full of great pity and compassion for him shining in her face. He gave a bitter cry and, like a man falling at the feet of a much-wronged, suffering mother, he fell on his knees on the threshold and clasped her hands, sobbing bitterly, unable to speak a word.

"I forgive thee, Michael," she said, softly,—he lifted his head striving to speak,—"I forgive thee from my heart." She bowed her head and kissed him, her tears now streaming down with his and blinding him so that he could not see her face, though he strove hard to read it for some small touch of the old wifely love; but the love was dead. He felt it was so; no use to search. She shook her head sadly, and went backward into her room, murmuring, "God give thee peace, Michael."

He crept away, white of face and sick at heart, but marvelling at her, and saying to himself,—

"The child will be safe in her keeping; I need not fear to look upon its face, but, ah! her love, her love for me is dead!"

Next day he was the self-controlled, self-centred man again. But Foka was sent away without his bride, and something like peace settled upon the house.

CHAPTER XXIII.

SPRING-TIME.

Spring was in the land! Spring, with its wild and jocund laughter, its trill of birds, its soft and tender hum of insect, its warm, caressing rain! Spring, with its perfume and joyance, filling the wind, as it swung to and fro, with all the breath of all the flowers, and the myriad sweet, green things which had lain beneath the brown old earth the winter through, and now, at her call, came stealing forth, leaf by leaf and bud by bud, till all the land was a very riot of colour! The snow was gone; the townspeople looked with smiling faces at the soft grey mud in the streets, a symbol to them of the fulness of the fertile fields, the promise of a rich harvest. Odessa, with her wide south front, was the first to feel the softening touch in the air. How the poor in the Jews' Quarter and the poor Russians who herd in the holes under the cliffs rejoiced at the mild, soft weather! The flowers were out, and soon the fruit would be coming into the port,—such fruit, too, they get in Odessa!—and everyone be glad at heart.

Who that has not lived in a country that is frost-bound for a good five months of the year can tell the big thrill of joy that goes through the hearts of the people from one end of the land to the other when

"Spring! spring! spring!" is the cry given from lip to lip, from throats young and old, from hearts beating high with hope! The children can once more bake themselves in the sun; doors and windows are flung open, the fresh wind rushing in and sweeping out from rooms and passages the sour, close odours with a swirl of its wings and a laugh, and away again to scatter the apple-blossom over the dewy grass. And then the cattle! What a sight it is to see them come out from the sheds, lean and soiled with the mire of their long imprisonment, and stand with extended necks and widespread nostrils, drinking deep of the pure, balmy air, their great eyes looking straight ahead, seeming as though they never can take in enough of the goodly sight and wholesome smell of sky and fields and honey-scented air!

So it comes that in spring-time in Russia everything is full of mirth and gladness; the ecstasy is in every breath that is taken, and it will enter into the most soured spirit and make it merry in spite of itself.

And thus it was with Ezra and his family. Though their hearts were still sad and aching for David, yet their spirits must up and sing with the rest. One morning close on the end of April, Judith was moving lightly about the room, making the beds and setting other things right, and singing Solomon's beautiful love-song. Salome was gone to her lessons at the house of Madam Golitzin, a Russian lady Daniel Pereira had induced to take the child, and who had consented on condition that Salome, being a Jewess, should come before the rest of the few pupils she gave instructions to. Belah always went with her, this morning carrying her shoes, for the dancing lesson was to follow, and this Kezia now gave at the theatre, wishing Salome to grow used to the downward slope of the stage. So Judith was alone, and she was lifting up her voice on the words,—

"'The fig-tree putteth forth her green figs, and the vines with the tender grape give a good smell. Arise, my love, my fair one, and come away,'" when there came a sharp knock at the door, and before she could stop or cry "Come in!" John Pemberton entered with,—

"A happy day to you, David Rheba! Where's my bowl and ewer?"

He stopped and let the door fall to behind him when he saw Judith, looking at her with a lift of his brows and a downward twitch of his mouth. So this was David's love! Well, he had expected something younger, at any rate. She had been pretty, he could see that,—in fact, one might say more than pretty,—but she was so thin the wind might blow through her and find no difficulty in it, either. And Judith stared at John Pemberton, wondering what country he could be of, that he stood so long with his hat on. At last she said, with a droll little note in her voice,—

"You are English?"

"Yes, I am, madam," bowing to her. "How did you guess that?"

"By your hat, sir," she answered, slyly.

"What—eh? Oh, the deuce!" Off came his hat in a twinkling, while Judith laid her sharpness to the spring, which must have taken entire possession of her, she told herself.

"Will you be seated?" she asked, her old, gentle self again, "and please tell me your business?"

"Well, I came to see David Rheba, but——" John Pemberton looked round to where David's work-bench and stool were standing in the window facing north. Both were covered; not a tool in sight, and not a trace of cinder on the forge. He looked at Judith, amazement in his eyes, then round the room once more. There were two beds in it now; children's clothing hanging behind the door, three more chairs, and a general air of filling up. The wide, airy space of the place seemed gone, though the windows were open.

The tears gathered in Judith's eyes.

"He is not here, sir, now, but we do pray for his return." Then she sat down and told John Pemberton the whole story, the tears falling unheeded upon her folded hands.

"Damn it! damn!" He cried in English, stamping about the room when she had finished, ramming his hat upon his head and mopping his eyes.

"The finest fellow that ever breathed! lost! wasted! sent away to rot—— I beg your pardon!" Off came his hat, flying onto one of the beds. "I wish I had the whole army of Russia here, I'd like to wring its neck. What do the people here know of the worth of that man? what do they care, or for thousands like him? But I'll have him back! I will, by Heaven!" Up went his hands through his thin hair till it stood on end like an infuriate broken-haired terrier's, and he rubbed the bridge of his nose with his thumb till it glowed like a beacon.

"What do they care that I've lost my bowl and ewer? What do they care that the finest brain in all Russia,—Russia—no, Russia be damned!—the finest brain in all the world is gone to be stultified, withered, ground down into insanity perhaps? No! not that, David, my friend, not that for you." He broke off, tears running down his wrinkled cheeks warm and swift as a girl's. "Not that. By Heaven!"—he was up again, flaming,—"I'll have him out of it if I have to sell my stupid old soul. Now tell me quick the date of his arrest," he asked, speaking again in Russian. "Yes, the 27th of February, on charge of perverting a Christian woman to the Jewish creed. Yes, go on," making short-hand notes in his pocket-book. "On the 26th he married Olga, a serf belonging to Michael Volkenoff, with the consent of her mistress. That'll do. No, stop. The mistress? Marya, Michael Volkenoff's wife. So, that's right." Putting the note-book in his pocket. "Now about this girl Olga; what's she like, eh?"

"Beautiful, and I think very good."

"Have you seen much of her?"

"Only once since David's arrest. Miriam Ludolfino tells me she is watched."

"What for?"

"I know not; unless her master fears she will follow David to Siberia."

"Well, she has got David into a nice muddle, and, for the present, I've lost my bowl and ewer"—he had taken up his hat to go; he dashed it down again—

"and the silver writing-set I promised the Princess Czartoryski. She told me she'd give her eyelashes for one of David Rheba's; and she has eyelashes, too, fine ones. She wants it for presentation to the Czarina next New Year's day; she'll go crazy. I promised it should be a masterpiece. My credit's gone for ever!"

He rubbed the bridge of his nose again violently and made for the door, forgetting his hat.

Judith ran after him,—

"You said the Princess Czartoryski!" hurrying her words one on the other fearful he might go before she had spoken; "she is the wife of the governor; cannot she——"

"Cannot she what?"

"Obtain a pardon for our David? She wants this silver writing-set. Well, is not the only way to get it to bring our David back?"

"God bless your wit, you dear woman! What a numskull I was not to think of it myself! Hooray! I'll be off this moment to the princess. . . . Bless my soul, where's my hat? Thank you. You may look upon David as good as free. I hold the ball in my hands." Away he went down the stairs like a boy, and Judith to walk about the room, laugh, sing, and weep; there was no resting, no work done until some of her dear ones returned to share the great news with her.

CHAPTER XXIV.

THE PRINCESS CZARTORYSKI.

John Pemberton got into the first empty drosky he met and told the man to drive fast. The man grinned all over his fat, good-tempered face. Round went the lash with a hiss, not touching his horses, and crying, "Heiugh! heiugh! my relations! my doves!" they were off, tearing along at break-neck speed. There is nothing the drosky-driver so loves as a customer who cries "Fast!" Then is his chance to show his skill, his power of sending on his cattle without once using his long, curling whip. John Pemberton held on to the sides. Twice he thought they were tumbled over into a mud-heap on turning a corner; but no, they shaved it, and in less time than it took him to get used to the pace the man pulled up before the princess's gateway.

"Wait!" said John to him. Then to the servant who opened the great doors to him, "Can I see her Excellency the princess?"

"Her Excellency does not receive at this hour," said the man, a big, bland-looking fellow, good-nature and laziness personified.

"Of course, I know that, but I am not a visitor. I have come on important business. Get that card carried in to her Excellency. I'll wait here." John slipped two roubles into the man's hand with his card, and sat himself down on a settee at the foot of the broad stairs with the air of one saying, "And here I remain until I see her."

The man beamed smilingly upon him and carried up the card, giving it, with half a rouble, to another servant who was waiting in the corridor, saying, "He is known to her Excellency."

This servant went up another flight of stairs, past the state apartment, and gave the card to the princess's maid. The woman laid the card on a dainty porcelain tray and carried it to her mistress.

The princess was in a happy mood. Her eyes were bright and her skin dazzling.

The windows of her boudoir were wide open to the sweet west wind, and she was floating about in a loose gown of clinging, apple-green silk, and apple-green slippers upon her tiny feet. She had just been examining her face in a silver hand-glass in the full, uncompromising flood of light from the window. She smiled. The long black eyelashes she was so proud of drooped softly over her clear grey eyes; her skin was like fine, new ivory, and her hair lay on her forehead in thick, heavy, lustrous waves and hung down her back in one big plait. She nodded as she laid down the glass; she was well content with herself.

The maid entered and gave her John Pemberton's card.

"What is his business?"

"Fedor did not say, Excellency."

"What can he want of me?" Suddenly she remembered the writing-set. "Bid him enter."

"Your hair, Excellency, is not arranged."

"It is becoming, is it not?" she smiled. The maid nodded approvingly. "Bring the man to me."

A few minutes later John entered the room. He bowed, looking dubiously at her, standing just inside the door.

"What has happened, that you seem afraid to approach me?" Then her face grew stern, anger in her eyes. "You have come to tell me that your David Rheba cannot fulfil my order."

"That is precisely what I have come to tell your Excellency," answered John Pemberton, advancing nearer. Then she saw that his eyes were red, as though he had been weeping. "David Rheba is now on his way to the mines, sentenced to twenty years' imprisonment."

"Explain," was all the princess said.

He told her in a few matter-of-fact words, no flourishes, his voice only shaking a little.

"Sit down," said the princess when he had finished. "If you please," she smiled when he hesitated. She rang a bell. "Bring wine," she said to her maid who entered. When it came she poured out a glass for him with her own hands and offered it, saying,—

"Drink this; you need it."

John rose and bowed, drinking the wine, wondering at her more than ever she had caused him to wonder, then, in obedience to a bend of her head, sat down again.

"So, unless I can obtain a pardon for David Rheba, I shall lose my writing-set. That is it, is it not?"

"There is no other alternative, your Excellency."

"And suppose I had not required the work of him, what would you have done then?"

"I should have come to you just the same."

"Thank you! That pleases me. So Michael Volkenoff has used his influence to send this Jew to the mines! The narrow, fanatical fool," she laughed, "who thinks he is using while he is being used! . . . You must forget that," she said to John Pemberton, with a change of mood bewitching enough to have made him forget a much more weighty thing. She rose.

"Come to-morrow, at this hour, and I may have good news for you."

John Pemberton bowed and left, feeling as happy as though he held David's pardon already in his hand.

The princess wrote a note and sealed it.

She sat biting the end of her pen considering it for a while, and thinking,—

"The Czarowitz has remained here nearly the whole of the winter. To see that the garrison be in a thoroughly efficient condition?" She shook her head and smiled, then rang the bell.

"Send that note immediately. I am not at home this afternoon to anyone but his Imperial Highness; and tell Ivan the ponies and carriage are to be ready by three o'clock."

At three o'clock the Czarowitz entered her boudoir. She was dressed for driving, in a close-fitting pelisse of mouse-coloured cloth, and a cunning little cottage bonnet of drawn velvet, the same colour as her pelisse, with violets nestling under the front round her face, and under the curtain at the back that drooped over the thick coils of her hair.

"I want you to see me try my ponies, will you come?" she asked, after greeting him.

"I am your devoted servant," he answered, bowing over her hand.

"Is that just a sweet little speech because you think me a pretty woman and say it to please me, or could I rely upon you to the death?" she asked, a dimple showing in her left cheek, but her voice vibrating with some deep feeling which made him look searchingly at her. Were they going to be something more than two friends with just enough affinity to make the time pass pleasantly for each other? Was she going to be that rare thing which he had not yet found, a loyal, staunch comrade for himself, not for his rank? Her eyes met his unflinchingly, with the frankness of a boy looking at a man he admired.

"Yes," he answered, satisfied, "to the death."

"Thank you," she said, simply, and turned away to take up her gloves from a table near. When she turned again she was all woman; a certain charming hesitation in her manner, her eyes shy as a girl's.

"We have been friends for nearly three years now, have we not?"

"Yes," he agreed, "three years."

"But it is only during this last winter that we have really come to know each other. In all that time——" She made a little movement with her shoulders and a sudden, hasty drawing on of her right glove, which said as plainly as words that she disliked what she was going to say. "In all that time I have not asked you to do anything for me; anything official, I mean."

"No." The lines of his face began to harden.

"Well, I want you to do something for me now. Not really for myself,"—he breathed more freely,—"but for a man who has been unjustly sentenced and exiled. Let us sit down and I will tell you." So they sat down in the open window, and she told him David's story, adding,—

"At first I thought I was merely disappointed that the work I had so set my heart on having was out of my reach; afterwards, when I had balanced things, I found my pity for the artist outweighed the other, so I felt I could ask you for help with a clear mind. There is, though,"—her dimple showed again bewitchingly, and she gave one rapid glance at him,—"a keen pleasure in hoping to outwit Michael Volkenoff."

The young man smiled; she was all gold right through, he was sure.

"What is it I am to do?" he asked, and the tone said, "Ask me to conquer the world and I'll do it."

"Obtain a pardon for the man. The affair has passed now out of Vladimir's hand; a revocation by him of the sentence would not be recognised by the officials in charge. The pardon must come from the Czar."

"Do you want me, then, to go to Petersburg?"

"Oh, that is so far away from Odessa," she murmured, with a little fascinating movement, as though she would have rather said, "I should miss you so." He sighed contentedly and understood.

A SON OF ISRAEL

"You may button my glove, if you wish." He bent over her hand, wholly her loyal servant. "A letter from you will be sufficient sent by someone who must start to-day, remember! Sit here now and write at once; you can leave it with your secretary with a note of instruction while we are driving."

He sat at her table and wrote the notes, she poised light as a bird at the window, a delicious feeling of conquest making her blood sing. She had gained what it had been her ambition to possess ever since she knew the meaning of the word power,—the friendship of the man who would one day be the ruler of her country. Her lover she knew he would have been long ago; it had only wanted a look to set him all aflame if she had desired it, but that way lay not her path, nor the way to help Russia. She wanted to be the one woman he could go to for advice, for rest, and guidance, and she knew she was the one woman who could give him all these without any ulterior object to gain, either for herself or her husband. He had been sternly suspicious of her at first. How he must have been deceived, she told herself.

"There, princess," he said, rising, "your first commission is fulfilled." He gave the letter addressed to the Czar into her hands, a question in his eyes.

"Yes," she said, answering it, her clear voice vibrating again, "all my commissions will be as impersonal,—nay, more impersonal than this, for you see I have something to gain by it,—the silver writing-set."

He sighed heavily. "Have I, then, found a comrade at last?"

"Yes, if you prove you know how to value her. Now seal the letter." She held the taper for him. The envelope was sealed and addressed. "Now come; I have kept the ponies waiting nearly an hour."

She darted to the door, then turned and stripped off her glove. "Comrade," she said, frankly, "you may kiss my hand." Then she went lightly down the stairs, drawing on her glove again. She felt that he, too, was all gold; the allowed kiss of her hand had been a test.

CHAPTER XXV.

A WOMAN'S CREED.

As John Pemberton had said, he held the ball in his hands; and when a note was given him next morning from the Princess Czartoryski, saying that a courier was despatched to Petersburg with a petition for David's release, the first thing he did was to dash off to Judith Manuelli, whom he found sitting with Ezra and the children at their midday meal. Only a meagre meal, even now, for nearly all the money Daniel Pereira had given them was gone with David. Somehow, little by little, he got that from them, and it was only by telling them that he was in David's debt, or would be when their friend was released, it was all the same, that he persuaded them to accept a little more than a third of what they had forced upon David. They wouldn't take the whole; they said they must have some share in providing for their beloved friend.

After their first burst of joy at his news, there was nothing for them but patience. The journey to Petersburg was a long one in those days. Then, even when the petition was granted, would come the long journey to David, now so many weeks on the march. And what if—— They all looked the question they dared not ask. But Salome answered it. She sprang up with,—

"No; our David is strong. He'll not die on the road."

"As thou sayest, my pigeon," murmured the silent Ezra, "David is strong. He can endure, thanks be to God."

So they waited patiently. John Pemberton went to the princess and begged for a letter authorizing him to travel with the bearer of the pardon, and started at once to Petersburg with it, never doubting that the release would be obtained.

The princess carried the news to Marya, and between the two it was arranged that when David was free the princess should obtain a passport for him and Olga and get them safely away. The princess rejoiced in the plot. She loved outwitting Michael Volkenoff, and there was no need to bind Marya to secrecy. Marya knew now it was no mere personal dislike to the Jews which made Michael so relentless to them. It was part of his religion to make them suffer. For every stroke he laid on them, he believed, he heaped up for himself rewards in heaven, and called down upon his head blessings from the merciful Christ, who had said, "Love one another;" for it happened one day she had pleaded with him to petition the Czar for a pardon for David, having great hope of his relenting, seeing that he had grown so gentle to her. At first his anger was terrible to see; then, putting great restraint upon himself, he said,—

"So you would have me be merciful to this infidel, and cheat myself of my reward when I shall stand up at the last day? Nay, more, you would have me imperil Olga's soul and her child's by giving her to this man. No, no; he shall remain where he is, and the child shall be mine, not the Jew's, to train as I choose. And I will train it to hate its father's race; to do as I do; to follow me in word and deed; and for every indignity, for every stroke they laid on our God Christ, this child of a Jew, when grown to man, shall make his own people suffer a thousand thousand pains and miseries, and atone with their sufferings for His."

Marya let his anger vent itself upon her in silence. Womanly pity and the compassion of a strong soul for a weaker one held her silent. She no longer felt intolerant of his fanaticism; he was to her as a child to be helped and guided silently to the good. Often he would go away and wonder at her, at her serenity, the quiet, all-conquering peace which breathed out from her, and he would hug the thought to himself that it was the child which had made this change. His child, which should be a wonder to the world. It should be dedicated to the church, for it would be an heir, and with his great wealth to help it what could stay it from becoming one of the heads of the Church of Russia, a bishop, why not?

Directly summer was come, and Odessa, with its heat and dust, became unbearable, he sent Marya to his estate on the northern uplands of the Crimea, above Livardia. The house stood among cool, green trees, with fragant orchards behind them, and a great wild garden that stretched away covering many acres on either side.

There among the beautiful flowers or in the shady,

quiet rooms Marya sat with Olga, making dainty little garments for the unborn children.

She had a store of knowledge to give the girl, knowledge that surprised even herself. She had not realised till then how much she had absorbed from the books she had read, and how deeply she had thought things out for herself on the subject of woman, and her great responsibility to God and to nature as the mother of the race. At first her mind and will were too benumbed to put in practice the theories she had cherished and felt so deeply to be true. But, now that she had schooled her soul to peace, she longed to tell all that she had learned to Olga, that she might benefit by it, and she began by teaching her what food it was best that she should eat, the amount of rest she must take each day during the first six months, and how to control her thoughts and temper, and to keep a clear, calm mind for the sake of the child she was bearing.

Olga opened her mild, dark eyes to their widest when she learned that a child takes the greater part of its spiritual and intellectual qualities from the mother.

"Yes," Marya smiled, and dropped the Liliputian shirt that she was sewing into her lap and took Olga's work away that the girl might listen more intently, "ever since I began to question the why and wherefore of things and discovered that the little children are not laid under the pine-trees by the angels for the mothers to find, I have had this subject most near my heart and have thought about it every day."

Olga made a movement of surprise.

"I know I have never spoken of it," Marya said, in answer to the expressive action, "because I have felt shy and fearful of myself, but now—— Well, now, my Olga, there is another woman concerned besides myself,—thou. And if I am right in all that I have learned from the many women I have questioned, from the numberless bits of silent information I have been able to gather from our own serfs, and from my friends, then I have discovered that woman's heritage is greater than a king's, for she may be the mother of great and noble women and men who shall be a lasting blessing to the earth."

"Tell me how that is possible," said Olga, eagerly.

"I will try," answered Marya. "Thou wilt understand——" She paused and smiled, then said, "These things have come to me only from time to time; from questions here, from observation there, and from books that I have read. And though I have had them all here in my mind growing little by little every day, it seems to me since my marriage, yet it is not easy even now to put them into words."

She paused again for a moment or two, and Olga pulled her stool closer to Marya's knees keen to hear. There was a hunger in the girl for knowledge, such as was rare among her class, and it was that craving which had made her education so easy for Marya.

"I believe," Marya began, half bashfully and fearfully, for the subject had been so cherished and loved by her in silence that to speak of it was like holding out a naked, newly born babe to the light of the sun and the sting of the wind,—" I believe that a woman, by the power and concentration of her thought, may make the child she is bearing whatever she will it to be in mind and soul."

"In soul!" whispered Olga.

"Yes, in soul. A woman may make her child's soul great, or weak and puny; true as truth itself, or false, mean, contemptible."

"But how can a woman do such wonderful things?" exclaimed Olga. "I know, because thou hast told me, how a child's body is built up bit by bit from the nourishment it receives from the mother,"—her eyes grew tender under her eyelids, the young mother nascent in her blushing face,—" but the soul, the mind——"

"They take their colour and strength from the mother. A child may have the noblest, bravest father that ever trod the earth, but unless the mother too be noble, or, lacking the fine qualities of her mate, fail to graft the father in her child by constant, concentrated thought, then the child comes hampered into the world, and it has to fight its way up and out of the bonds the mother has created for it when it has power to think for itself and the desire to grow in intellect and soul is come."

"Mistress,"—Olga took Marya's hand and pressed it to her cheek, then stroked it while she said, "do not think me a dunce to-day, but I wish thee to tell me again how a woman may do all this."

"Dear child," said Marya, "I fear I am not making the way so clear to thee as I think I am. It is so new and strange for me to be telling anyone of these thoughts that I grow excited and speak quickly, and so puzzle thee exceedingly. . . . Now let me try to be slow and calm. I know, I am sure,—as absolutely sure as though I had borne many children instead of only one, and had sent each one into the world filled with a different aspiration and talent,—that a woman by fixing her thoughts on all that is good and noble in the father of her child, on all that is best and highest in herself, and on all that is great and true and beautiful in the lives of the men and women who have made the world what it is, can so infuse its nature with good that for very lack of sustenance—of the food of thought, let us say—the grossness and evil it would otherwise have inherited from either side or both will be starved, and the child will come forth to begin life with its mind clear and healthy, and able to struggle victoriously with the follies and temptations that will beset it from its first years to its last."

"A mother can do that!" cried Olga.

"She can, indeed; and more, much more, than that, for that is only one of Nature's ways of providing for the progress and evolution of the race. Another is by making woman so delicate in body that she cannot go out and battle with the world by attempting work that is only fit for man and his coarser fibre and larger, less sensitive brain, without serious loss of the nervous energy and force that should go to her child. But, as recompense for the apparently restricted life she has to lead, Nature has made her strong in moral courage, love, and soul. Woman is the begetter of all that is great in man, for I have not found one instance of where a greatly gifted man has given an equally gifted son to the world unless the mother too was great at heart, and restful and self-contained, and had garnered up within herself all the expression of her husband's genius and her own latent capacity for the doing of glorious things. So from that I gathered there must be no mental strain upon a woman while she is bearing her child, but instead of giving out from her mind, she must hold fast to all her ideals and dreams of precious things, so that as she aspires will her child be filled full of her aspiration, and what was in her a dream shall be in it a reality. Nor must she let her vitality flow away in useless gadding and talking, in fits of passionate temper or selfish indulgence. Though we know the strain that is upon her at such a time is great and wearisome, she must be as reposeful and strength-giving to her unborn child as the warm, kind earth is to the germ of the tree or flower it carries in its breast. And so for the sake of the children, if not for the common right of human beings, a nation should cherish its women. It should give them of the best and highest it holds in its schools and colleges, for out from the mothers of the land spring the sinews that shall guard it from wrong, the genius that shall make it a joy to all the ages."

Marya's eyes were like two stars looking out over Olga's head into some fair and pleasant place. Her hesitation was gone; the words now flowed from her mouth as easily as the song from the throat of the skylark.

"No woman need crave or pine to be a man when

she holds within her the stuff that men are made of; when she holds within her two hands the welfare of the whole world. Woman alone can make the world or mar. The entire responsibility rests upon her shoulders. She cannot shirk it; every jot of the power that is given to her must be accounted for, and though the pain and travail may seem heavy enough of themselves to bear without the moral portion of the load, yet Nature has made it as easy and natural for her as it is easy and natural for her to love the helpless child when it is first laid in her arms. She has but to keep her thoughts on high things, and brave and sweet, not to fear child-bearing as a danger, but to welcome it as the joyful thing it most truly is, and she will bring forth children to bless herself, her husband, and the land they are born in. I would have," she added, her face now as bright as her eyes and as Olga had not seen it for many a long day, "this truth taught in every school, to boys and girls alike, that men may know what they owe to their mothers, and the women the great gift that is given them of God."

She smiled one day when Olga asked, with solemn eyes and serious face,—

"But what, Little Mother, of the women who have no children?"

"They can put all the dreams and ideals, all the strength and sweetness which would go to their children into the work it lies in their power to do, no matter how menial it may be, and so help the race that way; for work is prayer, and when a woman works with all her heart and soul and might she stands elbow to elbow with God, and he gives her of his wisdom and of his knowledge."

"But it is sweetest to be a mother," said Olga. "Dost not thou think so, Little Mother?"

"It is so to thee, is it not, child?" asked Marya.

Olga nodded, smiling brightly, and she pulled her stool closer to Marya's side.

"There is something I much want to know," she said, glowing rose-coloured. "David is, as thou knowest, a Jew, but I am a Christian; though now that I know Christ was a Jew, I cannot understand so well the difference; but this is what puzzles me, whether I ought not to read the Bible, the book, so thou hast told me, of Jewish law, so that should our child be a boy he may be like David, a Jew, and if a girl,"—she turned her eyes beaming upon Marya,—"then she, too, would be of his faith; for I could desire no other, being as it is, good, for it is David's."

Marya stroked the girl's hair, thinking of Michael and his purpose concerning the child; and presently she began to think of David, and wondered whether the law of Russia would give him, he being a Jew, the natural, common rights of a father.

"Little Mother,"—Olga had been wondering at her silence,—"is it not thy wish I should read the Bible? Thou hast one, I know, though the master made thee lock it up."

"No, it was not that, child. I was thinking of something else."

"But the book, may I have it?"

"Yes, thou shalt have it." Marya rose and unlocked a drawer in her writing-table. The book was there, lying in some rose-leaves,—leaves of the roses she had carried from the convent garden on her wedding-day. She took up the small, leather-bound Bible and kissed it.

"There, Olga, treasure it, for it is one of the mighty books of the world. I have had many a fight to keep it, for your master supposed—— Why trouble you with that?" She sat down again and took up her sewing, while Olga turned over the leaves reverentially, lovingly. It was the history of David's people. Presently she came upon a page which held her attention fixed to it. She read it over and over, and while she read Marya noticed that she constantly rubbed the ball of her thumb against her chin, an action Marya had often observed since her marriage to David, but had forgotten to speak of.

"Tell me, Olga——" she began, when Olga suddenly cried out,—

"Mistress, here is something written of David's own countrymen, the Nazarites. See." And she pointed to the thirteenth chapter of Judges, the fifth verse, reading, "'And no razor shall come on his head: for the child shall be a Nazarite unto God from the womb.' That is so; that is why my David hath long hair; he told me when I did ask him. And see, mistress, the angel says unto the woman that she beware, 'and drink not wine nor strong drink, and eat not any unclean thing.'"

The girl read on eagerly, and began again to rub the ball of her thumb against her chin.

"Tell me, Olga," smiled Marya, touching the girl's restless left hand, "why thou art always rubbing the ball of your thumb over your chin. Whenever thou art not sewing or occupied in some other way, thou art always rub, rub, rub, till I wonder thy flesh is not sore."

"I am thinking of David. He burnt his hand deeply in the ball of his thumb with some of the molten silver, and made a red wound like a triangle in shape; and I am always thinking of it, and unless I am at work I seem to feel the pain, and so rub it against my chin to soothe it."

"But when was that?"

"It was—on the day—he was arrested——" She could say no more; her eyes flooded and flowed over.

"Courage," whispered Marya; "remember what the Princess Czartoryski told me."

"But that is two months ago, and there is no news yet of the pardon."

"Yet it may be even now on the road to David. The courier will start from Petersburg, not here."

"And how long will he be before he reach David?"

"Let us consult my map." Marya took a page from an English atlas out of her pocket, worn and often fingered by the two women from its appearance, and they traced the journey up from Petersburg. Upon the maps were tiny dots to mark the distance between each, about ten miles as the crow flies; each dot meant to Marya and Olga the daily march of David and his fellow-prisoners since they had left Odessa. Marya measured the miles between Petersburg and the last halting-place. It would be well on into the month of August before they could hope the bearer of the pardon would come up with him. And then would begin the long journey back to Odessa.

"It will be the end of November," sighed Olga, "perhaps December, before he is here."

"And in November——" smiled Marya. "Keep a cheerful heart for his child's sake," she whispered, kissing Olga.

They traced the journey again upon the map, and it being now the cooler part of the day, they put away their needle-work and went out to walk in the garden until supper-time.

CHAPTER XXVI.

ON THE WAY TO DAVID.

Czar Nicholas granted the pardon. He knew that the thrifty, temperate Jew could be made the salvation of Russia. So when his son's letter was given to him, he consulted no one, but signed and sealed the pardon, and the next morning John Pemberton and a courier of the Czar's started on their long journey. John was all fiery impatience. He would have done, if possible, sixty miles a day, but, as the courier pointed out, it was madness to fret oneself to a skeleton under a hot sun because the horses that were made by God to go only five miles an hour could not be induced to go twelve. The courier lay back in the tarantass on the soft bundle of hay lazily smoking and swearing mildly at the flies and wasps, and John sat bolt upright grumbling in English and longing for the days of railroads in Russia. At last, after many days of useless worry, he followed the courier's example, and smoked, too, half lying, half sitting, on the hay, which they had heaped up in the bottom of the tarantass to save them from the jolts and jerks, which were sudden enough to dislocate each bone in their bodies, only occasionally lashing out into fierce invective when the driver, having fallen asleep and dropped his little whip, would have to turn back half a mile to pick it up; or when a wheel came off, or a trace broke, and the driver, smiling blandly, would proceed slowly to fix on the wheel, or, taking a strong needle and twine out of his pocket, would sit down on the roadside and proceed to sew the trace together again, alternately talking soothingly to John and his relations, as he called his horses. Telling John to thank the good Saint Nicholas for the medicine the delay was to his hasty spirit, and the horses that the Saint was merciful and had broken the trace, with a wink of his eye, so they might rest.

The heat was intense, the dust as thick and deep as the mud had been in spring, so that they travelled in a perpetual dun-coloured cloud. At last the courier suggested they should travel by night, starting at seven in the evening, and not stopping to rest until seven in the morning. John objected strongly, they would lose quite four or five hours by that. The courier assured him they would go faster, because the horses would suffer less from the heat, and so they would gain much time in the end. At last John was persuaded, and together they went to consult their driver.

"Yes," he nodded, looking highly pleased, "travelling by night will be best. There will be no difficulty in changing horses at the post station, because the Little Father's order" (meaning the Czar's) "makes the postmaster fly about like a spark from the devil's tail."

The courier was right, as the first night journey proved. The three horses went like the wind through the cool air, and though they had mosquitoes now instead of flies, the draught swept them away almost as fast as they settled. So on and on they journeyed through great dark forests, silent, sleeping villages, enormously wide, interminably long, white dusty roads, the air cool and balmy like milk against their faces. Three weeks and close on to the end of the fourth they journeyed, then they got news of David, and one day the last of the week they came upon David himself some miles above Viatka.

It was the noonday halt. The prisoners were sitting on some burnt-up grass by the side of the dusty road eating their ration of black bread. Some had cheese and milk, which they had begged or bought in the villages they had passed through since morning. A swarm of buzzing, maddening flies besieged them. There was not one whole pair of boots among the three dozen and odd men. Some had their old ragged boots slung round their necks, their feet too swollen and sore to bear anything but rags tied round them. Their faces were blistered by the sun and bitten by the flies. Some of them were so thin the skin hung on their cheekbones like shrivelled brown parchment; many of them were like living skeletons, save for the weary, piteous eyes which looked out, dumbly asking help of God and man. And each convict was chained from the ankles to the waist, so that each time one moved the irons clanked and kept up a constant noise.

David was at the end of the gang foremost along the road. He was worn to skin and bone. His thick hair was matted, his beard ragged and stained with dust, but his eyes looked out steadily over his lean face like the eyes of an eagle, unconquerable, unsubduable. The lines about his mouth were fixed and stern, save when he spoke to his mate, then they relaxed into a smile so tender the man half forgot the heat and sickly fatigue which had taken hold of him, and smiled, too. David saw the tarantass coming and rose, pulling his fellow-prisoner up with him, watching someone who was standing in it behind the courier shading his eyes with his two hands and eagerly scanning every face he passed. It was John Pemberton. David made a sudden spring towards him.

"Back, No. 27!" cried the guard. David paused and waited.

The tarantass stopped, and John stepped out, followed by the courier. He looked round for the captain of the guard, then saw David standing a little forward of the rest of the prisoners, waiting.

He suddenly felt weak at the knees. A lump climbed up into his throat; he gulped it down with a muttered "Hang it, I feel like a woman!" and got to David, how he never knew; it seemed to him he stumbled like a blind man in the dusty road, and, gripping hold of David's hand, tried to say, carelessly, "All right, old fellow, eh?" when suddenly the mother's nature in him bore down the man's; he hid his face on his friend's neck and wept like a child. The captain stepped to interfere, but the courier stepped up and showed him the Czar's order.

John's tears were sweet as spring rain to David. He put his arms about him, his heart leaping high, and he laughed aloud for joy, saying,—

"Said I not my cause was in the hands of the God of Israel and could not fail!"

A SON OF ISRAEL

The courier was now showing the pardon to the captain, who shook his head, saying,—

"You must come on with me to the next town to have that verified by the governor. I have no power to let the man go." It was useless protesting; they had to submit.

The hour's rest being up, they started on again, John tramping by David's side and telling him the good news he had brought.

CHAPTER XXVII.

FOLLOWERS OF CHRIST.

DAVID was not released till the next morning, only a short time before the gang started once more upon the march. All the men clustered round him, rejoicing for him, but sorrowing at their own loss. His mate couldn't let go his hand; he clung hard to it, as though it was his one stay of strength. At the Ostrog door one of the convicts cried,—

"Show us Little Father, mate, before you go."

Out came the little mannikin. It was passed round, the men kissing it and letting it go again reluctantly, saying, "God rest thee, Little Father, God rest thee." When it came to David's own mate, he held it close and looked hard at David. David took it from him, brushed it tenderly with Olga's kerchief, kissed it, then laid it back in the man's hands, saying,—

"It is thine, mate; keep it." Then they started on the march, he walking beside them till they came to the open country outside the town, where he said good-bye for the last time, and stood awhile in the road watching them tramp along the parched and dusty way, driven along like cattle. When they came to a turn in the road, where a few trees were growing, they looked back at him, nodded, his mate gave him a wan smile, then they were lost in the shade of the trees and the thick cloud of dust their dragging feet made.

David walked on to the inn, where John Pemberton was waiting for him, his heart heavy under all its joy. He had starved and suffered with them. He was going back to love and life, they were going to perpetual night and suffering in the silver-mines. They were being swept away out of touch with kindred and friends; some would drop dying on the road from utter want of strength to drag themselves on, as he had seen five fall and die, and be kicked aside by the guard and left on the chance of someone putting them under the ground. It was terrible and strange, and he wondered, as he had never ceased to wonder since he was first brought face to face with it, at the want of true charity and forbearance shown by the Christians one to the other. If they loved, then it was well, then they would help, they would work, would give their very lives; but to those who had done them wrong, so far as he had been able to judge, they had no mercy, no pity. It seemed to him they were still savages and knew it not, for what merit is it to be kind where one loves? The very barbarians and beasts of the fields do not less than that.

He felt the Christians still held to the creed an eye for an eye, a tooth for a tooth. The teaching of the man Christ, whom they worshipped as their God, they despised, or why not follow it? He turned and looked back again along the road. The convicts were out now in the sunshine. He knew that by the thick, heavy, trailing line of yellow dust which floated lazily through the air. What would their Christ say to such a sight? What would their Christ say to the tortures these, his brothers, were going to, and on some inflicted in his name?

"An eye for an eye and a tooth for a tooth, that is their creed," he muttered. "So why should we Jews be blamed for being even as they themselves? And if they have injured thee, my Olga, they shall repay. As they, when they are wronged, strike, so will I. That is justice as they by their deeds prove, but with their tongues preach 'Love your enemies,' even while they flay them."

He was come by now to the inn, and there, in the cleanest bedroom the place possessed, he found John Pemberton waiting for him with fresh, comfortable clothing laid out ready for him to put on. And, miracle of miracles, in the centre of the room a big pail of water with John's own towels and soap lying by its side. John's sun-blistered, mosquito-bitten face beamed on him when he entered.

"What do you think of that?" asked John, as he waved his hand proudly towards the pail.

"That my body will be grateful," answered David. "It hasn't known water for nearly four months."

John looked despairingly at the pail.

"You'll have to make it do," he said; "it's the largest thing they possess, and I believe if we ask for more water they'll think me a madman and send me off. They already look upon me as a kind of witch-doctor or something worse." Then he went out to order the breakfast.

The sweet, cool water was a benediction to David's parched body. He threw open the shutters of the room and lay on the boarded floor in the full flood of sunlight to dry himself and purify himself still more that way.

He could understand now the intense joy the trees must feel when the cool autumn rains dash against them after the fierce, scorching heat of summer. He sang praises to God for it, he prayed, he sang again. The people of the inn thought the witch-doctor's pardoned convict was a madman, but when David came out of the room radiant and clean, such an atmosphere of gladness came with him all were infected. His swollen, blistered feet were bare, his head still unwashed; his beard he had been able to cleanse, but his hair being so thick was more than he could manage. The woman of the house took compassion on him; she swathed his feet in cool, clean, wet rags, and then sat him down in the court-yard while she combed out lock by lock his long hair. She was used, she said, to tending her husband's hair, who was a hide-dresser, and who would always wipe his hands upon his head, so that her task with him each week was no easy one. After an hour of rubbing and brushing and pouring some wash made from herbs upon his head, David's hair shone and glistened soft as silk and fell on his shoulders in heavy waves and curls.

The woman lifted her hands in wonder at it. "Thou hast hair like the Christ," she exclaimed, "in my icon there."

David smiled. "I, too, am a Nazarene."

"What may that be?" she asked.

"A native of the place where your Christ was born," he said. She shook her head, not understanding, and went away to see that her girls had made the breakfast ready.

Anton Nevski, the Czar's courier, had supped and slept at the house of the governor of the little town, and was already on his way back to Petersburg in the tarantass he had come in, so David and John hired a fresh tarantass, and just before noon they started. David was too impatient to wait for the cool of the evening.

He said, "We will travel to-day and all night, rest to-morrow, and then start at evening time. Think, friend, we have nearly two months' hard travelling before we shall reach Odessa; we mustn't waste a moment."

During the heat of the middle of the day John noticed that David suddenly looked tired and pinched about the face.

"Oh, it is nothing," he laughed. "There was an outbreak of cholera among the men; a third of them died; I got a touch of it and am not strong yet; it is no more."

"Take a pull at my flask," said John.

"No; we will ask that old woman for a cup of milk."

They were passing through a village. All the villagers, men, women, and children, with the exception of an old woman bent nearly double, were working in the fields carrying the corn. The old woman looked at David and John with bright, kindly eyes beaming on them from under her coloured kerchief.

"Will you give us a cup of milk, little mother?" smiled David.

"Aye, aye," she nodded in answer to him, and went into her hut. Presently she returned with a small basin of milk, cool from the cellar, in her brown hand, the beads of moisture glistening on the outside. John refused it with a shiver, but David took a deep drink, saying, as he gave back the empty basin,—

"That is good."

Then on they sped again, with a smile and a blessing from the old woman.

CHAPTER XXVIII.

IN DANGER.

It was November. The rain was over; the roads were hardening under the frost and the snow was spreading her fair white mantle over the face of the country. In the house of Michael Volkenoff, in the servants' quarters, there was great rejoicing and merry-making, for a son was born to the master. Outside Marya's room Michael walked noiselessly up and down, and there he had walked since ten the night before, unable to rest, to eat, until he had seen the child. All his old fears had returned to him,—what manner of child would it be? The doctor opened the door of Marya's dressing-room and beckoned to him. He drew his breath with difficulty and went in. On the nurse's knee before the fire lay his son. He made the sign of the cross and went forward. He stooped over it, staring at its puckered brows and dark, blinking eyes, not yet used to the light, then he made a feverish sign to the nurse. She lifted the soft flannel covering and showed him the child's straight, rosy little limbs. It gave a strong, protesting cry, for, though the room was almost at summer heat, it missed the warm covering. Michael stood gazing at it; he felt he could never satiate his eyes with looking on that morsel of flesh, his son, his heir. After a while he went towards the door leading into Marya's room, but the doctor stepped between, saying,—

"She is asleep." Michael nodded and went back to the child, stooped again and felt all its limbs through the covering, then he crept softly away to his rooms, seeming to walk on air, to be drinking in some rare, etherealized wine. "Thank the Lord and all the saints," he repeated over and over again. "I knew my child would be safe in her keeping. My son, my son!" Then he lay down upon his bed and slept for hours.

Olga was in a room in the outdoor servants' quarters on the north side of the court-yard. It was by Michael Volkenoff's orders. He had said Marya must have perfect peace and quiet. Olga went gladly. If it was for her dear mistress' sake, she was ready for far more trying things than the leaving of her cosy room for a cheerless, ill-furnished one, with many uncouth, unaccustomed sounds breaking in upon her peace from the kitchens underneath. Anna, the serf who was to attend her, grumbled loudly at the room; she declared it gave her goose's flesh. She devoutly crossed herself when Olga wanted to know the reason why, and replied, "Never mind, my pigeon."

Two of the women had died there in childbed, and Anna knew the mistress had said it was not to be used again. Why, then, had Nadeja Saviska put Olga into that room?

But though Anna was ignorant, she was too wise to fill Olga's head with her own fears, and in a day or two she herself forgot them.

And there in the dull, sunless room Olga's child was

born, a sturdy, strong-limbed boy. Anna was amazed at her endurance, and could not cease exclaiming at it.

Olga laughed. "Why should I suffer? My dear mistress told me that fear was the cause of nearly all the agony women bear. Each time the mother shrinks and cries she draws back the little life, and thus she stays the course of nature, causing herself great pain.

"Well, all I can say is that thou art a wonderful one. Dost thee not feel tired?"

"Maybe. I feel I only want to lie here and look at David's son."

So she lay quiet, watching the woman wash the child. When it was swathed in the soft woollen garments she had made for it, Anna laid it, clamouring, in her arms.

"That's good," said Anna; "it didn't cry half enough to please me. Now it's all right. Now thou canst feed it." She put the hungry, complaining little mouth to Olga's breast. It began to draw lustily. Olga winced and bit her lips.

"That hurts greatly," she whispered.

"Shows how strong the rascal is," smiled Anna. "But it's a pleasant pain and will soon pass."

"It is almost gone already," said Olga, smiling, but with the sharp tears under her eyelids. Anna prepared a posset for her, and soon after she had taken it she was asleep with the child in her arms.

Anna sat at the side of the stove watching her, nodding with intense satisfaction, and the natural, happy content a good woman always feels when a child comes safely into the world.

During the few days Olga was lying in bed she made what were to her three great discoveries,—first, that the child had her eyes and brow, but David's hair and chin; and, lastly, that on the ball of its left thumb was a red, triangular-shaped mark like the wound she had bound up on David's hand.

Anna didn't share her enthusiasm about its hair. It was soft and silky and golden at present, no doubt of that; but, then, the first crop of hair often changed, and no doubt it would in time come dark as Olga's own. And the mark on its thumb. She looked up from her making of the bed. "Thy fault; it fretted thee, and thy child hath a mark that comes not from nature. Now let that teach thee mothers should not fret."

Olga laughed happily; then she looked longingly across to the window. She wondered whether Marya had received any news yet of David.

"Might I go to the house to see the mistress, Anna? I long to show her my boy; and oh, I do so long to see her! It is the first time since she came here that I have been parted from her for so many days."

"Then you shall," said Anna, decisively.

She had noticed that Olga's face had lost some of its natural colour, and she was anxious to get her away from the place as quickly as possible.

Olga was out of bed in a moment. "See, I am strong; I am sure I am strong, and I do so long to get away from this room."

"Not more than I do," cried Anna, while she helped Olga to dress. "No sun! Ugh! This room was not intended for the winter. Mistress said it was only for summer, that the women might be cool; but after Katenka died—— Why, thou art strong, indeed. Hi! hi! hi!" she cried, interrupting herself. "Why, thou art strong, indeed!"

"Did Katenka die here?" asked Olga, catching her by the arm.

"Well, she did," said Anna, bluntly, "and we are not going to stay here for thee to do the same. We'll leave it to-morrow. It's bewitched. I know, for I saw Nadeja Saviska looking at it over her crossed thumbs and muttering. Thou shalt have a share of my bed, and Mikej can sleep on the oven. So come along, my pigeon."

The child was wrapped in a blanket and Olga in her sleeved, fur-lined cloak, the warm hood over her head, her thick overshoes on. Anna went with her, carrying the child. They crossed the court-yard and went in by the eastern door, that was always left unlocked for the serfs to pass in and out during the daytime, and into Marya's rooms that way.

Nadeja Saviska, a tall, bony woman, head of the female serfs and chief nurse when any of the family fell ill, frowned when they entered the dressing-room. She was jealous of Olga, and angry that her son Foka had been cheated of the wife he had wished for.

She rose to close the door of Marya's room, but Marya had heard the little stir and had caught Olga's whisper to Anna, bidding her make no noise.

"Is that Olga?" she called, faintly. "Let her come to me."

Without waiting Nadeja's permission, Olga snatched the child from Anna and ran in to Marya, her cloak and the blanket from the baby falling on the floor of the room as she went.

Anna picked up the cloak and blanket, and, with a defiant, belligerent toss of her head at Nadeja, said,—

"That's my patient. How is thine?"

Nadeja gave her a black look and closed the bedroom door, answering not a word. Anna, with a shrug of her fine shoulders and a grand swing of her full, round body, sat down in a chair opposite Nadeja's and began a long, glowing recital of Olga's courage and endurance, the woman Nadeja growling and grunting out her spleen and impatience between every sentence.

"So that is thy child," Marya was saying to Olga. She was already feeling stronger; Olga's coming had invigorated her and made the very air of the room seem lighter.

Olga displayed the boy's legs and arms, laughing proudly at their round, firm rosiness; then she showed Marya the triangular-shaped red mark on the ball of his thumb.

"There, mistress, see; that is like the wound the silver burnt in David's hand. Isn't it wonderful that it be here on the child? I only discovered it yesterday, for he hath been so red and kept his little fist doubled up so tight there was no seeing it."

"His brows are straight and dark like thine, Olga."

"And his eyes, too, as thou wouldst see if he were awake. He hath done nothing but sleep and eat since he was born. Do all children sleep so long?"

"If they be healthy."

"Little Mother—David—hath any news?" whispered Olga, speaking last of what lay nearest to her heart. Marya shook her head. Olga crossed herself and rubbed the red mark on the child's hand, her heart too full for further speech. The silence oppressed Marya. She feared it, lest in her weakness she should tell Olga Michael's plans with regard to the child.

"Dost thou not want to see my child, Olga?" she asked.

"My beloved mistress, it is what I have been longing to ask. But it is not here nor with Nadeja Saviska, and I feared——"

"He is with Wanda in the room beyond my boudoir. We have made that into a nursery because I wished him as near as possible. I have been weak and not allowed to see him. But go, Olga; go and bring him to me. Do not mind what Nadeja says; I want him. Lay thy child here by me."

Olga laid the little bundle of baby and flannel on the bed and went through the rooms without a word to Nadeja, who followed her with frowning looks into the room where Marya's child was lying. Wanda, a fine, healthy young serf, who had been taken from her own child to suckle the master's, was sitting by the fire, knitting and swaying the child to and fro on her knees. She nodded smilingly when Olga took it from her lap and carried it to Marya.

Nadeja followed Olga when she came back carrying the child, protesting against the disobedience to the master's orders, but Anna pulled her away and closed the bedroom door, placing her back against it and saying,—

"It can't hurt the mistress to see her child for five minutes; it will do her much more harm to be hungering after it." Nadeja fell into a fury, whispering savagely at her; but Anna laughed, holding her ground, saying she wouldn't budge an inch until the mistress bade her. After some little time Olga came out again with the baby. To her great surprise Wanda was fast asleep.

"Pardon, pardon," mumbled Wanda. "The child is so restless, I get so little sleep."

"Best lay him in his cradle, then, lest you fall asleep while he is on thy lap." Wanda obeyed sleepily, and settled once more to her knitting.

"Come again to-morrow, my pigeon," Marya said when Olga took up her child to go. "I feel so well and strong for seeing thee."

"That will be easy now," said Olga. "We do not go back to the outdoor servants' quarters. Anna says I may share her bed."

"But why shouldst thou share Anna's bed?"

Olga was silent, understanding that Marya hadn't been told that she was moved to the outdoor servants' quarters, and it might distress her to learn it, so she began to move as quickly as she had strength to the door, saying, "Yes, to-morrow, Little Mother."

"Answer my question," said Marya, firmly.

Olga turned, saying frankly, feeling it was best,—

"I was put in the outdoor servants' quarters, mistress. It is best for thee. This rascal here might have been noisy."

Marya set her lips close together and rang her bell. Nadeja entered, looking back triumphantly at Anna. "Tell Mimi to light the stove in Olga's room and prepare it for her instantly. I expect it ready within an hour. Is Anna there?"

"Yes, Excellency."

"Bid her help."

Nadeja went away looking sullen and angry. Anna, who had heard all, went like a whirlwind into Olga's room, and in less than an hour it was ready.

"How cruel! how wicked! By whose orders was it done?" asked Marya, her cheeks burning.

"Dear mistress, see, I am well and strong, and so is the child, therefore it has been good. Do not distress thyself, it may be ill for thee," said Olga, brightly.

"Yes, my Olga, yes, I will be calm. Go into the dressing-room and rest now, and send Nadeja to me."

When Nadeja entered the room, Marya said, "Close the door and come here."

The woman closed the door, leaving Olga in the dressing-room.

"By whose orders was Olga removed to the outdoor servants' quarters?"

"The master gave the order to the steward, Excellency, thinking it would be best for you in case her child should disturb you."

"Which room was given to her?"

"I put her into the room that is always used for the

house servants in childbed." Nadeja lowered her eyes; there was a wicked look in them.

"That room!" There was a long pause, then Marya said, slowly and quietly, "You are a cruel, vindictive woman, Nadeja Saviska. You are still angry with Olga because she would not marry your son. I told you that room would be dangerous to any woman in her present condition. You know why."

"Because the coachman's wife died there of the mother's fever," answered Nadeja, with the wicked look still under her eyelids.

"Was the bedding burnt?"

"I gave the order, but I do not know whether it was done, Excellency."

"Come here." Nadeja went slowly to Marya's side. "Look at me," said Marya. The woman trembled, tried to raise her eyelids, then turned suddenly away, her fingers twitching.

"Go away," said Marya, sternly; "you are not fit to have charge of the women. Never let me see your face again. Natalia shall attend me."

Nadeja went out of the room, her face dark and twisted with passion. She noticed as she passed through the dressing-room that Michael Volkenoff was standing there looking at Olga, whose face was set and white and full of trouble.

He had been to look at his boy, and passing through from the nursery to go to Marya he found Olga. He looked sternly at her and was going, when he seemed to remember something. Returning and pointing to the baby, he asked,—

" Your child ?"

" Yes, master."

He touched the flannel over its head. " Let me see it."

Olga threw back the covering. The little fellow was fast asleep, sucking his rosy fist.

" A boy or girl?" asked Michael.

" A boy, Excellency," said Olga, proudly.

Michael's face softened wonderfully. He made the sign of the cross above the child.

" Has your mistress told you that I intend to consecrate him to the Church ?"

" No, Excellency." Olga watched his lips anxiously.

" Yes, this little soul shall be dedicated to the service of Christ. At the end of this month he shall be sent to the good sisters of St. Barbara, to stay with them until he is old enough to enter the monastery."

" You will not take him away from me, Excellency ?" cried Olga, feeling suddenly sick and faint under the shock.

" Could you desire any other life for him?" asked Michael Volkenoff, in great surprise. " What else can cleanse his soul of the sin you yourself have clogged it with? At the end of this month he will be taken away. Be ready to part with him," he said, making again the sign of the cross, his lips moving as though he were praying.

Just then Nadeja passed through to the corridor. Michael turned and went on tiptoe into Marya's room, closing the door after him. Olga crept away, hugging the child to her breast, and when she came to the little flight of stairs leading up to her room she sank down on them with her head against the wall, feeling stunned and sick, a strong rigour seizing her and making her icy cold from her feet upwards. When Anna came running out, all being now ready, her eyes were like the eyes of a poor, hunted animal. She neither spoke nor moved, but sat sighing piteously.

Anna first took the child and laid it down before the stove, then she lifted Olga and half carried her into the room and made her lie upon the bed. Olga held out her arms for her boy, looking fearfully at the door. She hugged him up to her breast again; then Anna covered them with the warm blankets and rushed away after Nadeja, whom she saw from the window crossing the court-yard to the outdoor servants' quarters. Anna came up with her as she was pushing open the door.

"Now, Nadeja Saviska," cried Anna, clutching the woman by the shoulder and pulling her round, "what have you done to Olga Ivanna?"

Nadeja jerked her shoulder out of Anna's hand and muttered, sullenly, "Nothing."

"You lie!" cried Anna. "You were mad because she was so well and strong, so you cast your wicked spell upon her, you old witch! Everybody knows you have the evil eye." Anna crossed herself rapidly, and again in the air between them she made the sign of the cross.

"It were better for you to repeat all this to the master," said Nadeja, scornfully. "He'll know more about your wicked spell than I do." She folded her arms and stuck out her lips at Anna.

"If you were not Nicolinka's mother I'd beat you," muttered Anna, savagely. "But wait; I'll be even with you." She flung up her head and went with a free, swinging, defiant stride back to the house, Nadeja Saviska watching her, shaking with silent laughter, and muttering,—

"If I were not Nicolinka's mother! So that's your secret! That's why you quarrel so with Mikej!" She shrugged her shoulders contemptuously. "It is always the fool that hath the widest mouth," she sneered, her voice sinking into a snarl. She walked into the kitchen, and, taking a seat near the stove, sat there eating her heart out at her self-imposed degradation, saying to the outdoor servants when they entered at sunset, "I am no more now than the least of you." In that way nursing her spite till chance should show on which to let it fall, Olga or Anna.

Two days after, at the same hour, when the men were coming in from their work, chance showed Nadeja the way to satisfy her grudge.

CHAPTER XXIX.

ANNA'S HUSBAND.

Early next morning Marya sent Natalia to Anna to enquire how Olga had passed the night. She had been restless and strange; she refused to answer any question that was put to her, thinking only of the child, talking and whispering continuously to it.

Doctor Stodham, Marya's doctor, came in soon after the woman had delivered her message. Never had he seen any face light up at sight of him as Marya's did when he entered her room. She briefly stated the case to him, making him promise to attend to it himself and send his assistant to her. He looked relieved after seeing Olga; it was not so grave as he had feared.

"You say she was out yesterday? Did she complain of feeling cold when she came in?" he asked Anna.

"No," she replied.

"Had she any shock?"

"Yes," cried Anna; "Nadeja Saviska hath cast an evil spell upon her."

"You must be quiet," said the doctor, "or I can't trust you with the case." He was an Englishman, but he knew the Russian peasant nature well. "No spell has been cast upon her. She was put into the room where Katenka, the coachman's wife, died of what you know as mother's fever; the cold and shock, for there must have been a shock of some kind, have hastened the attack."

"But Olga isn't going to die?" whispered Anna, and stopped; she could say no more. She looked into the inner room where Olga lay muttering to the child, and twisted a corner of her apron, striving not to cry.

"No, certainly not. She is young and healthy; the infection has not had time to get much hold of her. Do as I tell you,"—he gave her a few simple instructions,—"and she'll be all right. Keep her warm, give her the medicine I will send, and warm rice and barley-milk; and you mustn't let her leave her bed, mind, nor must you let the heat in the stove go down; another shock of cold might kill her. Take the child from her and send for one of the women to nurse it."

"She won't let it out of her arms. I've tried and she holds to it like death. I've had to attend to it as best I could."

"Then let it remain with her while she is quiet, but keep it clean. Don't neglect that. Another thing, no one who has been in this room must approach your mistress, or she may take the fever. It is impossible to remove her," pointing to Olga, "without great danger, so we must take all the precautions possible. Some one shall come to help you, and one of you must sit up all night with her." He went in again to look at Olga, who was still muttering and whispering to the child, but so low he couldn't catch the words. "You must keep the child well nourished; have milk and water standing in the stove, and give it a teaspoonful every fifteen minutes. Not more," he said, sharply; then, after giving Anna further instructions, he went to the house steward, muttering, "Old Simmelweiss is right, it is infectious."

One of the women, after he left, came to help Anna, soon followed by another with barley-milk and the warm rice, which was placed in the stove. They all stood in wholesome dread of the English doctor, who held threats of whipping over their thick heads if they neglected anything he said. The whole day Olga talked or muttered, sometimes laughing loudly, many times springing up to leave her bed, and weeping bitterly when she found that she had no milk to feed the child.

About four next day Anna saw Mikej, her husband, cross the court-yard to the servants' quarters and stand talking awhile with Nadeja at the door. Nadeja tossed her head and walked abruptly away into the kitchen, Mikej following her. Just then Nicolinka came into the yard from the stables, and Anna saw Nadeja looking at him from the kitchen window. A wild gleam of mischief came into her eyes. Saying to the woman who was helping her nurse Olga, "I'll be back before supper, as I'm to sit up with her to-night," she snatched up her cloak and darted out, taking a pail from the kitchen on her way.

Nadeja stood in the window looking absently at Nicolinka brushing the dirt from his boots, fighting on the one hand with her love of ease and comfort, on the other with her pride. Should she go back to the house and be jeered at by the girls in the maids' room, or remain where she was among the dirty, disorderly field and yard hands? Mikej was smoking by the stove and talking to two of the men. He had brought a message from old Nicolas, saying unless Nadeja cared to go to him she might stay where she was. He preferred his own warm room.

"Well, I will return," she thought, "and if Mimi and the rest sneer at me let them look out. "Ha! ha!" she gave a sudden, harsh laugh as Anna, rolled up in her sleeved cloak, with the pail in her hand, came from the house and stopped to speak to Nicolinka. "Come here, Mikej! poor Mikej! come here," she said. Mikej slouched over to her. "Look there," she said.

Anna was standing close to Nicolinka, swinging her pail and laughing and giving wicked sidelong glances at the kitchen window.

"She loves him, Mikej, poor Mikej, that's why she quarrels so with thee; she confessed it to me yesterday." Just then Anna bent her head forward and touched the collar of Nicolinka's coat, as though whispering something in his ear. With a howl of rage, Mikej bounded out of the place and over to Anna. He seized her by the back of her cloak and dragged her along into the kitchen, followed by Nicolinka, Nadeja quietly watching.

"Now, cat! black she-goat! I've caught thee, and I'll whip thee severely for this," he shouted.

"Yes, do, do, Mikej, and we'll help thee," laughed some of the men, who knew how he feared Anna; but Mikej was not afraid now; he was beside himself with rage and mad with jealousy.

"Thou'lt not dare touch me!" cried Anna, flinging off her cloak and shaking her fists at him.

"What dost thou say?" howled Mikej, cutting her across the arms with the strap he snatched from round his waist. "What's that, then?"

"Well!" Anna stared at him. "Why, thou hast some spirit in thee."

"Try some more," he jabbered, with his face stuck into hers. "Love-making before my eyes." Anna began to laugh, and she looked wickedly at Nadeja.

"Aye, but only so thou'lt be angry and whip Nicolinka there to spite his mother for me, if thou hadst any spirit in thee, for I knew thou wert here." Nicolinka's laughter died. "I knew he could give as good as he got, so I chose the best man among ye," she flashed out at the servants, who were grinning.

"That tale won't do for me," said Mikej. "I'll not let thee out of my sight again to-night. Get up there." He pointed to the broad shelf over the oven.

"I'll not," cried Anna. "I'm an indoor servant, as thou art. Come to the house."

"While thou slip away"—Mikej shook his head cunningly—"or send some crafty tale to the mistress? Get up! get up!" He flourished his strap.

"But I will not!" screamed Anna. "I have to attend Olga Ivanna; she is sick; I dare not leave her."

"Thou couldst leave her to go sweethearting; now thou must leave her for me." Without more ado, he seized her in his strong arms and flung her onto the shelf, then scrambled up beside her, and sat there cross-legged, twirling his strap. Nadeja Saviska walked over to the oven, and thrust up her face into Anna's with a snarling, impudent laugh, then went out of the kitchen with a backward, contemptuous movement of her left hand.

The men set about making their tea. Nicolinka threw himself on the floor with his back to the wall and lighted up his pipe, wondering what effect Mikej's sudden display of courage would have on Anna's love for him, and Anna lay along the shelf, hoping Mikej would fall asleep, that she might slip away to Olga; but she didn't know the power jealousy has for keeping a man awake, and fell asleep herself. But not an eyelid did Mikej close till the sun set next afternoon. When he had escorted Anna to the house, still flourishing his strap, he saw her safely through the door leading to Olga's room, then went back to watch Nicolinka.

CHAPTER XXX.

OLGA.

The woman who was watching Olga waited a long time for Anna, and after a while fell asleep. When she awoke the room was dark; it seemed to her that it must be very late. She threw some pieces of wood into the stove and left the door open, that the flare might light up the room. Then she offered some food to Olga, who turned her head from side to side, impatiently refusing to take it. The child was asleep. The woman walked over to the window and stood there looking out. The house seemed strangely quiet. She strained her head sideways to find out, if possible, whether the lights in the wing of the house where the indoor servants slept were still burning. There was no reflection from them on the snow, but the rooms were parallel with the one she was in, and were, moreover, too far away for her to find out. The flare in the stove died down to a dull red glow. She began to grow nervous of the shadows. Why did not Anna return?

Olga's muttering and laughter made her tremble; not knowing the nature of her illness, she began to fear that she might take it. She crept away out of the room to the end of the passage, where a sheet was hanging saturated with a solution of sulphurous acid.

She would wait there for Anna; she was afraid to remain in the room. Olga's whispers came sharply to her strained sense of hearing. The child woke and began to wail faintly; she half started forward to go in to feed it, but she shrank back farther and farther from the room, it was so dark, and to her ignorant mind it seemed to be full of malicious goblins dancing and gibbering at her. The wet sheet shook with the excessive trembling of her body, and flapped once against her cheek. To her excited sense it was like a cold, dead hand. With a half-smothered cry she dashed past it, and rushed on blindly down the long corridor and up a flight of stairs to the maids' room. It was empty and dark, save for a red glow that came from under the door of the stove. She was sobbing with terror, and stumbled on up to the bedroom she shared with some of her fellow-servants. They were all fast asleep. With her teeth chattering, she flung herself down on her bed, dragging the blanket over her head, and lay there praying to St. Nicholas to protect her, and thankful for the moon that was rising, and now began to shine on the window. Presently she, too, slept.

Olga talked on, cooing and laughing to the child. The glow in the stove died out, and soon there was only the light from the stars falling across her bed. She began to talk more rapidly and her voice came more clearly.

"David's child! David's child! dost thou hear the stars singing to us? Listen now, little one; listen! There! then it was the big white star. The swallow flying over it said we are sad down here, so the star answered with a song to cheer thee. Now, hark! the swallow is flying higher, right into God's garden, for the swallows are the souls of dear, dead children. But thou shalt not die, no, nor be taken from me." Her words broke off into hysterical laughter and frightened the child, who began to cry grievously. "Hush thee, hush thee," she whispered, "or the master will snatch thee away."

She held its little mouth to her breast, but still it cried. She watched it, terror making her face grey, and dark shadows gathered about her eyes. "My milk is dried up," she moaned, "and my babe will perish!" Suddenly her cheeks flushed and she lifted herself on her arm, a cunning light creeping into her eyes. "Wanda, yes, Wanda," she whispered, nodding her head; "she shall feed thee."

She slipped out of bed onto the floor, with the child in her arms, and walked unsteadily into the outer room. She paused at the door, the cunning, anxious expression of her face changing to a wild, exultant one; then she sprang back to the bed and laid the child in it, looking watchfully over her shoulder the while.

"No one saw me! No one saw me!" she laughed. Then she covered the child and crept away, smiling and nodding, "Mother will save thee, mother will save thee," until she came to the door of the room where Wanda and Marya's child were lying. Wolf came down the corridor wagging his tail and licked her bare feet. She neither felt him nor saw him. Silently, like a ghost, she entered the nursery, then paused, holding her hands tightly over her heart, as though she feared Wanda would hear its bounds and waken. But Wanda slept on heavily, and the child, too, slept. Olga crept forward and lifted it from its cosy nest of lace and silk and flew with it to her room. She closed the door and locked it, laughing gleefully. The child began to cry. Singing to it and cooing, she began to strip off its night-clothes; then she laid it naked in her bed and as swiftly stripped off her own child's clothing. It complained bitterly; it was hungry and chilled, the fire was out, and the air was cooling rapidly.

"Hush thee, hush thee, my dove; thou wilt soon be warm and some food will be given thee,"—her voice rang out with shrill laughter,—"though my breasts are dry." When it was dressed she laid it for a moment by the side of the other child, scanning their faces closely by the light from the stars and the soft white light the moon made in the court-yard below her window. She laughed and clapped her hands. "The same dark brows," she cried, "and they each do pucker them in the same way. Come, then, my bird; his own child he shall make a monk, and thou shalt be safe,—safe till thou art big and strong and canst fight thy way to thy father. Come, then, my dove, my sunshine; come!"

She flew again down the passage with the crying child in her arms, its little mouth crushed against her breast, that no one but she might hear it. She paused an instant at the door where Wanda lay. The woman's breathing came evenly and deep. "She is still asleep,"

Olga said, and, giving a low, cunning laugh, she entered, laying her child carefully and tenderly in the cradle. It set up a louder crying. Olga stole to the door and stood in the corridor listening. She heard Wanda mutter, "Hush thee, little one; hush." Still the child wailed. Then she heard the bedclothes moved, the creaking of the cradle, and after a moment more the child's cries quieted into a satisfied mumbling; he sighed happily, and Wanda began to croon to him. Clapping her hands noiselessly together, with a wild, triumphant flash in her eyes, Olga ran back to her room. The other child was crying complainingly under the blanket. She went to the window and looked out.

"The morning is coming up from the east," she whispered, "and David is thinking of me. He will be starting soon. I must hurry, hurry, or I shall lose him." The child began to cry more loudly. "I must tell him, too, of our child."

She pulled on her thick snow-shoes and tied on a petticoat over her night-dress. After a long pause, as though she had forgotten what she had intended to do, she flung on her big-sleeved cloak and warm hood; then she gently took up the child, muffling its cries under the blanket she wrapped round it.

"Thou must go with me," she muttered, "or they will know,—they will know." She stopped, with a puzzled expression on her face, struggling, striving to remember. "What is it they will know?" She shook her head, the whole forgotten, and she laughed. "The stars are calling,—come, then; come!" She opened the door and sped down the passage, this time to the "Little Mother's door." Wolf followed her. She stumbled once or twice, and a deathly feeling of faintness made her face and lips white.

"Come," she muttered, as though cheering someone; "come, David is waiting, David is waiting."

She went out into the court-yard and staggered on blindly through the snow, driving back the dog and closing the gate softly, saying,—

"Hush! Hush!"

CHAPTER XXXI.

THE WOMAN KEZIA.

On the morning that Olga was seized with the fever Ezra, Judith, Salome, and Belah were fluttering about David's room like four birds preparing for flight. A letter had come from Daniel Pereira, saying that he wished Salome to be in Milan by the beginning of spring. Following the instructions in the letter, Ezra, accompanied by Kezia, had gone down to the harbour to secure berths in a ship bound for Genoa, that being the best and most comfortable way, in those days, to get to Italy from Odessa. The captain of the ship had also received a letter from Pereira, so the negotiation was made easy to them. They were to sail at seven on the morning of the 30th,—just two days only ahead. Kezia and Salome went out to the shops to buy the necessary things for the voyage, while Ezra and Judith, more hindered than helped by Belah, put all David's things back, as far as they could remember, in their old places, even to his leathern apron lying over his workstool.

"If we could but see his face before we start," Judith kept sighing.

"It is possible we may," said Ezra, once, consolingly. "The time that we allowed for the journey is up by fifteen days."

The 26th passed and the 27th was come, and they were sitting at their last supper in Odessa. It was about seven o'clock. They were going on board at nine.

"Who will take care of David's room when we are gone?" asked Belah, anxious for his friend.

"Kezia," said Judith, resolutely, looking at her.

Kezia was seated on the floor by the stove with her lean arms clasped round her knees. She made an impatient movement with her head, and spoke not a word.

"I say again, Kezia," repeated Judith. "There is no one else I will trust it to."

"Then hang the key inside my door and leave a slip of paper tied here to the handle telling him where he will find it," said Kezia. "But what of the rent?" she added, sharply.

"That is arranged for," Ezra assured her, "up to the beginning of December;" and then he rose and spread out his hands, speaking the blessing in a low, earnest voice, and after that they prepared to start. Everything was cleared away, the table covered with a fresh white cloth, the tall silver candlesticks placed in the middle, and David's favourite book at the side.

This being done, they walked slowly round the room hand in hand, murmuring prayers and blessings on David and weeping many tears for him, the silent Ezra weeping most. But the time sped; he and Belah shouldered the blankets and pillows, Judith and Salome carrying some shawls and a basket containing a few things too precious to Ezra to be trusted to the trunks, and so they started on their way to the ship. All their friends and neighbours were waiting at the door and along the street for them, and thus escorted they went on board, Kezia clinging hard to Salome's hand. The last bit of her youth seemed going with the child; she felt she must hold to it to the last.

She went on board with them, and lingered talking with Judith and helping her arrange the things in the tiny cabin till she was almost forcibly sent off the ship by the captain's orders. But still she lingered on the quay, looking through her tear-blurred eyes at the lanterns as they were put out one by one till only the watch-light at the head remained. She stamped about to keep her feet warm, resolved to conquer the cold and stay till the time for sailing, but the icy air conquered her at last, and she was compelled to go. With a savage gesture for the climate of Russia and all the country contained, she turned sullenly away with a bitter feeling against Daniel Pereira for robbing her of Salome, though she had been begged by him to accompany her pupil and had refused. She hugged her thin arms close under her long cloak muttering angrily to herself, and went back to her room.

An officer stopped her on her way and demanded her business out of doors at that hour.

She told him she had been down to the "Wanda" to say good-bye to her friends. He pulled her under a lamp and studied every line of her face, she cursing him softly under her breath in Italian the while, which he, mistaking the beautiful, liquid sounds for a blessing, prayed the saints to guard her, and let her go.

Kezia laughed under her breath and went home. Arrived there, she sat down on the threshold of her door to think. She felt desolate, suddenly years older; the little, feeble glimmer of pleasure that had lighted up her life gone out with Salome.

"Why should I stay here," she began to mutter, "while she, in whom I could re-live my life, see all my triumphs over again, is there in my Italy, thousands of miles away, while I stay here teaching stupid fools with legs and arms like sausages, and with just as much soul in them, my divine art? I can go, too, if I choose. What kept me back when Pereira said, 'Come with her,' but pride? Hate that anyone should recognize in this old grey bag of bones La Meldola? Ha! ha! ha!" she laughed, bitterly; "that was it, and I said I could not endure it. That loneliness! the snapping of my very heart-strings was as nothing to it, and now —— Let me look at myself," she said, abruptly, rising. She unlocked her door and went into her room. She laid aside the thick, woollen shawl that had been wrapped hoodwise about her head, lighted a candle, and, holding it above her head that it might show up every line and shadow in her face, patiently studied herself in a bit of looking-glass.

"Hideous! hideous as hell!" she cried, passionately, with a savage snarl at her poor, wrinkled, pinched face. She flung down the candle and tossed the looking-glass onto her bed, and began to walk up and down the room to keep herself warm, muttering curses at the ill luck that had stolen her beauty.

"And yet,"—she paused and again took up the looking-glass and candle,—"with my hair washed and brushed, a rich velvet bonnet and mantle, a purple silk gown, what then? These hard lines and shadows would be softened. The papers should say that I, La Meldola, the great, the famous La Meldola, was come to Milan to see the *début* of my pupil, Salome Manuelli. ... Shall I go? Shall I go? Spend some of my hoard to buy these things? Feast my eyes upon her, hear the cheers that used to be for me, then go to Rome, look once upon the Ghetto, and creep away into some corner up in the hills and die? Yes, why not? One short, glorious retaste of Italy, its sun, its flowers, its speech, then nothing. Yes, yes; it shall be done," she cried, her withered cheeks flushing.

She flung aside her cloak, her body suddenly aglow with the thought. She tore open with her teeth and hands the head of her straw mattress, where it had been ripped and stitched together again. She was about to thrust in her hand, but the old habit came over her. She peered into the corners of the room, fearful that some one might be watching her, rose and locked her door, then she returned, and, thrusting her hand into the mattress, pulled out a small bag of roubles. She sat down cross-legged on the floor and poured them into her lap. She began to count them, testing some on the bare boards of the room. Once she thought she heard a movement on the stairs. She covered the pieces with her arms and listened. Old Zebudah was coughing in the garret overhead; it must have been that she had heard. She began to count again.

"Three hundred!" she whispered, exultantly. "Three

hundred!" Then she sneered, "Three hundred only in ten years, and I once had as many thousands in as many months, fool that I was, to waste! And what would this journey to Italy be but to waste? Was starvation so sweet to me that I should be keen to taste it again? Have I forgotten binding my scarf tightly round my waist, almost crushing my ribs in, to keep me from crying out for bread in the streets while I hoarded you? No, no!"—she began to shovel the money back into the bag with her hand,—"La Moldola knows now how to be prudent."

When all the money was back in the bag, she tied the neck up with a piece of string, saying again, "No, no! I will be prudent."

After that she sat a long time with her chin on her clenched hands, thinking, alternately pulling the bag towards her, then pushing it away again. At last, with a defiant look at the walls of her room, as though they had been restraining her, she said,—

"And yet wherefore not? Better a swift, sharp death than this slow, desolate death in life. Come, then!" she cried, lifting the bag in her right hand and holding it high, the full length of her thin arm, above her head. "Come to Italy, Salome, and the sun, and when thou art empty, there is old Father Tiber for my bed. He will but tumble me over awhile with his turbid yellow waves, then I shall sink and sleep, the fear of starvation far behind."

She rose to put together her few things for the journey, half singing to herself, and picturing Salome's surprise and delight, for the child loved her.

Someone laughed softly outside her door, then came a little gliding sound and a deep sigh, followed by the sudden cry of a young child.

Kezia's lips went white. Had someone been watching her? Someone who would perhaps seize her money?

Again the child cried, and again came the deep sigh. Kezia suddenly puffed out her candle while she thrust the bag into the head of her mattress, then she lighted the candle again, and quickly unlocked and threw open her door.

Olga was sitting on the stairs just above, with her head drooping heavily against the wall, her hood off, and her long, dark hair sweeping over her shoulders. Her arms were hanging loosely down; the child was in the blanket lying across her knees.

Kezia crept up the stairs and held the candle to her face. It was white as new snow; her eyes were closed.

"Father of Israel!" whispered Kezia; "it is the wife of David Rheba."

Again the child cried. She opened the blanket with the tips of her fingers and peeped at it. She could just see its puckered brows and red little face. It gave a gasp when the air reached it, and cried again lustily. A wistful look came into her eyes.

"So God hath given him a child." She suddenly put out her hands to raise Olga's head.

"No, no!" she muttered, drawing them back. "He would say my touch had defiled her." She rose abruptly and sprang down to the door on the opposite side of the landing to her own and rapped sharply on it, then listened. Someone was asleep within, snoring loudly. Again she rapped, this time with the heel of her shoe, which she had stooped and pulled off her foot. The snoring ceased. She rapped again, hard and fast, crying,—

"Wake up! wake up, Samuel Jacobi! Leah, wake up! Here is a woman lying on the stairs; she seems to be dying. Wake up! wake up!"

She put her ear to the key-hole; she heard a deep grunt, followed by a softer one, and a gruff voice say,—

"You are not going to catch two old birds with that sort of chaff." Then the snoring began louder than before.

"Swine!" she hissed through the key-hole. "Miserable swine! You are fearful that I am come to beg some wood of you. Misers!" She heard a muffled laugh, then again the snores.

She went back again up the stairs to Olga.

"Defile her or not in his eyes, I must do what I can."

She touched Olga, shook her by the arm. Olga's head only drooped lower. Was she dead? Kezia slipped her hand into the breast of Olga's cloak. Her heart seemed still, and yet she imagined there was a little trembling under her hand like the wing of a frightened bird. She snatched the key of David's room from where it was hanging inside her own door, took the child from Olga's lap and carried it into his room. There was a faint glow from the door of the stove. She laid the child on his bed, heaped on more wood, then hurried back down the stairs to Olga.

Kezia knelt beside her and carefully examined her hands and face; they were not frost-bitten, but they were deadly cold.

"I must get her to the warmth; this icy draught will kill her," she muttered. She put her arms round Olga, straining her strength to its uttermost to lift her up stair by stair to David's room, but she couldn't move her an inch. Kezia shook her fist in the direction of Samuel Jacobi's door.

"Inhuman pigs!" she called; then she set her teeth hard together and tried once more to lift Olga. It was useless; she was heavy as lead, no life or spring in her. Kezia thought of the "Wanda;" it was to sail at seven. It must be now nearly four.

"I will do what I can," she muttered, "then at daylight I must leave her. I can do no more than that."

She began to rub vigorously at Olga's hands and neck to get some heat into them.

About a quarter of an hour had passed when the house door opened and a police officer on his round of inspection entered. He flashed his lantern up the narrow stairs, and seeing Kezia's candle and the women two flights above, he immediately made for them.

Kezia looked hopefully at him as he came up. It was the officer who had stopped her on her way from the "Wanda." He smiled when he saw her, remembering gratefully her "blessing." He imagined it had kept him warm ever since.

"Your good Saint Nicholas watch over you," said Kezia, "and soften your heart to this poor woman here. She is the wife of a man who lives in that room when he is in Odessa. She is sick and hath fallen here in a faint."

"Her name?" asked the officer, taking out his note-book.

"Judith Manuelli," answered the quick-witted Kezia. "She was to have gone with her husband to Genoa, but, poor soul, as you see, she is sick."

"Her husband is Ezra Manuelli?"

"The same. As I told you, I went to see him and the children on board. Will you help me carry her up to that room?"

The man looked over the banisters at his mate, who had come in from the next house and was resting contentedly on the bottom stair, half dozing.

"Well, let's be quick about it. Stand aside; I'll do it quicker alone." He picked up Olga and carried her, breathing heavily under her weight, up to the room. Kezia ran on before him and stood the flaring candle on the landing, while she ran into the room and caught up the baby. She laid it down behind the stove, where it was completely hidden. Fortunately, it was quiet. Kezia nodded approvingly and said,—

"Now, if this man takes my word and makes no enquiry at the ship, the wife of David Rheba can remain here as Judith Manuelli." Kezia's hand went into the bosom of her gown, where a few small pieces of silver were lying tied in her handkerchief. "Everyone is precious to me," she muttered; "and yet if I do not give to this man——" She set her teeth together, as she had set them when she tried to lift Olga, and untied the corner of the handkerchief. She took out the pieces without looking at them, and held them tightly in her fingers.

The officer entered.

"There," she said, pointing to the bed. He laid Olga upon it, all huddled together as she was, and turned, wiping his forehead, and saying,—

"She's as heavy as the dead."

Kezia started. What if Olga were dead? She went anxiously over to the bed and threw back the cloak from Olga's breast, then stooped and slipped her hand in through the neck of the night-gown.

"It is well; she is recovering," Kezia whispered to herself; then she gave the money to the officer, saying, "It is all I have."

He slipped it into his pocket, nodding carelessly; he was used to taking bribes.

"You said Judith Manuelli?"

"Yes, Judith Manuelli," repeated Kezia.

He nodded again and tramped heavily down the stairs; Kezia followed after him, nodding pleasantly and saying,—

"Peace be with you." She went into her own room, took some bread and a little bowl of milk from her cupboard, then up again to Olga, after closing and locking the door. The first thing she did was to set the milk to warm, and while it was warming she picked up the baby and laid it in front of the stove; after that she went to Olga and felt her arms and hands: they were still deadly cold. With a quick, deft movement she stripped off Olga's cloak, got her straight upon the bed, and began, softly and skilfully, to rub her from her hands to her shoulders. This she did for fully half an hour, then she covered Olga closely with the cloak and tried to pour some of the warm milk between her lips, but her teeth were clenched and her jaws rigid, so Kezia left her for a while and sat down on the floor by the child and fed it with the milk, a drop at a time. When it had taken about a tablespoonful she lifted it on to her knees and opened the blanket. She started when she found that its little body was naked.

"What has been the trouble?" she asked, half aloud. Olga was in her cloak, night-gown only, and petticoat. Why had she fled like that?

Kezia now let her hands pass with a slow, soothing action over the child's limbs, for it was whimpering. Presently its cries ceased, and it snuggled its helpless head close to Kezia's breast. A thrill went through her like a knife. Something strange began to tingle in her blood; an odd, queer feeling of heartsickness and longing came over her. It was the first time she had ever held anything in her arms so young and so appealing in its utter dependency.

She looked yearning upon it; then from it to the helpless woman upon the bed, then back again her eyes came hungrily to the child, and only knew then, for the first time, what all the passion and unrest of her life had meant; what the hunger, the desire. It had been for a child; something she could fend and fight and work for; something wholly her own. The heartsickness grew, a pain as keen as sweet. She drew the child up close to her neck and covered it with the blanket, her thin bosom seeming to grow round and full again under the warmth from its young limbs, and she stroked its rosy chin and traced her finger along its dark, straight brows, and began to croon a lullaby. Presently her voice cracked; a big lump rose in her throat. It was the lullaby she had often heard her mother sing when sitting with the children on the floor of the old sunny, wooden balcony that overhung the river Tiber.

She rose suddenly and laid the child on the floor in the glow from the stove, and leaned against the wall with her arms folded, her face turned sternly away from it. The heartsickness grew; the yearning, the hunger. She bit her lips and dug her nails into the palms of her hands and beat her foot fiercely against the floor to silence the cry in her heart, but it cried out the more loudly for her resistance to it; and then again as suddenly as she had risen she was down on her knees again by the child, her hands going out to snatch it up to her breast.

"No, no," she muttered, springing away from it. "I have myself to think of!"

She rose and went resolutely to the door and opened it.

Olga moved her head feebly from side to side, sighed deeply, then was still.

"No, no," said Kezia, again; "I must think of myself. The 'Wanda' sails at seven, and I go with her." She stepped through the door and turned to draw it to, and in turning looked towards the bed. Olga's great, dark eyes were open and staring vacantly at her.

As though strong hands pushed her forward, Kezia went slowly and reluctantly to Olga's side, and stood by the bed with her hands hanging loosely clasped below her waist. Olga smiled a wan, piteous smile, lifted one of her weak hands and caught hold of Kezia by the wrist, then her eyelids fluttered down, and she lay muttering under her breath, and now and again laughing softly to herself.

The hold on Kezia's wrist was as weak as a child's. She could have shaken it off with a single movement of her arm, yet there she stood as though held with the grip of a strong man, with no power left in her to loose it or draw herself away.

The sun began to colour the clouds in the east. Kezia turned her head and looked at the growing light; in another hour the "Wanda" would sail, and with it her hope of seeing Italy, yet she had no strength to release herself from Olga's hand. Suddenly Olga's hand slipped and of its own weakness fell and hung over the side of the bed, and she lay there white and silent, helpless as a child.

Then all Kezia's heart was turned to pity and to woman for her. She set no bar, no stay, to the sudden uprush of tenderness and love that swept through her like a flood; she let it flow in through all her being and take possession of it, trembling under its impetuosity and the strange, new sweetness that came with it.

The great sun came up over the house-tops and filled the room with his golden light, and making the He-

brew characters on the disc over the eastern window
shine out like flame. Kezia saw them, and they brought
back the morning in the Ghetto when her father had
bidden her go and darken his house no more, and he
was dead and could never know how she had hungered
for her home.

She gave a bitter, wailing cry, and sank on her knees,
the tears welling up and gushing out of her eyes in big,
round, scalding drops that tasted salt as brine upon her
lips, and in that moment, sudden and fierce and passionate as she was in all her actions, she put from her
thoughts the desire of seeing Salome, and the place of
her longing, and her arms went round Olga and held
her tightly and close, breast to breast, for a moment,
saying,—

"Thou, too, art desolate." Then she laid Olga back
on the pillow and sat on the floor looking up at her.

Presently Kezia gave a grim, chuckling laugh.

"So I am held here by the wife and child of the man
who despises me! and I feel I must work and fend for
them till he comes."

She rose, with a queer ironical smile, and gave Olga
a few spoonfuls of the warm milk, which Olga drank,
then closed her eyes and seemed to sleep. Kezia peeped
at the child, it was still asleep; so away she hurried to
her own room, tied her mattress and bedclothing together in a blanket, then she staggered up the stairs
under the load and threw it down in the corner by the
forge, heaped more wood in the stove, and lay down to
rest, with the child safe and warm in her arms, but
with the queer, ironical smile still on her lips.

CHAPTER XXXII.

OUT OF SUFFERING COMES STRENGTH.

"A NOTE, sir."

Minchington, Doctor Stodham's man, laid a soiled, folded sheet of note-paper tied round with a piece of cotton by the side of his master's plate and waited.

"Immediate?" asked Doctor Stodham, looking up. He was at breakfast, which he always took English fashion, though he had lived so many years in Russia.

"The messenger, sir, said you was to go at once." Minchington filled his master's cup with fresh, hot coffee, and placed it by his side with the air of saying, "But please take your second cup before you go, sir."

Doctor Stodham opened the letter and read, written in badly spelt English,—

"I want you to come unto me now soon. Someone I have care to very ill sick, so come here directly, if you please.   LA MELDOLA."

Meldola! La Meldola!

Doctor Stodham stared at the common sheet of note-paper. A mist came between his eyes and the delicate, shaky, pointed handwriting. His dining-room with its heavy furniture and thick curtains faded away; he was in a sunny, dainty boudoir, all rose silk and white lace, and filled with the perfume of lilies and roses that were scattered here, there, everywhere, on the table, the sofa, the floor, the mantelpiece; some in jars, and bowls, and jugs, some loose, just thrown down, and dancing in and out among them a tall, slender woman, wonderful in her grace and beauty, laughing, clapping her hands, and saying,—

"All these last night and this morning from your countrymen, so much do they love me."

He must have sat a long time thinking. The discreet Minchington at last ventured to say,—

"Your coffee is nearly cold, sir."

Doctor Stodham looked up, half smiling. Minchington had been a "handy" boy about his father's house, and had carried many a love-sick letter to the Meldola during the opera season for him when he, an infatuated young medical student, used to spend all his allowance on flowers and presents for her. And she was alive and here in Odessa, and not dead, according to the sensational obituary notice he had read in a London paper. He felt half inclined to tell Minchington, who used to be as much in love with her as he was, and who used to say,—

"Crikey, sir, ain't she a one'er?"

But Doctor Stodham looked again at the soiled, flimsy wrapper and the bit of sewing cotton that had been tied round the note. So she had neither sealing-wax nor wafers. Was she poor? He sighed and put her letter in his pocket.

"Who brought the note?"

"A boy, sir. A Jew boy."

"Bring him in."

"Yes, sir." Minchington went to the door. "Shall I make you some fresh coffee first, sir?"

"No; I have finished."

Minchington went into the hall, and, taking the boy by the shoulder, sent him into the dining-room. The boy was about seven years old, with cropped head and long side curls, in the fashion of the Polish Jews. He was wrapped in a ragged caftan many sizes too big for him, and he was blue with cold and hunger. And when the doctor looked at his hands he was not surprised the outside of the note had been so soiled.

"Who gave you this note?" He took the note from his pocket and held it up.

"Kezia," said the boy, solemnly.

Doctor Stodham smiled, remembering the many futile guesses made by the newspapers in his day at her first name, which she had kept so jealously secret.

"You are to take me to her?"

"Yes, Excellency," answered the boy.

"Minchington! Give this youngster something to eat while I pull on my boots. Is the carriage at the door?"

"Yes, sir."

Though the boy was on the verge of starvation, he shook his head at the food.

"Thought it was pork, I s'pose, sir," Minchington afterwards said to the doctor; "but I give him some kopecks, knowing that would be your wish, and told him to get some 'kosher,' and you should have seen him, sir, and seen him grab that money!"

A SON OF ISRAEL

Kezia was standing in the middle of the room when the doctor arrived. She was in her old red flannel gown, her hair twisted carelessly up. There was only one dainty thing about her,—her long, thin hands, which she always kept spotlessly clean. She stood there like the dethroned queen of some barbaric race. At first he started, then he bowed, wondering who she might be. She smiled at his bewilderment, some of her old devilry and bewitchment lighting up her face.

"La Meldola!" he exclaimed.

Kezia nodded, went to him, and gave him her hand, which he, with a sigh, bowed over, as he had been used to do in his boyish days, then he looked straight forward into her eyes, asking mutely why she had allowed herself to come to such a pass.

"I know," she whispered, flushing hotly; "but it is not of myself we must talk. See here!" She pulled aside a curtain from the bed which she had roughly contrived out of an old table-cover, and showed him Olga lying there white and still, just breathing, no more.

"What is her name?" he asked, in amazement.

"Olga. It is all I know."

"How did she come here?"

"I found her sitting on the stairs this morning about four with the child."

"And where is the child?"

"Overhead, in the garret, with old Zebudah's daughter, who had a child of her own, but it died a few weeks ago, and she has promised to feed him for me if I will give her money to buy a little extra food for herself."

After a close and thorough examination of his patient Doctor Stodham asked,—

"Have you any idea how she got here?"

"No. All I know is that I found her on the stairs. Is she very ill?"

"Dangerously. After such an exposure to the cold, there is no hope for her unless a miracle happen, and they don't happen nowadays."

"You know something about her?" said Kezia, quickly.

"Yes. I attend her mistress, and I was attending her only yesterday."

"Then I am sorry that I did ask you to come."

"Why?"

"Why! Because now you will say where you have found her, and that man her master will order her back, because she is a runaway. He is cruel, cruel, I know. Miriam Ludolfino hath told me."

Doctor Stodham looked steadily at her. There was the old, fiery impetuosity flaming in her eyes.

"Trust me to get my patient well first, if it be possible," he said, calmly. "We can think of Michael Volkenoff by and by. Do you suppose I would endanger this woman's life still further by telling that fanatic where she is? Now, listen quietly to me." He gave her some minute, particular instructions, and ended with, "Understand, if she have a chance of recovery, it lies with you."

"With me!" cried Kezia.

"Yes, with you. Be restful and calm; have no fear, and we may conquer, and what a victory it will be if we do!" he said, glowing to his finger-tips with enthusiasm of his subject.

"I'll send Minchington to you for two hours every day, to carry up water and wood and to run any errands you may require him for. Remember that you always have plenty of hot water ready. I'll be back in half an hour with the medicine. Is the child all right?"

"He seems very hungry."

"Then he's safe, but I'll have a look at him when I return." Once more he repeated his instructions, then made for the door. He paused on the landing and asked, suddenly,—

"How did you know I was in Odessa?"

"I saw you one day, years ago, passing along the street, and took the trouble to find out whether you were living here."

"Do you know why I came?"

She was silent, but smiled, and with a twirl of her skirt and a backward glance went into the room and closed the door, while he walked down the stairs, frowning and growling,—

"Hang the woman! what is she made of? There is the same witchery about her, though she is a withered old bag of bones? What is it? Fineness of nerve, strength of will, or animal magnetism,—which?" he mused.

* * * * * * * *

Through many weeks Kezia tended Olga. It was wonderful to see her fierce, haggard face soften day by day; to watch her tender care, her calm, strong restfulness. Her body began to fill out, and a gloss came to her dry, faded hair. It was the first time in all Kezia's life that she had felt a deep, unselfish love for anyone outside herself.

One by one the hoarded, precious roubles were taken from the little bag hidden away in the straw mattress. At first Kezia had closed her eyes when she took them out, that the shining of the silver might not whisper to her of the bread it was to buy when she was too old and weak to work. At last, in desperation, one day she hissed at the money,—

"I wasn't born to hoard. I must spend! I must!" And then again, another day,—

"Well, and if I have starved myself for years to lay you by, what then? It was my own body I made to suffer, not the bodies of others. She must have bread, and the child must be nourished. He has been sick, and will die if I hold you back." And she would thrust the bag back, giving it a smart blow with her hand, because the roubles would chink and seem to laugh,—

"The wife and child of the man who calls you harlot."

One day, standing by Olga, watching her in sleep, she said,—

"If this, O God of Israel, be what mothers feel for their children, why didst not thou give to me a child? Then I should not now be this that I am." Olga moved a little, saying something softly under her breath. "And if, when David Rheba return, he should send me away because I am unclean in his sight,"—

her hands worked nervously and her brows,—" nevertheless, he cannot take away these days, or this new sweetness which is come into my heart. It may even be I shall feel soft to others as I feel to her; and if that be so, for all thy grace, O Lord, will I praise thee."

* * * * * * * *

Meanwhile, on the road, making slow and difficult way over the deep, hard-frozen ruts the snow had not fallen heavy enough to fill and make into the smooth, white, easy way, David and John Pemberton toiled along, groaning in spirit, disheartened and weary. It would be spring, they feared, before they could reach Odessa.

CHAPTER XXXIII.

THE CHILD.

THREE weeks after Olga left the house, Marya was sitting in the cedar room. She was spreading out her hands in the sunshine and feeling to the full the sweetness of returning strength. It was the first day she had been allowed to leave her room. Almost every hour she had asked for Olga, and the same answer given was,—

"She is better, but may not see you yet." In this way they kept from her that Olga was gone and no trace of her could be found. Michael Volkenoff thought that in the delirium that was upon her Olga had started to follow David Rheba, and had fallen somewhere by the wayside and had died, her child with her, and that the snow had hidden them from sight. When he spoke of this to Doctor Stodham, the doctor agreed with him, and at the same time gave strict orders that no word of Olga's disappearance was to be carried to Marya until she was strong again. He argued that he could tell Michael Volkenoff the whole truth when Olga was safely out of Russia with her husband.

The child was in the cradle at Marya's feet, fast asleep. Presently he woke and kicked out his chubby arms and legs, puckering up his brows and blinking at the light. Marya was down on her knees by his side in a moment, cooing to him and singing little snatches of song, pursing up her lips and whistling to him, a sound which interested him greatly. He watched the little round hole the noise came from with his great, dark eyes, looking out steadily from under his straight brows, filling Marya with amused delight at seeing them now in the strong light look so like to Olga's.

"It must be because I had her always by me," she said to herself. After a while she took him in her lap, talking gravely to him in happy make-believe that he was now a tall, strong man, and must be very tender and careful of this little mother of his.

The child still looked steadily at her with the wise, solemn gaze most babies have. Marya paused and said, half aloud, "I wonder whether babies think us foolish for saying such absurd things to them? I am sure you do, my son," she said, earnestly. She sat after that looking at him silently awhile. He gave a contented little sigh, and seemed more than pleased to just lie and look at her.

"Oh, thou art an odd one!" she exclaimed, catching up his small hand and mumbling it with kisses. "I love thee, I love thee so dearly."

She rubbed the tender morsel of flesh and bone against her chin, merrily at first, then musingly, thinking,—

"That was what my dear Olga used to do so often. Oh, how long it is since I last saw her, my poor girl!"

She looked absently at the child's hand as she spoke. Suddenly she started and passed her hand rapidly over her eyes, then looked again at his hand. There was a red triangular-shaped mark on the ball of his thumb.

"Oh, I must be dreaming, or I am dazzled by the sunlight!"

She rang a bell that was near. Nicolas answered it.

"Come here," she said to him. "Can you see a red mark on the child's hand?"

"Yes, mistress, plainly."

"And the shape?" Her nerves were in a strange whirl.

"Like something with three corners," he answered. She drew in her breath sharply, saying, "Bring Olga's child to me."

"Excellency! mistress!" stammered Nicolas.

"I wish Olga's child brought to me at once."

Nicolas went bewildered from the room to his master and told him Marya's request. Michael Volkenoff looked up from the letter he was writing.

"Tell your mistress that the child might carry infection to her in its clothing. She cannot see it." Nicolas bowed, and, returning to the cedar room, delivered the message.

"That will do; you may go," she said, quietly. When he was gone she went down the long corridor to Olga's room. Presently returning with a white face and anger in her eyes, she rang the bell. Nicolas came hurrying from the servants' room. She met him half-way down the corridor. "Tell your master I must speak with him instantly."

Nicolas went away with a relieved expression. "She has discovered for herself," he muttered, and, going once more to his master's room, delivered Marya's message, adding, "I think, Excellency, the mistress has been into Olga's room."

Michael rose with a troubled look upon his face. If Marya had discovered that Olga was gone, what effect would it have upon her?

"What is it?" he said, anxiously, not going farther than the door of the cedar room.

She was sitting in the window, the child on her lap, no anger now in her look, only determination. "Where is Olga?" she asked, calmly.

"In her room," he replied.

"I have just been there, and it is empty, even of furniture."

He started and pulled at his beard. "We feared the infection for thee," he said, hastily.

"Please tell me the truth, Michael. Thou hast sent her away." Marya could see that he was greatly distressed. Just then Doctor Stodham appeared, following Nicolas. Michael went quickly forward to meet him, and stood whispering earnestly to him.

"Let her know the truth? Certainly!" said the doctor. "To keep her on the tenter-hooks of suspense would do more mischief than the whole thing put together. Go back to your work; I will tell her."

"Doctor Stodham," said Marya, when he entered the room, "before you ask me a single question answer mine. What have you done with Olga?"

"I will answer your question first, certainly," he said, cheerily, sitting down by her side. "Olga is gone, gone to her husband. She crept out of the room while

Anna was asleep,—at least so Anna reported,—taking the child with her, and by now she must be a good many miles on the road." He looked at the nails of his beautifully kept hands, then brushed some imaginary specks from his rather shabby but perfectly speckless coat, and looked up smilingly at her.

"Doctor," said Marya, quietly, "you are not speaking truthfully. Now tell me just exactly what you know, not what you imagine."

He put his fingers on her pulse, and kept them there while he repeated what he had already told her. Marya's pulse bounded wildly when he said Olga had taken the child with her.

"Not strong enough to be trusted with the truth yet awhile," he thought.

Marya leaned back in her chair feeling sick and cold. The doctor took the child from her knees and laid it in the cradle, then he rang for wine.

"You say," said Marya, faintly, "that she was very ill when you left her in the afternoon. Do you know whether she had been frightened about her child?"

"I fancy she was. She had been told that it was to be sent away to the sisters of St. Barbara. That, perhaps, preyed upon her mind."

"Do you think the shock caused her illness?"

"Yes; that, the chill, and the infection there was in the room where she was confined, no doubt caused her illness."

"And at such a time do you think a woman capable of—of——" Marya dared not ask. Suppose he should guess what Olga had done and tell Michael, who would

A SON OF ISRAEL

at once, she felt, take Olga's child away. Perhaps, in his grief, anger, and disappointment, do some fearful thing to it.

"At such a time," said the doctor, not waiting for her to finish the sentence, "it is not possible to set a limit to what a woman may do. The possibilities are practically illimitable; she is absolutely irresponsible, and cannot be held accountable for anything she may do."

"She was very ill, was she not?"

"Well, I have known worse cases than hers. When I left—here on the afternoon—of the day——" He grew confused. He had almost committed himself by saying, "When I left her this morning," but paused in time.

"But tell me, it is not possible that she is dead? And the child! Ah, tell me! tell me! My heart is bursting! The child! the child! is it dead?" Marya cried, with the tears streaming over her face, and caught hard at his hand, looking appealingly at him.

"No, no," he said, soothingly, "she is all right; and the child, too, I assure you. We shall find her at one of the farm-houses on the road. She was young and strong. She'll pull through."

"But it is three weeks since she left," interrupted Marya, "and you have not found her yet." Presently she thought of David's room in the Jews' Quarter; Olga must be there. She grew calmer; she almost smiled. Why had she not thought of that before?

"Were any enquiries made in the town?" she asked, cautiously.

"I really don't know; but, of course, enquiries would be made there. I will ask——"

"No, please do not! Let that wait until I can enquire for myself. If you please, doctor," she said, firmly, seeing that he seemed a little puzzled at the change which had come over her so suddenly. After a short talk about her own health she asked, carelessly, "How soon may I go out?"

"Not for a month," he said, energetically.

"But I feel quite well. I want to go out to-day."

He felt her pulse. "Out to-day! You are as weak as your baby there. One moment you are crying like a woman who has lost the most precious thing she had in the whole world, the next smiling. No, you do not leave the house for a month."

"Oh, if I might tell you," she exclaimed, "why I wish so much to go out!"

He made an expressive action, saying, "You may trust me," and thinking, "I wish I could be sure of trusting you."

She shook her head. "It is not my secret. But if I tell you that the more quickly you let me go out the more quickly I shall be strong, will you give your permission to my going out in—say a week? You know you have always said I am the most sensible patient you have ever had. Will you trust to my sense now?"

"Yes; if you are sure to get the thing you want by going out, go! but if there is the smallest doubt of it being the reverse of what you wish, no! emphatically no! Can you assure me it will be exactly what you hope?"

"No, I cannot," she sighed; "and yet I feel it must be as I think. It is the only explanation."

Soon as the doctor was gone Marya sent a note to the Princess Czartoryski, asking, merely, "Is John Pemberton in Odessa? If so, the date of his return?" The reply came in about two hours: "No; not yet returned." Marya gave a glad little cry. She was sure she would find Olga, and the child with her, waiting for David's return in David's room.

Hope gave a strong impetus to Marya's strength. She grew well rapidly, and in a week she was allowed to drive out, but Michael went with her, and the next time and the next, till she grew impatient and restive. She thought he had heard of David's pardon and was watching her, but he was only trying in a silent, humble way to win back her love.

At last one day the mother's hunger in her bore down all her caution, her fear for Olga, and when he told the coachman to drive through the public gardens and round by the cliffs, she cried out, impetuously,—

"No; to David Rheba's, in the Jews' Quarter."

"To the Jews' Quarter," said Michael, gravely, to the man, then stepped into the carriage beside her, asking no questions, but sitting silent, guessing that she hoped to find Olga in David's room. Presently he turned to her and said,—

"Perhaps she is there; I had not thought of enquiring. Strange that I should have forgotten such an obvious thing."

Marya looked at him in amazement.

"Thou canst understand, then, why?"

"Yes, I understand," he answered, quietly.

She took his hand gratefully, thinking what a wonderful change was come over him.

When they came to the house she flew up the stairs, her face bright with the foretaste of the joy that she felt was so soon to follow. She tapped on the door, and in her keen desire opened it. Kezia was just in the act of putting out her hand to lift the latch. She remembered Marya's face and stepped back, pointing with a warning action to the bed. Olga lay there, turning her head constantly from side to side, her lips moving, though no sound came from them. Marya put Kezia gently aside, and looked searchingly round the room; then seeing the place was empty of what she sought, she caught Kezia by the hand and drew her on to the landing.

"Where is the child?" she whispered.

Kezia started, then answered, in a low voice, "I know not." Had not Olga's one cry been that the child must be kept from Michael Volkenoff, and was not that the man standing behind Marya?

"You can trust me," pleaded Marya; "I am Olga's friend; I only wish to help her. Where is the child?"

Kezia shut her lips resolutely; not a word would she utter.

"Tell me, I beg of you," whispered Marya in her ear, guessing at the woman's silence. "I am his mother,—believe me, I speak the truth. He is my child."

"Up there," said Kezia, bewildered into answering, and pointing to the narrow, rickety stairs that led to the garret where Zebudah and her daughter Naomi lived.

Marya sprang up them, Michael following.

She didn't pause to knock at the door; she pushed it open and entered.

Zebudah was a rag-picker and collector of broken bits of metal and bones, and the place was foul with a stale, musty odour, and littered with refuse. The old woman was kneeling under the window, coughing and sorting the white pieces of rag from the coloured, and her daughter was sitting by a small charcoal stove with the child at her breast. He looked white and sickly, and his little lips were blue with cold. The blanket that he had been wrapt in when Olga carried him away had been cut into two gowns for him, and he was now dressed in one of the rough, ungainly things.

With a strange, low, quavering cry, Marya stumbled forward and fell on her knees by the young Jewess, and snatched up the child, covering his face and hands with kisses, and moaning and making little foolish laughs and cries over him, saying to the bewildered woman before her,—

"He is mine! mine! Olga took him and left hers in his cradle, because she feared he would be taken from her, and in her madness did that to save him. And mother thought thou wast lost, dead. How thin thou art and pale!" She sat on the dirty floor and rocked him in her arms. "And what a rough, coarse gown thou art in!" she cooed to him.

"He was naked when he came to me," said Naomi,

thinking of the two precious hours she had lost from her work while making the gowns.

"Naked!" Marya's eyes grew wet.

"And he has been sick, nigh to the point of death."

"To the point of death! Oh, my child!"

Suddenly Michael Volkenoff's hand was laid upon Marya's shoulder. She had forgotten him. His face was white, horror was in his eyes. He thought that she was mad. He stooped and lifted her to her feet.

"Take your child," he said to the young Jewess. "Cannot you see that she is ill?"

"He is not my child," answered Naomi; "he belongs to the sick woman in David Rheba's room."

"No, no, he is mine; thy son, Michael, and mine!" cried Marya. "Let us go home, and I will tell thee how I think it all happened; and I will tell thee, too, how I discovered what Olga had done." She looked appealingly at him, and held tight to the child, which was crying feebly.

"You say that this is the child of the sick woman in David Rheba's room?" Michael Volkenoff asked Naomi.

"Yes, that is her child. Mine is dead," she answered, and turned suddenly away, one hand lifted to hide her eyes.

"Then, as her master, it belongs to me," he said, looking coldly at her thin hand and arm that the loose, ragged sleeve of her gown had slipped from. Then he said, tenderly, to Marya, "Come, it shall go with thee." He put his arm round her and led her to the door. There she turned and looked at Naomi, who was weeping silently, with her back to them. Marya gently slipped her shoulder from under Michael's hand and returned.

"You would like to say good-bye to him?" she whispered.

Naomi turned, and her arms went out hungrily to the child.

"I have grown to love him," she sobbed.

Marya put her arm on Naomi's, the child between them.

"You shall see him again, and more than once, trust me; he owes his life to you." She kissed Naomi lovingly on the cheek, then, with a bright smile at Michael, went before him down the stairs.

Outside David's room she paused.

"No," he said, firmly; "it is not safe for thee to go in."

"Thou wilt not take Olga away from here?"

"Not until she is well again."

Marya stretched out her hand and knocked. "I wish to give the woman who is nursing her some money," she said, in explanation to Michael's look.

Kezia opened the door.

"For your patient," said Michael, holding out some money in notes, the old feeling of loathing for the Jewish race strong within him.

Kezia felt it, and, without looking at the money, said, proudly,—

"My bag is not empty yet." Then, with a deep curtsy to Marya, she was closing the door, saying, "My patient must have quiet."

"One moment," Marya begged. "Tell her, when

she is well, that her child is with me, her mistress; that I will keep him safe from all harm until she is strong. Tell her that she is not to be anxious or grieve for him in any way. Say that I will be surety for him."

Kezia curtsied again to her and went in hastily, closing the door. Olga was moving restlessly, as though Marya's voice had pierced through the fever that held her.

With a bitter feeling of resentment, Michael rolled the notes into a ball and threw them upon the landing. They had been offered to one of the accursed race, and therefore were polluted in his eyes. He was angry, too, that they had been refused. He had been taught and believed that a Jew could no more resist money than a tiger the taste of blood, and he found they could be proud, the curs! Well, there they were, for whichever of the vermin to pick up that found them.

When they were seated in the carriage, he sat with his back to the horses, looking curiously at Myra. Her face was radiant, and she kept kissing and saying sweet, foolish things to the complaining baby in her arms. It was pale and sickly looking, not over-clean, and its gown was soiled. Presently he leaned forward, saying,—

"Tell me how this strange, mad notion that this child is ours came into thy mind."

Then Marya told him.

"And is the mark on the child's hand all thou hast of proof?" he asked, impatiently.

"No. Anna told me only a few days ago that she

had found some of our child's clothing on Olga's bed the morning after she had disappeared, but feared to speak of it."

"But what reason could Olga have had for changing the children?"

"I can only suppose that she did it to save her child from thee, Michael."

He frowned and said no more. He sat back, striving to recall to mind the words he had spoken to Olga on the day she was stricken with the fever. The doctor had told him there had been some great shock to her nervous system. So, then, it was he, himself, who was to blame, to blame all through, for it was by his orders that she was moved into the outdoor servants' quarters, he caring little whether she suffered or not; and he had told her of his intention of taking her child away to have it reared for the Church, and had endangered the life of his own child thereby, if it were true, if this wretched, puling creature, wasted almost to skin and bone, lying there before him, was his son. His son, and he had seen him in the arms of a Jewess, feeding from her breast. . . . The thought made his blood sing and buzz in his ears. His child! a Volkenoff! nourished by one of the race he spat upon and hated! No, no! it was not true! It was David Rheba's whelp. A wave of venomous hate rushed through his heart, and he had to turn his eyes away and grip his hands hard, one within the other, to restrain the horrible impulse which tempted him to pluck the helpless babe from Marya's knees and fling it into the street. . . . But if he were his own son? . . . Had not the Jewess said that he was naked when he was taken to her? . . . He might have died! . . . His son, his heir! No, no! he was not his child! Marya was weak and hysterical; she was not yet strong.

He looked at her. Her face gave the lie to his thought. It was rosy with renewed health and joy.

Suddenly he leaned forward and said,—

"What, then, shall we do with the child that you say is Olga's?"

"Take it to her the moment she is recovered from her sickness," she answered.

He leaned back, half smiling. How confident she was that he would do this! It was as though she regarded Olga as a free woman; and yet his heart warmed to see that she believed he would do what she thought the right and good thing, and yet the right and holy thing was to dedicate the child to the Church. He had vowed that, and he must not go back from his word.

When Marya arrived at home, she had her child washed and dressed in his own beautiful, dainty clothes, then she carried him triumphantly in to Michael, Wanda following, bearing the son of David Rheba.

He looked at the two children in amazement. There were the same dark brows and great, earnest eyes, and they were both like to Olga, but the child that Marya held was scarcely half the size of the rosy, sturdy boy that Wanda was carrying and that he had been so proud of. It must be his,—it must! There was some terrible mistake that he must set right.

Day after day passed. He noticed that Marya gave most of her time to the child he called Olga's. He would come upon her at odd, unexpected times, and, though motherly to both children, it was the one she called her own that she held most close and had by her at night; yet still he doubted.

*   *   *   *   *   *   *   *

And nearer and nearer over the frozen roads came David Rheba,—nearer to the place of his soul's desire.

CHAPTER XXXIV.

DAVID COMES HOME.

Six days after Marya's visit Olga woke from a deep, silent sleep that had lasted from twelve the night before to noon the following day. Kezia had sat by her side watching trustfully, blessing the hours as they passed, and still she slept. It was the turning-point of the fever, and the doctor had said it meant life to her.

Olga stretched her limbs, moving her hands feebly to and fro upon the blanket. Kezia rose quietly and went over to the bed with a cup of cool barley-water in her hand. Kneeling by the side of the bed, she passed her left arm under Olga's head and held the cup to her lips.

Olga drank it thirstily, then gazed intently at Kezia as she laid her head back again upon the pillow.

"Who art thou?" she whispered.

"The Meldola," Kezia replied, spreading out her hands in deprecation of herself; the bitterness of shame for the first time filling her heart. Olga strove to rise and look round, but fell back, too weak to do more than lift her head and shoulders.

"Have I been sick?" she asked, faintly.

"For many weeks," answered Kezia.

"What, then, is the month?"

"We are nearly at the end of January."

"January," she repeated, vaguely, too weak to realise the length of time. She lay silent awhile, and presently slept again, not waking until early morning on the following day. Her first words were, "What room is this?"

"David's," said Kezia.

"David's," whispered Olga. "I know——"

Kezia watched the expression of her face anxiously, but it was calm, the skin pale and healthy-looking, the livid colour gone. She drank from the cup Kezia held, and then lay quiet while her face, and neck, and hands were washed with vinegar and water.

Presently she said,—

"Have I had strange dreams?"

Kezia nodded "Yes," then added, "but I must not let you talk any more to-day."

Olga gave her a little smile. She felt like a child with all things yet to learn. She let the thoughts come flowing back, and her gaze go from thing to thing that she barely as yet recognised, then after a while she slept again.

Next day she said to Kezia,—

"It is strange; I dreamed I had a child."

Kezia busied herself with the pillow, pretending not to hear.

"Did I go away with my mistress, or have I been here since David was arrested?"

"You have been here," answered Kezia, judging that it would be best not to tell her the whole truth until she was stronger.

At the end of an hour Olga said,—

"Art thou quite sure I did not go away with my mistress?" She looked troubled and flushed. "The thought is beating so hard against my brain it hurts me."

"Yes, you did go away with your mistress, and when you are strong and can bear to listen I will tell you all that has happened, but now obey me and rest."

"That will I," said Olga, and troubled no more till at the end of some days she said, quietly,—

"Everything is come back to me up to the time a great black cloud seemed to settle down upon me and my child. Where is he?"

"Quite safe with your mistress," said Kezia, soothingly; "and she left word with me that she will keep him from all harm until you are strong again. She said you were not to be anxious or trouble for him in any way. She will be surety for his safety."

Olga's face cleared and glowed with deep content and joy.

"With my beloved mistress," she whispered; "Holy Mother of Christ watch over her and give her of thy peace."

* * * * * * * *

A few mornings after, while Kezia was out buying fish for the noonday meal, David returned.

Odessa was white and smiling under a heavy covering of snow that the sun danced and shone upon, lighting it up with a thousand sparkles.

David's spirits went up, and the swiftest drosky seemed all too slow. He laughed at John Pemberton, who warned him not to be too sure of finding Olga waiting for him.

He cried, "My heart has not once sagged; our cause was in the hands of God, and he has carried it through thus far! why should I doubt now?"

But John still growled, "Don't be too sure, don't be too sure."

He left John at the door of the hotel and went on foot to the Jews' Quarter, saying to him,—

"She is there, waiting for me; and if thou hadst ever been a lover thou wouldst understand why I know." He kissed John fervently on the cheek and was gone. Gone with his love welling up in his heart and making his eyes overflow with gladness. The people stopped to look at him striding along with his bright hair flowing out behind, the joyous tears running over his gaunt, hollow face. He felt her breath in every gust of wind that swept along; he saw the glow of her cheek in the light from the sun; he saw the sparkle of her eyes in the glistening snow that lay on the roof-tops. On, swifter than any drosky could have carried him, he went; on into the old familiar ways of the Jews' Quarter. Heads were thrust out of doors after him as he passed.

"It is David Rheba!" cried one, and "David Rheba!" cried another. The cries were taken up, and swelled into a hubbub of voices; his people began to follow till at the door of the house they closed round him, a great, struggling crowd, each one there striving to get nighest to him, to grasp his hands, with cries of welcome and gladness. They were gesticulating, laughing, some weeping, and all chattering at once. Old Isaac tottered down from his garret and clasped him round the neck, saying,—

"Now will the starving find food again to their hands as though fallen as the blessed manna dropped from heaven."

When he had greeted them all he was left free to go, and crying, "God's blessing be upon ye all!" sprang up the stairs and into his room.

Olga had heard the cries, for David's north window jutted out over the door of the house.

She listened. Then came the sound of his step, the sound that would have had power to strike through the dark earth and rouse her even from death had she been in her grave. She slipped out of her bed and stood there swaying by the side, with her arms stretched out, waiting for him.

* * * * * * * *

When Kezia returned she found David sitting by the bed, holding Olga's hand. He looked up when she entered and stood waiting with the basket in her hand.

"Kezia Meldola," he began,—the masterful ring of his voice made her weep in her heart, for she thought her service was to end,—"you have tended her, you with your care have saved her, you and the God of our people, for she hath told me of all her sufferings and of all your goodness unto her."

Kezia let the basket of fish slip to the floor. A bird seemed fluttering in her throat. He rose and went to her, taking her, brother-like, by the hand, and continued,—

"Will you, then, as you have been her friend in her sorest need, continue and do such things for her as will be necessary for her till she be strong again, and for me whilst I work?"

"I will," she answered, simply. Then she went suddenly away down to her room, and wept such tears as she had never wept before in all her life; and they seemed to wash all her sins from her soul, for her face had a touch of beauty when she returned to pick up the forgotten basket of fish such as never had been seen upon it even when she was called "Meldola, the most Beautiful among Women."

CHAPTER XXXV.

THE REDEMPTION OF MICHAEL VOLKENOFF.

It was the afternoon of the same day, and David was sitting by Olga's bed, saying,—

"And so a child hath been given to us,—a son?"

"Yes, a son," answered Olga.

"And Michael Volkenoff hath taken him?"

"Kezia told me that my mistress carried him away."

"And I will go bring him here again to his home," said David, resolutely. He rose and looked about for his pelisse. Olga caught his hand, her face pale with fear.

"Remember, I am not free. He has power to carry me away from thee. He has the right to keep our child."

David laughed, a hearty, ringing laugh, and kissed her and went, no misgiving in his heart. He would so set the strength of his will against Michael Volkenoff's that there could be no saying nay. Looking on David's face, he should remember all the shame and suffering he had been the cause of, and if he were a man, not a devil, if he had human blood in his veins, his heart must be softened, and he would hold his hand from further wrong. Thus David thought, his spirit light within him. He passed the porch of the old wooden house where he had found Olga hiding on that first divine morning, when, with the sky singing in rose and gold over their heads, the wind stinging and sweet with kisses from the mouth of the sea, they met and scarce spoke, and yet the air seemed eloquent with their murmured speech. He saluted it and passed on. Away in the west the sun was sinking, and in the purple and amethyst mist the slender, feathery moon, not three days old, was hanging.

"I take thee for a sign of good!" he cried. "Thou singest of happy things."

* * * * * * * *

Michael was with Marya in the cedar room, when to them came Nicolas, saying that David Rheba was waiting in the master's room, and would not go without speech with him.

Michael Volkenoff knew already from the Princess Czartoryski that she had obtained a pardon for David, and that he was protected from further arrest or danger at his hands. He rose and walked impatiently about the room, biting at his finger-nails.

"Bid him wait," he presently said to Nicolas. Then he sat down again, staring into the fire.

Marya crept round behind him and bent her face close to his.

"He has come for his child, Michael."

He made no reply.

"And thou wilt give it to him."

"Marya, let me be; let me fight this thing out for myself. Whatever I do, let it be of my own will."

Marya drew away to the window and prayed, and let the struggle go on within him undisturbed by further word from her. Presently she saw his hands clench themselves upon his knees and shake there like aspen leaves. After a while he turned and looked at her, all the hunger in him for her love speaking in his hard-drawn face and pale lips, and she knew it meant life or death for his soul. A light like morning shone out from her face. She smiled and moved her hands softly and gravely in assent.

Then he rose and passed from the room, silent and uplifted, and went straight to David Rheba.

David was standing in the window, where he had stood with Olga on the day he asked Michael Volkenoff to give her to him for wife. He was looking out over the snow-fields. He turned when Michael entered, and the two men gazed eye to eye. There was no mistaking David's look; he was come for his child, for the flesh of his flesh, for the bone of his bone, and he would not go hence with empty arms.

At sight of the Jew all the bitterness of Michael's hate for the unfortunate people began to seethe and burn afresh in his heart, blurring Marya's image and filling him with gall. And at sight of the man who had brought so much suffering upon him and his, David's blood drummed in his ears and a red mist came between him and Michael's face.

Neither spoke. The battle was silent and close-waged. And yet Michael Volkenoff knew David was ready to spring upon him and pin him by the throat if all else failed, and wring the right by force from him. And his pulses began to beat hotly. What if they two should fight it out, foot to foot, within those four walls? Why not end it thus, and let the Jew squeeze the life out of him? There would be then no sin of unfulfilled vows and faith broken with the Church. He clenched his hands and moved forward, breathing hard. He would do it! He would end the Jew's life, and then his own. Suddenly laughter—children's laughter, fresh and shrill and glad—rang out in the court-yard under the window. Some of the little serfs were playing snowballs, and had run thither out of bounds. The music of their sweet young voices mounted up into the room, and the evil spell was broken. The sound brought back Marya's face. He felt her tender arms clinging about him; he saw her appealing eyes looking deep into his, and like a perfume round about him stole the sense of her returning love. And to gain it wholly, to make life sweet as it had never yet been to him, he had but to give the Jew his own. The tension of his nerves relaxed; he let the softening influence flow through and possess all his being.

Without a word, he sat down at his table and wrote rapidly a few words on a sheet of note-paper. At the end, while he dried the ink, he looked up at David. David gave him look for look, and Michael Volkenoff had to confess that the Jew was every inch a man.

"Wait," he said, abruptly, and left the room.

Through the long corridors he strode, putting aside all the thoughts that strove to beset him about his vow to the Church with,—

"For Marya! for Marya! It is for her!" and into

the cedar room without a pause he went, and placed the paper in her hand, saying merely,—

"Read."

She read; then her breast rose high,—

"Michael, my husband!"

A dry, tearless sob broke in his throat; it was the first time she had called him by that name since the night he had so wronged her.

"Come," he said, tenderly. "Let us go to the child."

They went into the nursery hand in hand. A grim smile came to his lips when she took up Olga's child, the sturdy, splendid-limbed boy with the fine, earnest face and eyes, the child he had cherished, and thought, even till now, his own, and wrapt it warmly in a cloak and a fur above that, while giving Wanda instructions to pack a box with the rest of its things.

When the child was dressed she set him on her arm, and there he balanced himself as straight and strong as though he had the spine of a young Samson.

Michael Volkenoff looked from him to the weak and sickly child that he knew now, past doubt, was his; for what mother would give away her own flesh and blood? And again the wave of bitter hate for David and all his race swept over him, and he put out his hands to snatch the child from Marya's arms.

But she, divining what was come so suddenly to him, held closer to the babe and asked, quietly,—

"Shall we go now?"

"Marya, my wife!" he cried, with a revulsion of feeling as keen and swift as the flood of hate had been, "teach me to be like thyself."

"There is better in store for thee to learn than that," she said, joyously.

"What could be better?"

"To be thine own true self. Come, let us go."

She ran lightly away, and he followed her to the room where David was, opened the door, and gently put her in, then turned and walked away back to the cedar room.

Marya went forward and stood just within by the table, her glowing face turned to David. He came forward and held out his arms.

"Take him," she said, "and this." She placed the paper in his hand. "It is Olga's freedom."

Then she gave a queer, rippling little laugh, filled half with joy and half with tears, and could say no more; all she could do was to motion him dumbly to the door of the room.

David's arms closed tightly round the child and his hand on the precious paper; then he bowed low and passed out silent, being, like herself, too full at heart to speak.

But when he was come to the great door that led into the court-yard, Marya sped after him, and fingering the child's clothes, mother-like, she said,—

"Keep him close covered from the cold; the air is sharp."

"May the blessing of the Eternal rest upon thee and thine forever!" said David, fervently, and bent and kissed her hands. Then he pulled on his cap and went carefully down the steps, one foot at a time, with an odd feeling of fear that he might break the dear burden he was carrying, and so, slowly on over the frozen road. And yet it seemed to him that the door of Michael Volkenoff's house had hardly closed upon him than he was kneeling by Olga's side, laughing at her joy when he laid the child within her arms, and gave her the paper which made her free, so swiftly had gone the time.

THE END.

By Marie Corelli.

Barabbas:
A Dream of the World's Tragedy.

12mo. Red buckram, $1.00.

During its comparatively brief existence this remarkable book has been translated into French, German, Swedish, Hindoostani, and Gujerati. In England and America, the phenomenal demand for the work still exhausts edition after edition in rapid succession.

"Tragic intensity and imaginative vigor are the features of this powerful tale."—*Philadelphia Ledger.*

"A book which aroused in some quarters more violent hostility than any book of recent years. By most secular critics the authoress was accused of bad taste, bad art, and gross blasphemy; but, in curious contrast, most of the religious papers acknowledged the reverence of treatment and the dignity of conception which characterized the work."—*London Athenæum.*

The Sorrows of Satan;
Or, The Strange Experience of One Geoffrey Tempest, Millionaire.

WITH FRONTISPIECE BY VAN SCHAICK.

12mo. Red buckram, $1.50.

"A very powerful piece of work. A literary phenomenon, novel, and even sublime."—*Review of Reviews.*

"She is full of her purpose. Dear me, how she scathes English society! She exposes the low life of high life with a ruthless pen. The sins of the fashionable world made even Satan sad; they were more than he could bear, poor man! The book is lively reading."—*Chicago Tribune.*

Cameos.

12mo. Red buckram, $1.00.

"Marie Corelli possesses a charm as a writer that perhaps has never been better displayed than in her recent work, 'Cameos.'"—*Burlington Hawk-Eye.*

"As long as Miss Corelli can write stories like these she will not lack readers. In this volume she gives new and convincing proofs of versatility, spirit, tenderness, and power."—*Chicago Tribune.*

J. B. LIPPINCOTT COMPANY, PHILADELPHIA.

By Marie Corelli.

The Murder of Delicia.

12mo. Red buckram, $1.25.

"The story is told with all the vigor and command of sarcasm which are peculiar to the author. It is a most interesting story, and the moral of it is a wholesome one."—*Buffalo Courier.*

"Her style is so clear-cut, keen, and incisive, so trenchant and yet so delicate, so easily wielded—so like a javelin, in short—that one cannot but be fascinated throughout the book."—*Philadelphia Record.*

"A more powerful invective against the reigning and popular society evils has rarely been written, with so fine a blending of the elements of reproach and condemnation, rage and pity, sarcasm and pathos."—*Boston Courier.*

The Mighty Atom.

12mo. Red buckram, $1.25.

"Such a book as 'The Mighty Atom' can scarcely fail in accomplishing a vast amount of good. It should be on the shelves of every public library in England and America. Marie Corelli has many remarkable qualities as a writer of fiction. Her style is singularly clear and alert, and she is the most independent of thinkers and authors of fiction; but her principal gift is an imagination which rises on a bold and easy wing to the highest heaven of invention."—*Boston Home Journal.*

Vendetta ; or, The Story of One Forgotten.

12mo. Buckram, $1.00.

"The story is Italian, the time 1884, and the precise stage of the acts, Naples, during the last visitation of the cholera. A romance, but a romance of reality. No mind of man can imagine incidents so wonderful, so amazing, as those of actual occurrence."—*Washington National Republican.*

ISSUED IN THE LOTOS LIBRARY.

Jane.

16mo. Polished buckram, 75 cents.

"It is a sympathetic tale, full of admirable contrast between the old-fashioned and the new."—*Washington Times.*

J. B. LIPPINCOTT COMPANY, PHILADELPHIA.

By Charles Conrad Abbott.

A Colonial Wooing.

A Novel. 12mo. Cloth, $1.00.

"Those of our readers who remember Dr. Abbott's 'Travels in a Tree-Top,' published about a year ago, will be glad to get this new volume from his pen. It is a study of social life during the early Colonial period in this section of New Jersey. The story is a charming one, and will add very much to Dr. Abbott's literary reputation."—*Trenton True American.*

When the Century was New.

A Novel. 12mo. Cloth, uncut, $1.00.

The books by Dr. Charles C. Abbott which appeal most intensely to our hearts are those in which he sketches the familiar character of the Jersey neighborhoods he has made his own. In this charming novel we have the best of his character-drawing up to date, and the plot is exceptionally well planned. The tale deals with our forefathers, and is therefore in the vein which best pleases the reader of to-day.

Recent Rambles; Or, in Touch with Nature.

Illustrated. 12mo. Cloth, $2.00.

"In the literature of nature Dr. Abbott's books hold a peculiar place. With all their close application they are not too technical, and their charm for the general reader is the more potent in that this is so. We all love nature, but we do not all care to embark in a study of ornithology, botany, and zoology in order to appreciate it; and in this new volume we find how keen our enjoyment can be, even if we do not possess such scientific knowledge. Those, on the other hand, who are already students of nature, will be fascinated by the wide and accurate information gained for them by the Doctor's numerous tramps and multiplied hours of observant idleness. The book is full of touches of humor, unexpected turns, and pungent sayings, and should be perused by every one of our readers."—*Commercial Advertiser* (Detroit).

J. B. LIPPINCOTT COMPANY, PHILADELPHIA.

By Charles Conrad Abbott.

Travels in a Tree-Top.

12mo. Cloth, $1.25.

"Mr. Abbott is a kindred spirit with Burroughs and Maurice Thompson and, we might add, Thoreau, in his love for wild nature, and with Olive Thorne Miller in his love for the birds. He writes without a trace of affectation, and his simple, compact, yet polished style breathes of out-of-doors in every line."—*New York Churchman.*

Bird-Land Echoes.

Profusely illustrated by William Everett Cram. Crown 8vo. Cloth, gilt top, $2.00.

"The birds are grouped 'geographically' and not 'systematically.' He has allowed eye and ear to revel in what the wild birds do and say. The triumph of his spontaneous art in writing is to impart to the reader a goodly proportion of the love he bears to all birds, 'whether they are commonplace or rare, stupid or entertaining, gentle or vicious, large or small.' The volume is further enriched by about a hundred portraits of birds from the skilful pencil of William Everett Cram."—*Philadelphia Press.*

The Birds About Us.

Illustrated. Crown 8vo. Cloth, $2.00.

"This book is one of the most complete and interesting studies of the birds of our country that has ever come to our knowledge, and must be valued by every lover of our feathered friends. Its style is familiar and genial, and it is not burdened with technicalities, while its descriptions are perfectly accurate."—*Boston Home Journal.*

Abbott's Bird Library.

THE BIRDS ABOUT US.   BIRD-LAND ECHOES.

Two volumes in a box. 12mo. Cloth, gilt top, $4.00.

J. B. LIPPINCOTT COMPANY, PHILADELPHIA.

By Capt. Chas. King, U.S.A.

Under Fire. Illustrated.   The Colonel's Daughter. Illustrated.

Marion's Faith. Illustrated.   Captain Blake. Illustrated.

Foes in Ambush. (Paper, 50 cents.)

12mo. Cloth, $1.25.

Waring's Peril.   Trials of a Staff Officer.

12mo. Cloth, $1.00.

Kitty's Conquest.

Starlight Ranch, and Other Stories.

Laramie; or, The Queen of Bedlam.

The Deserter, and From the Ranks.

Two Soldiers, and Dunraven Ranch.

A Soldier's Secret, and An Army Portia.

Captain Close, and Sergeant Crœsus.

12mo. Cloth, $1.00; paper, 50 cents.

"From the lowest soldier to the highest officer, from the servant to the master, there is not a character in any of Captain King's novels that is not wholly in keeping with expressed sentiments. There is not a movement made on the field, not a break from the ranks, not an offence against the military code of discipline, and hardly a heart-beat that escapes his watchfulness."—*Boston Herald.*

J. B. LIPPINCOTT COMPANY, PHILADELPHIA.

By Mrs. Alexander.

A Golden Autumn.
12mo. Cloth, $1.25.

"This author's stories are always worth reading."—*Boston Congregationalist.*

"Mrs. Alexander's novels are decidedly of the higher order. They reflect the lives and sayings of wholesome people, carry a healthy moral, and convey valuable lessons to enlightened readers."—*St. Louis Globe-Democrat.*

A Fight with Fate.
12mo. Cloth, $1.25.

"This is Mrs. Alexander's best story, and readers of her two previous novels, 'For His Sake' and 'Found Wanting,' will at once recognize this as high praise. It is an English story. The plot is good, is skilfully developed; the dialogue is bright, the situations, many of them, dramatic. On the whole, it is a bright, entertaining novel, and one of the best of the season."—*Boston Advertiser.*

Found Wanting.
12mo. Paper, 50 cents; cloth, $1.00.

"This author's stories are always worth reading, and her new one is no exception. The heroine is fascinating and noble, and all the characters are well drawn, and the dilemma on which the plot hinges is handled well."—*Boston Congregationalist.*

For His Sake.
12mo. Paper, 50 cents; cloth, $1.00.

"Mrs. Alexander is always successful in tasks such as she has set herself in this novel,—the portrayal of character in English middle-class life. In dealing with domestic complications and the interaction of characters upon each other she is very skilful, and she contrives to divide our sympathies pretty equally between her heroine and her two lovers."—*Charleston News and Courier.*

J. B. LIPPINCOTT COMPANY, PHILADELPHIA.

By John Strange Winter.
(Mrs. Arthur Stannard.)

A Magnificent Young Man.
12mo. Paper, 50 cents; cloth, $1.00.

"There is a happy mingling of comedy and tragedy in *A Magnificent Young Man*. It is a story with an original plot, involving a secret marriage, the mysterious disappearance of a bridegroom, and the experiences of a young girl, who refuses to clear her reputation, even to the mother of her unacknowledged husband, until such a time as he shall give permission. The plot is well sustained, the incidents and dialogue are entertaining, and the mystery is kept up long enough to hold the close attention of the reader to the last chapter."—*Boston Beacon.*

Every Inch a Soldier.
12mo. Paper, 50 cents; cloth, $1.00.

"Of the incidents of the work before us, the plot is highly entertaining, and incidentally we meet the Bishop of Blankhampton, whose matrimonial affairs were ably discussed in a book previously written. It is a very pleasant and readable book, and we are glad to see it."—*Norristown Herald.*

Aunt Johnnie.
12mo. Paper, 50 cents; cloth, $1.00.

"Mrs. Stannard preserves her freshness and vivacity in a wonderful way. 'Aunt Johnnie' is as bright and amusing a story as any that she has written, and it rattles on from the first chapter to the last with unabated gayety and vigor. The hero and heroine are both charming, and the frisky matron who gives the story its name is a capitally managed character. The novel is exactly suited to the season, and is sure to be very popular."—*Charleston News and Courier.*

The Other Man's Wife.
12mo. Paper, 50 cents; cloth, $1.00.

"The hero and heroine have a charm which is really unusual in these backneyed personages, for they are most attractive and wholesome types. Indeed, wholesomeness may be said to be the most notable characteristic of this author's work."—*N. Y. Telegram.*

Only Human.
12mo. Paper, 50 cents; cloth, $1.00.

"A bright and interesting story. . . . Its pathos and humor are of the same admirable quality that is found in all the other novels by this author."—*Boston Gazette.*

J. B. LIPPINCOTT COMPANY, PHILADELPHIA.

By Joseph Hatton.

WHEN GREEK MEETS GREEK.

A Tale of Love and War. With ten full-page illustrations by B. WEST CLINEDINST. Large 12mo. Cloth extra, $1.50.

"The present story is one that is calculated to stir the deepest feelings that enter into human experience. It is of the masterly order, and therefore will confidently command readers even while inviting them."—*Boston Courier.*

"Joseph Hatton has written many successful volumes of incident, but in none of them has he given us a more stirring romance than in his latest novel, 'When Greek Meets Greek.' The characters are drawn with a skilful hand, and the scenes follow each other in rapid succession, each teeming with interest and vigor."—*Boston Advertiser.*

THE BANISHMENT OF JESSOP BLYTHE.

In LIPPINCOTT'S SERIES OF SELECT NOVELS. 12mo.- Cloth, $1.00; paper, 50 cents.

"It is one of the strongest stories of the year, remarkably graphic in its descriptions of the wild and wonderful scenery amidst which its action is located, and equally remarkable for the character drawing of the real men and women who figure in it."—*Boston Home Journal.*

"The author has depicted clearly a true socialistic organization on a small scale, which seems as though it might have been founded on fact. It is a strong story, extremely well told, and will attract attention as much for its socialistic ideas as for its romantic features."—*San Francisco Chronicle.*

CIGARETTE PAPERS.

12mo. Cloth, $1.75.

After-dinner chats they certainly are, such as congenial comrades over the nuts, etc., utter in fragmentary sentences between the long contemplative puffs of a cigar. The illustrations throughout the text add to the beauty of an already attractive volume.

J. B. LIPPINCOTT COMPANY, PHILADELPHIA.

ISSUED IN

Lippincott's Series of Select Novels.

12mo. Paper, 50 cents; cloth, $1.00.

"'Lippincott's Select Novels' is a series that is most properly named. The reader may select at random from the long list of titles with the certainty of getting a good novel."—*N. Y. Bookseller.*

Lady Val's Elopement.
By JOHN BICKERDYKE.

"The story is full of the brightest interest throughout, and several charming romances are interwoven with the main tale. The author shows remarkable skill in the formation of his plot, and several delightful characters are introduced. The bright spirit of the story does not lag for a moment."—*Boston Home Journal.*

The Failure of Sibyl Fletcher.
By ADELINE SERGEANT.

"This new novel by Adeline Sergeant, whose previous works have attracted more than usual attention, is a story of English life, and is a fascinating study of character. The plot is original, is ingeniously developed, the dialogue bright and sparkling, and the situations artistically arranged. On the whole it is one of the best of the select novel series."—*Boston Advertiser.*

Heavy Odds.
By MARCUS CLARKE.

"The story is good, running along with thrilling enough interest to keep the reader's attention faithfully unto the end. It is just the book to take with one on a journey or to spend an evening with. We recommend it heartily to the lover of an entertaining story."—*Cleveland Critic.*

J. B. LIPPINCOTT COMPANY, PHILADELPHIA.

WILSON BARRETT'S GREAT NOVEL.

The Sign of the Cross

WITH FRONTISPIECE BY B. WEST CLINEDINST

12mo. Cloth, extra, $1.50.

"You seem to me to have rendered a great service to the best and holiest of all causes,—The Cause of Faith."—RT. HON. W. E. GLADSTONE.

"Mr. Barrett has succeeded admirably in placing a strong and intense story before the reading public."—*Cincinnati Commercial Tribune.*

"Mr. Barrett has treated his subject with reverence and dignity. The brutal, licentious Nero and his ribald drunken satellites make an admirable foil to the spiritual Mercia and the other followers of Christ; and throughout the book the nobility, the simple faith, and the steadfastness of these last are dominating notes. No more impressive lesson of the power of the doctrines of Christianity has been given in fiction than the conversion of Marcus, Nero's Prefect, through the example and fearlessness of the girl Mercia."—*Philadelphia Evening Bulletin.*

"'The Sign of the Cross' is an historical story of the first Christian century which in a forcible way portrays the conflict between the religion of the Cæsars and that of Christ. It is crowded with picturesque personages, some of them historical, and it is provided with moving scenes and dramatic situations. The triumph of the Cross is set forth in a manner to make vivid the odds it overcame and the force of its influence. Mr. Barrett, in making fiction out of drama, shows himself to possess a decided literary ability (not necessarily to be found in the writer of a good acting play), and he tells the story with keen instinct for its dramatic value. The result is a readable and impressive novel whose action is swift and whose interest is sustained throughout. The book is a justification of the experiment of turning stage literature into closet reading."—*Hartford Courant.*

J. B. LIPPINCOTT COMPANY, PHILADELPHIA.

BILL NYE'S POSTHUMOUS WORK.

A Comic History of England.
From the Druids to the Reign of Henry VIII.
By BILL NYE.

Profusely illustrated by W. M. GOODES and A. M. RICHARDS. Crown 8vo. Cloth, $1.25.

JOAN OF ARC INDUCES THE KING TO BELIEVE THE TRUTH OF HER MISSION.

"It is Nye's masterpiece."
St. Louis Post-Dispatch.

"It is written in the author's best vein."—*Pittsburg Chronicle Telegraph.*

"The fun of the book is good and well sustained, and the illustrations are amusing."
—*Boston Congregationalist.*

"There is a vast amount of fun to be found between the covers of this book. Many a hearty laugh will end in a sigh of regret that the time is past when any new work from Mr. Nye's pen will move the world to laughter. How surely does he find the weak spot and dance upon it to the delectation of his crowd of admirers! How absolutely absurd he makes those ancient monarchs and their reigns! What fun history is viewed across the pages of this humorist's book! His satire is so keen, so amusing! W. M. Goodes and A. M. Richards have added greatly to the humor of the book by their illustrations. Twenty pages of these complete the work left unfinished by the illness and death of the author."—*Cleveland Critic.*

"This comic History of England was evidently written in the author's best vein of humor, as well as with the strong attempt of making a funny history an instructive one; for, throughout, he follows and adheres to dates and events with an historian's accuracy. The illustrations are no small portion of its attractiveness, adding greatly to an appreciation of the text, as they certainly do."—*Boston Courier.*

J. B. LIPPINCOTT COMPANY, PHILADELPHIA.

A Comic History of the United States

By BILL NYE.

With one hundred and fifty illustrations by F. OPPER.

12mo. Cloth extra, $2.00.

CLUB LIFE IN EARLY NEW YORK.

"The author's satire is keen, his humor unceasing; but he never has forgotten the requirements of good taste. The book will induce many a smile and not a few uproarious laughs."—*Philadelphia Evening Bulletin.*

"Those who admire the funniments of Bill Nye will enjoy many a hearty laugh at his quaint and curious way of presenting historical facts."—*Boston Saturday Evening Gazette.*

"One cannot forbear a smile over these truly comic sketches."—*Public Ledger*, Philadelphia.

"Everybody with any sense of humor in their souls will be entertained—and instructed, too—by its perusal."—*Boston Home Journal.*

"The greatest enjoyment will be derived from it."—*Chicago Journal.*

"The book is bound to be a great success."—*New York School Journal.*

"The best thing Bill Nye has ever done. There is real worth in it."—*Philadelphia To-Day.*

J. B. LIPPINCOTT COMPANY, PHILADELPHIA.

The True George Washington.

BY

PAUL LEICESTER FORD,

Author of
" The Honorable Peter Stirling," etc.

With twenty-four full-page illustrations. Crown 8vo. Cloth, deckle edges, $2.00; three-quarters levant, $5.00.

" This book is a monument of industry."—*New York Nation.*

" This is a wonderfully interesting book."—*Buffalo Commercial.*

" Mr. Ford's book is rich in new matter which commends itself as interesting as well as valuable."—*Washington Times.*

" Mr. Ford has delved with diligence and with rich reward into contemporary records, correspondence, and traditions, and gives an entertaining account of colonial times and of the personal traits of the Father of His Country."—*Chicago Advance.*

" Mr. Ford's book is important out of all proportion to its size, and will probably be read so long as the name of Washington continues to be revered. Brushing aside the hysterical panegyrics of would-be biographers and historians as well as super-laudatory passages in works otherwise trustworthy and meritorious, Mr. Ford resolutely set out to acquire real knowledge of the man, George Washington. Few of the other heroes of history could pass unscathed through an examination so thorough and so rigid. Every attainable fact that helps to show the Father of His Country as he was in his social and family relations has been carefully considered."—*Boston Evening Gazette.*

" This work challenges attention for the really valuable light which it throws upon the character of George Washington. The picture which Mr. Ford here draws of him is careful, life-like, and impressive in the extreme. While his exhaustive researches have resulted in humanizing Washington 'and making him a man rather than a historical figure,' a fair and intelligent reader, we submit, will arise from the glowing chapters of Mr. Ford's work with a larger conception of the character, endowments, and equipment of the first of Americans. . . . The work embodies a surprising measure of information on a most important as well as interesting subject."—*Philadelphia Evening Bulletin.*

J. B. LIPPINCOTT COMPANY, PHILADELPHIA.

BY
ANNE HOLLINGSWORTH WHARTON.

Through Colonial Doorways.

With a number of colonial illustrations from drawings specially made for the work. 12mo. Cloth, $1.25.

"It is a pleasant retrospect of fashionable New York and Philadelphia society during and immediately following the Revolution; for there was a Four Hundred even in those days, and some of them were Whigs and some were Tories, but all enjoyed feasting and dancing, of which there seemed to be no limit. And this little book tells us about the belles of the Philadelphia meschianza, who they were, how they dressed, and how they flirted with Major André and other officers in Sir William Howe's wicked employ."—*Philadelphia Record.*

Colonial Days and Dames.

With numerous illustrations. 12mo. Cloth, $1.25.

"In less skilful hands than those of Anne Hollingsworth Wharton's, these scraps of reminiscences from diaries and letters would prove but dry bones. But she has made them so charming that it is as if she had taken dried roses from an old album and freshened them into bloom and perfume. Each slight paragraph from a letter is framed in historical sketches of local affairs or with some account of the people who knew the letter writers, or were at least of their date, and there are pretty suggestions as to how and why such letters were written, with hints of love affairs, which lend a rose-colored veil to what were probably every-day matters in colonial families."—*Pittsburg Bulletin.*

For sale by all Booksellers, or will be sent, post-paid, upon receipt of price,

J. B. LIPPINCOTT COMPANY, Publishers,
PHILADELPHIA.

www.ingramcontent.com/pod-product-compliance
Lightning Source LLC
Chambersburg PA
CBHW022020240426
43667CB00042B/1004